EVERYONE'S MONEY BOOK

ON COLLEGE

JORDAN E. GOODMAN

Dearborn™
Trade Publishing
A **Kaplan Professional** Company

Vice President and Publisher: Cynthia A. Zigmund
Editorial Director: Donald J. Hull
Senior Managing Editor: Jack Kiburz
Interior Design: Lucy Jenkins
Cover Design: Design Alliance, Inc.
Typesetting: the dotted i

Published by Dearborn Trade Publishing, a Kaplan Professional Company

Printed in the United States of America

02 03 04 05 06 10 9 8 7 6 5 4 3 2 1

Library of Congress Cataloging-in-Publication Data

Goodman, Jordan Elliot.
    Everyone's money book on college / Jordan E. Goodman.
        p.   cm.
    Includes bibliographical references and index.
    ISBN 0-7931-5381-6 (pbk.)
    1. College costs—United States.   2. Student aid—United States.   3. Finance,
Personal—United States.   I. Title.
    LB2342 .G76 2002
    378.3'8'0973—dc21

           2002007870

Contents

List of Figures

Preface

Once upon a time, attending college was regarded as a luxury—something for a relatively small, privileged few. Well, those days are gone. Now, if you want a decent job, you need at least a bachelor of arts degree, or BA, and maybe more.

Not that it's easy getting in. More and more students are going to college, so many that even second-tier institutions find themselves deluged with applications. And the competition for the top, prestigious institutions is even fiercer.

Still, with more than 3,600 colleges and universities in this country, you have quite a few potential choices. If you intelligently select a roster of potential candidates and systematically go about the application process, your child stands a good chance of getting in—somewhere. Maybe not the dream school. But somewhere.

No, the larger problem, the really big Kahuna, is another matter: how to pay for that education. The average four-year private school, including room and board, supplies, and other expenses, costs $26,070 a year. For a family with two or three children, that adds up to a big chunk of change—probably the biggest expense you're likely to face next to your mortgage. In the current volatile economic climate, coming up with the money may be an especially big worry.

But, we know something you may not: Most people *do* have the means to send their children to college. People like you. Even in today's shaky economy, and even if you don't get started when your offspring are just out

of the delivery room, there are still many ways for you to scrape together the
money you will need.

Still, you won't get there without a lot of work. This isn't a fairy tale.
Planning, saving, and a clear understanding both of how to find financial aid
and the mistakes to avoid are all necessary elements in your strategy.

And that's where this book comes in. We aim to help you learn how to
tackle the college-financing monster—and we aim to do it in a form that's
clear, concise, and easy to read. After all, while we know it's a subject of
vital importance to you and your children, we also realize something else:
You're busy. And what you need is one place where you can get all the information you need.

To that end, we've assembled a soup-to-nuts guide to everything you
need to know, from estimating costs to finding potential scholarships your
child might be eligible for. It's all here. And, because we know that half the
battle is having the right resources at your fingertips, we've included lots of
comprehensive tables and a host of invaluable books, software programs, associations, and Web sites you can turn to along the way.

Specifically, we'll show you:

- How to determine what costs are likely to be at various kinds of
  schools and how much you'll need to save to pay them.
- How to invest wisely in funds earmarked for college tuition
- All about the latest savings plans, including the new 529 state plans
- Which government grants are available and how to apply for them
- All about scholarships—who offers them, where to find them, how to
  win one
- The lowdown on loans, both government and private
- What financial aid officers are looking for
- How to apply for federal aid
- Ways to reduce costs
- How to use the Internet in your financing efforts

Whether you assemble the money to pay for your children's college education from savings and investments, grants, scholarships, or loans, the
costs are burdensome. The earlier you develop a plan to fund college, the
lighter the burden will be. Ultimately, however, it's important to keep your
eye on the prize. Indeed, while the sacrifice of paying for college is great, the
reward—a bright future for your children—can be even greater.

Acknowledgments

Everyone's Money Book on College would not have been possible without the extremely hard work of financial writer Anne Field, who expertly pulled together the threads of this book into the most comprehensive resource on financing college ever created.

I also want to thank Jack Joyce, Director of Guidance Services at the College Board, who gave generously of his time and ideas to make this book as complete and accurate as possible. I also want to thank Tasheem Lomax for all of her hard work on this book, and Barbara Wagner for her sage advice throughout the project. Roselle Weingart's help is also much appreciated.

These organizations also were very helpful and gave me permission to use some of their explanatory materials:

- BabyMint
- Commonapp.org
- eStudentLoan.com
- FastWeb.com
- FinAid.org
- FleetBoston Financial Corporation
- Morningstar
- Sallie Mae
- Savingforcollege.com
- Scholarship Resource Network Express
- Scudder Investments
- Upromise

CHAPTER 1

You *Can* Pay for College

Remember the 1990s, when all those dot-com entrepreneurs, barely out of high school, made millions almost overnight? Seemed likely they'd beat the system. Without a college degree, they'd struck it rich.

Well, we all know what happened. The market tanked and dot-com heaven evaporated. Almost as quickly as they'd made it, they were out on the street, looking for a job.

More than anything else, that dramatic rise and fall underscored one of the unavoidable facts of life today: To get anywhere, you need a college education. Unless your last name is Rockefeller or Gates, there's no magic pill—not now, not ever.

A BACHELOR'S DEGREE MEANS A BETTER JOB

As the world continues to grow more competitive and technologically sophisticated, most of the high-paying jobs will require skills learned in college and graduate school. Want to be a computer programmer? An engineer? A corporate vice president? Years ago, employers generally expected workers to have at least a high school diploma; today, a college degree, such as a bachelor of arts (BA) or a bachelor of science (BS), is considered a minimum requirement for most well-paying jobs. Even occupations, like farmer or factory worker, that once seemed unlikely candidates for requiring technological savvy, now call for some level of computer literacy.

In fact, as Figures 1.1 and 1.2 show, the gap between earnings of college and high school graduates has widened every year for decades. According to the U.S. Census Bureau, the average income for high school graduates is $26,099; for those with a BA, it's $48,517. (With an advanced degree, you can expect to make an average $71,905!) Over a lifetime, the gap in earning potential between someone with a high school diploma and someone with a college degree is more than $1 million, according to the College Board.

Figure 1.1   Average Income Table, 1975–1999

Year	High School Diploma	Bachelor's Degree
1975	$25,758	$40,500
1976	26,067	40,477
1977	26,283	41,430
1978	26,644	41,429
1979	25,873	40,217
1980	24,265	38,766
1981	23,538	36,944
1982	23,004	37,129
1983	23,147	38,209
1984	23,637	39,254
1985	23,754	40,875
1986	24,381	42,749
1987	24,793	41,872
1988	25,034	42,361
1989	25,084	43,821
1990	24,105	42,086
1991	23,698	40,649
1992	23,601	41,099
1993	23,763	42,970
1994	24,144	44,386
1995	24,857	42,892
1996	24,964	42,946
1997	25,209	44,570
1998	25,604	47,512
1999	26,099	48,517

Source: "Figure 12. Income by Educational Attainment for Persons 18 Years Old and Over, 1975–1999 (Inflation Adjusted for 2001)." *Trends in College Pricing 2001:* 19. ©2001 by College Entrance Examination Board. Reprinted with permission. All rights reserved. <www.collegeboard.com>

Figure 1.2   Average Income Chart, 1975–1999

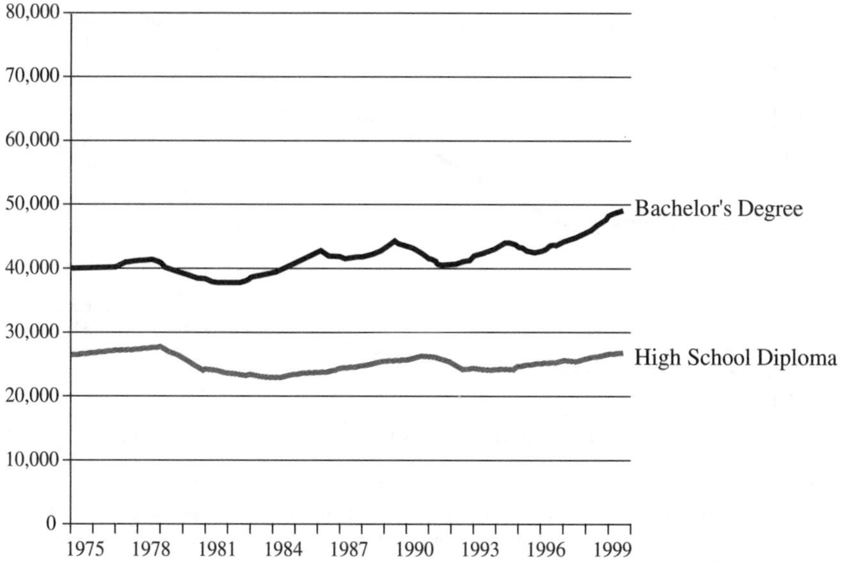

Plus, more and more people are attending a postsecondary institution (college). About 75 percent of all high school graduates go to college, compared to 50 percent just 20 years ago. So you're really at a competitive disadvantage if you don't get a BA. It's no wonder that the number of applications to Ivy League schools has skyrocketed in recent years. At the same time, the sheer number of applicants will rise even more dramatically, as the new baby boomers, who are the offspring of the children born from 1946 to 1964, reach college age.

COLLEGE COSTS KEEP ON RISING

Okay, so you have to go to college. At the same time, however, as Figure 1.3 demonstrates, costs keep going up. According to the College Board, growth in tuition has outpaced household income growth by more than fivefold since 1980. Four years of tuition, fees, and room and board at a public university in your home state can easily run between $20,000 and $50,000, and the cost of four years at an Ivy League school ranges from $100,000 to $150,000. That's

Figure 1.3   Average Tuition and Fees, 1971–2002

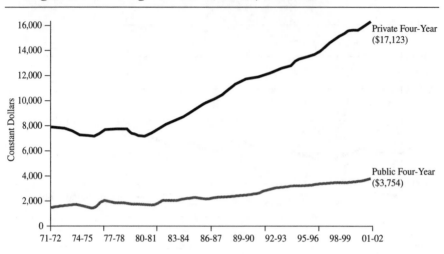

for now. With college costs expected to increase between 4 percent and 7 percent a year, today's prices could look like bargains 20 years from now. For example, unless the pace of college cost inflation dramatically slows, parents of a baby born in 1998 should expect to pay a whopping $100,000 to $150,000 for their child's public education and a mind-boggling $300,000 to $400,000 for four years at a top-ranked private university. As if that weren't enough of a financial burden, you also may be saving for retirement, or taking care of an elderly parent, at the same time that the college tuition bill comes due. This is often called the "Sandwich Generation Squeeze."

PLANNING WILL PAY OFF

Most people look at the math and go bug-eyed. It just seems impossible to ever be able to afford that kind of money. But, before you become discouraged and convinced that you could never amass such a sum, take a deep breath and stop a moment. The fact is, despite the obstacles, millions of people finance their children's college education every year—and you can be one of them.

Chances are likely you won't end up paying full freight completely on your own. More than 60 percent of students at four-year private colleges and universities receive some type of financial aid, while 75 percent get aid at four-year public colleges and universities. According to the College Board, approximately $75 billion in financial aid is available to students and their families each year.

We're not saying that paying for college will be easy. It won't. You will need a lot of discipline in the form of long-term saving and investing in the years before college, combined with borrowing from several sources once your children enroll. Indeed, you'll need to put together many pieces—investments, grants, financial aid, loans—to solve the college payment puzzle. But, if you develop a realistic plan and commit seriously to it, you can meet most or all of the massive expenses.

Don't put off planning. It's important to start as soon as possible. If you ignore or postpone the problem, the challenge of college funding becomes only more daunting. So, bite the bullet and get started. Clearly, it's worth the effort.

CHAPTER 2

Estimating
College Costs

A mbiguity drives most of us crazy. In other words, it's always easier to deal with what you know than what you may imagine. So, rather than dwelling on the hundreds of thousands of dollars that college could cost, your first step should be getting a rough idea of just how much money you'll really need to spend annually, quarterly, or monthly. With that in mind, you can create a realistic plan that you can live with.

Of course, you never can be sure if, or when, fate will do a number on your blueprint. There's no way of knowing whether your child will win that coveted violin scholarship or decide that a college on the other side of the country is the only place to go. So, remember that your estimates are not carved in stone.

The bottom line: It's best to be as conservative as possible when estimating your costs. Plan for the worst and hope for the best.

FIRST ASSUMPTIONS

If you're starting early, it's hard to know what school your toddler might aspire to more than a decade from now. Although you might suspect that adorable child taking his or her first steps will be a genius, you just can't be sure. Nevertheless, it's important to consider some preliminary questions. Your answers to these questions will have a direct impact on how much you'll have to spend:

- Is he or she likely to attend a public university in the state where you live or an out-of-state public institution?
- Is there a chance he or she might want to enroll at a top-ranked private college, such as an Ivy League university or its equivalent?
- Might a junior college, or community college, be the most realistic choice?

Though you cannot answer these hypothetical questions with much certainty, you force yourself to confront the reality of how much to save. Most parents save far less than they ultimately need for college costs. And what's the worst that could happen if you save too much? In the unlikely event that you accumulate more than enough money for college tuition, room and board, and other expenses, you will have plenty of other uses for the assets—your retirement, for instance. However, if you save too little, you and your child will be forced to assume debt that will take years to repay and cost thousands of dollars in nondeductible interest.

PRIVATE VERSUS PUBLIC

The more prestigious the school on which your child sets his or her sights, the more it will cost, of course. But, that by no means implies that you shouldn't try. While private colleges are expensive, they may be able to give you more in aid than a public school. The financial aid officers at a private college will typically figure that the difference between their tuition and what you can pay will be larger than what their counterparts at a public or less prestigious private school might determine. The more you can show that there's a gap between what you can pay and the costs, the bigger the amount of aid you may get.

At the same time, many schools charge far less tuition than Ivy League universities or their equivalents. These schools also provide high-quality education, though they may not have as prestigious a reputation. For example, while tuition, fees, and room and board at Harvard cost more than $34,000 a year, at the University of Massachusetts–Amherst, they're around $10,000 for state residents and $18,000 for nonresidents. Sending your child to one of these institutions may very well ease some of the financial pressure. For a better idea of what colleges cost, take a look at Figure 2.1, which includes tuition and fees at various colleges and universities. While the list is a sampling, it should give you a good feel for the differences.

Remember: If you choose a public school, you're in good company. Forty-five percent of all first-year students attend public two-year colleges,

Figure 2.1   College Tuition and Fees at a Sampling of Schools

College, State	Tuition and Fees
Amherst College, Massachusetts	$27,258
Athens State University, Georgia	2,430 (state residents)
	4,800 (nonresidents)
Babson College, Massachusetts	24,544
Butler University, Indiana	18,230
Drake University, Iowa	17,790
California Institute of Technology, California	21,120
College of Santa Fe, New Mexico	17,154
Connecticut College, Connecticut	33,585
Emory University, Georgia	25,552
Johns Hopkins University, Baltimore	26,710
Lake Forest College, Illinois	22,206
Northwestern University, Illinois	25,839
Prescott College, Arizona	13,990
Seattle Pacific University, Washington	16,335
Stanford University, California	26,192
Tuskegee University, Alabama	10,496
University of Alaska Fairbanks, Alaska	3,420 (state residents)
	8,340 (nonresidents)
University of California: Berkeley, California	4,407 (state residents)
	14,221 (nonresidents)
University of Colorado at Boulder, Colorado	3,223 (state residents)
	16,541 (nonresidents)
Wichita State University, Kansas	2,759 (state residents)
	9,374 (nonresidents)
Yale University, Connecticut	26,100

according to the College Board. And only 6 percent of all students attend schools where tuition is $24,000 or more.

What Is Included in the Cost

When people talk about the cost of college, they mean a lot more than just the tuition. The full cost also includes room and board, books, supplies, transportation, and a variety of other things, depending on your child's lifestyle. Some of these costs include:

- *Full-time tuition.* It's less expensive at public institutions, because they are subsidized, although nonresidents are usually charged more at state schools.
- *Part-time tuition.* May work out to be more costly, if the school charges per credit.
- *Fees.* At many schools, there will be extra fees for items like library or gym.
- *Books and supplies.* One of the few areas where there's not a big difference in cost between a private and public school: $704 at a four-year public school, $730 at a four-year private institution, according to the College Board.
- *Room and board.* Costs, obviously, will be greater if you're not living at home.

How to Calculate Costs

For a rough idea of how much college might cost and how much you must save, you have a few choices. You can ask a financial planner to calculate the amounts. Or, you can use one of the software programs on the market or the many calculators on college financing found in related Web sites to figure it out for yourself. (Some of these sites are listed in the "Resources" section of this chapter.) For most of these calculators, you enter the number of years until your child starts college, your assumed inflation rate, your estimated return on investment, and some additional factors, to arrive at likely college costs. As you change your assumptions, note how the cost of college and the amount you must save change. Figure 2.2 shows you what one such calculator looks like, from the Web site of the College Board (www.collegeboard.com). A similar exercise is also available in such software packages as Quicken and Microsoft Money.

Figure 2.3 provides a worksheet that will help you estimate college costs and your savings needs. It assumes that your child is 2 years old and will

Figure 2.2   Sample Cost Calculator

PLANNING FOR COLLEGE | TAKING THE TESTS | FINDING THE RIGHT COLLEGE | GETTING INTO COLLEGE | PAYING FOR COLLEGE | MY ORGANIZER

collegeboard.com

Paying > Financial Aid Calculators

College Savings Calculator

Do you like to plan ahead? Use this calculator to get an estimate of the amount of money you would have at the time your child enters college, if you begin saving now. Then, add these additional savings to your current savings and investments. Complete the brief form below and submit it for analysis.

**Do not use commas when entering dollar amounts
(2000 - not 2,000).**

$[   ]   Total value of your current savings and investments (stocks, bonds, etc.)

$[   ]   How much per month do you think you might be able to save for college between now and the time your child enrolls?

[5]   % Annual interest rate you expect to earn on your savings and investments (you may enter a percentage other than the one shown).

[   ] Numbers of years until your child enters college.

[Send data]   [Reset]

enter college at age 18, that you will continue to save throughout your child's college years, and that education costs will escalate 5 percent a year. It also assumes that you earn 8 percent per year after taxes on your investments and are in the 31 percent federal tax rate bracket. To complete the worksheet, you must know the current annual cost of a school your child might attend. Take a look back at Figure 2.1. If you don't find your choice, you can locate this figure in the book *Meeting College Costs: What You Need to Know Before Your Child and Your Money Leave Home.* (For more information, consult the "Resources" section at the end of this chapter.)

As you will see by trying various combinations of factors on the worksheet, the earlier you start to save, the less you must put aside each month or each year. And, of course, the longer you wait, the more you must save every month. A rule of thumb is to set aside between $2,000 and $4,000 a year, if you

Figure 2.3   College Costs and Savings Needs Worksheet

Step 1: Estimate Your Child's College Costs

Enter the Following Information	Example	Your Child
1. Your Child's Age	2	
2. Years Until College	16	
3. Current Annual College Cost of Preferred School	$ 22,533	
4. Inflation Factor (see Table A)	2.18	
5. Anticipated Annual College Cost (Multiply line 3 by line 4.)	$ 49,121	
6. Total Cost of College (Multiply line 5 by the number of college years planned.)	$196,487	
7. Estimated Amount of Future Income, Loans, Work-Study Income, and Other Sources of College Expenses	$ 50,000	
8. Net Cost of College (Subtract line 7 from line 6.)	$146,487	

Table A: College Inflation Factor

Years to College	1	2	3	4	5	6	7	8	9
Inflation Factor	1.05	1.10	1.16	1.22	1.28	1.34	1.41	1.48	1.55
Years to College	10	11	12	13	14	15	16	17	18
Inflation Factor	1.63	1.71	1.80	1.89	1.98	2.08	2.18	2.29	2.41

**Figure 2.3   College Costs and Savings Needs
                 Worksheet (continued)**

Step 2: Calculate Your Regular Investment Amount

9. Investment Factor (Enter the
    appropriate factor from
    Table B.)   29.18   _____

10. Annual Investment Amount
    (Divide line 8 by line 9.) $ 4,027   _____

11. Monthly Investment Amount
    (Divide line 10 by line 12.) $ 336   _____

12. Quarterly Investment (Divide
    line 10 by line 4.) $ 1,007   _____

Table B: Periodic Investment Factor Table

Years to College	1	2	3	4	5	6	7	8	9
Inflation Factor	1.07	2.21	3.42	4.72	6.11	7.59	9.17	10.86	12.66

Years to College	10	11	12	13	14	15	16	17	18
Inflation Factor	14.58	16.64	18.83	21.17	23.67	26.34	29.18	32.23	35.47

Source: Reprinted with permission of Scudder Investments.

begin when your child is a newborn. If you start saving when he or she is in second or third grade, you'll need to reserve between $4,000 and $8,000 a year.

CONSISTENT SAVING HELPS

Perhaps you've heard financial advisors talk about how saving a little bit consistently goes a long way over time. They're right. Figure 2.4 gives you an idea of how much money you will accumulate if you save $100 a month. In the left column, find the number of years until your child enrolls in college. Across the top, you can see how your money will compound at different after-tax rates of return. If you save more than $100 a month, multiply

Figure 2.4 Money Accumulated by Investing $100 per Month

Number of Years until College	Rates of Return					
	5.5%	7%	8%	9%	10%	12%
1	$ 1,236	$ 1,246	$ 1,253	$ 1,260	$ 1,267	$ 1,281
2	2,542	2,583	2,611	2,638	2,667	2,724
3	3,922	4,106	4,081	4,146	4,213	4,351
4	5,380	5,553	5,673	5,795	5,921	6,183
5	6,920	7,201	7,397	7,599	7,808	8,249
6	8,546	8,968	9,264	9,572	9,893	10,576
7	10,265	10,863	11,286	11,730	12,196	13,198
8	12,080	12,895	13,476	14,091	13,740	16,153
9	13,998	15,073	15,848	16,672	17,550	19,482
10	16,024	17,409	18,417	19,497	20,655	23,234
11	18,164	19,914	21,198	22,586	24,085	27,461
12	20,425	22,602	24,211	25,964	27,874	32,225
13	22,814	25,481	27,474	29,660	32,060	37,593
14	25,537	28,569	31,008	33,703	36,684	43,642
15	28,002	31,881	34,835	38,124	41,792	50,458
16	30,818	35,432	38,979	42,961	47,436	58,138
17	33,793	39,240	43,468	48,251	53,670	66,792
18	36,936	43,323	48,329	54,037	60,557	76,544

these numbers by the appropriate multiple of $100. For example, if you save $400 a month, multiply these numbers by four.

RESOURCES

Books

Meeting College Costs: What You Need to Know Before Your Child and Your Money Leave Home (The College Board, 45 Columbus Ave., New York, NY 10023-6992; 212-713-8000; www.collegeboard.org). Includes information on current costs of colleges and universities.

Funding a College Education: Finding the Right School for Your Child and the Right Fit for Your Budget, by Alice Drum and Richard Kneedler (Harvard Business

School Publishing, 300 N. Beacon St., 4th Floor, Watertown, MA 02472; 800-988-0886; www.hbsp.harvard.edu). Targeted to parents, this book explains how to negotiate the maze of available education choices and financial aid options. Provides worksheets to help assess family resources and explain the different types of colleges and the different types of aid, loans, and scholarships.

Last Minute College Financing: It's Never Too Late to Prepare for the Future, by Daniel J. Cassidy (Career Press, P.O. Box 687, Franklin Lakes, NJ 07417; 201-848-0310; www.careerpress.com). Explains how to save for your child's college expenses, how to make your savings grow, how to estimate how much money will be needed, how to locate sources of financial aid, and how to find low-cost, high-quality colleges.

Software Programs

Financial Aid (EFC) (Octameron Associates, P.O. Box 2748, Alexandria, VA 22301; 703-836-5480; www.octameron.com). A simple software program designed to help you compute your expected family contribution to college costs. By changing the income or assets that your family reports, you easily can see how your expected contribution changes. May also help you find ways to lower your expected family contribution and, thus, qualify for more student aid.

Microsoft Money (Microsoft Corp., One Microsoft Way, Redmond, WA 98052-6399; 425-882-8080, 800-426-9400; www.microsoft.com). A simple program designed to track your income, expenses, and net worth; keep your checkbook; and pay your bills electronically. Also helps you estimate the cost of college and how much you need to save for it.

Quicken (Intuit, 2535 Garcia Ave., Mountain View, CA 94043; 650-944-6000; www.qfn.com). When you must make a financial decision on investments, taxes, or other matters, this program allows you to track every aspect of your personal finances and analyze alternatives using color graphics. Offers six software packages: Quicken Basic to start organizing your finances, balance your checkbook, and bank online; Quicken Deluxe, same as Basic plus you can enter transactions via the Web, you can download stock quotes and news, planners for retirement, college, home purchase, and savings, and track basic tax data; Quicken Suite with TurboTax and Family Lawyer allows you to do banking, investing, planning, taxes, and legal applications in one integrated program; Quicken Financial Planner helps plan for retirement; and finally Quicken Deluxe for Macintosh.

Trade Associations

The Financial Planning Association (FPA) (3801 E. Florida Ave., Suite 708, Denver, Colorado 80210; 800-322-4237; www.fpanet.org). A membership organization for the financial planning industry. Offers a free brochure, *Planning for the Costs of Higher Education.* Send a self-addressed, stamped envelope to the FPA or go to <www.fpanet.org/plannersearch/brochures/FPAEducationBro.pdf>.

The National Association of Student Financial Aid Administrators (1129 20th Street, N.W., Suite 400, Washington, DC 20036; 202-785-0453; www.nasfaa.org). Represents more than 10,000 financial aid professionals at more than 3,000 colleges, universities, and career schools.

Web Sites

Collegeboard.org. Helps with the financial aid process. This site offers, among other things, calculators and worksheets for figuring out college costs. <www.collegeboard.org>

FinAid. A public service site that provides information about college loans, scholarships, and grants. Includes calculators to help determine how much money you will need and what loan payments will be. <www.finaid.org>

CHAPTER 3

Stock Mutual Funds

I t would be nice if we could send our children to four years of college on a full scholarship. But that's not likely. Most people pay for at least part of college through money they've invested.

One of the most effective ways to invest is in the stock market. Even given today's volatile market conditions, the experts advise you put at least some of your savings there. After all, over time, the stock market has been shown to outperform all other investments.

Still, most people lack the knowledge to invest in individual stocks. So, instead, they put their money in mutual funds. A stock mutual fund is a pool of money that a fund manager invests in stocks to achieve a specific objective. It's quite possible to save a large portion of total college costs using this tool.

CUSTODIAL ACCOUNTS

Before examining the appropriateness of specific investments for funding college, let's look at whose name the investments should be held in. Under the Uniform Gifts to Minors Act (UGMA) or the Uniform Transfers to Minors Act (UTMA), you set aside money in your child's name until he or she reaches the age of majority, which is 18 or 21, depending on the state. (In a few states, you can choose an age between 18 to 21 or 18 to 25.) Note that, while many states have changed their rules recently, you will be governed by the age stipulated under the previous law. Figure 3.1 provides a list of states and their age of majority.

Figure 3.1   Age of Majority by State

State	Age of Majority	State	Age of Majority
Alabama	21	Montana	21
Alaska	18–25	Nebraska	21
Arizona	21	Nevada	18–25
Arkansas	18–21	New Hampshire	21
California	18–25	New Jersey	18–21
Colorado	21	New Mexico	21
Connecticut	21	New York	21
Delaware	21	North Carolina	18–21
District of Columbia	18	North Dakota	21
Florida	21	Ohio	21
Georgia	21	Oklahoma	18
Hawaii	21	Oregon	21
Idaho	21	Pennsylvania	21
Illinois	21	Rhode Island	18
Iowa	21	South Carolina	18
Kansas	21	South Dakota	18
Kentucky	18	Tennessee	21
Louisiana	21	Texas	21
Maine	18–21	Utah	21
Maryland	21	Vermont	18
Massachusetts	21	Virginia	18–21
Michigan	18–21	Washington	21
Minnesota	21	West Virginia	21
Mississippi	21	Wisconsin	21
Missouri	21	Wyoming	21

What's the advantage? Before the Tax Reform Act of 1986, it made sense for parents to fund college trusts, because all assets held in a child's name were taxed at the child's low income tax rate. Tax reform limited the amount of income that could be taxed at the child's rate. Currently, for a child younger than age 14, the first $750 of income from interest and dividends is totally tax-free, and the second $750 is taxed at the child's tax rate, usually

10 percent. Any earnings exceeding that amount are taxed at the parent's rate, which may be 28 percent or more. The limit is indexed upward for inflation annually. Once the child turns 14, all earnings above the first tax-free $750 are again taxed at his or her rate.

But putting assets in your child's name has a few disadvantages. Once your child reaches the age of majority, he or she has full discretion over how to use the money in the UGMA account. In other words, if your child spends it on a sports car instead of college tuition, you can't do anything about it. You hope your child would never squander all this carefully invested capital, but you never know by looking at your two-year-old what that little darling will do in the future. That's less of a concern in states where the age of majority is 21, but it's still a consideration.

Another downside of building a child's portfolio is that if your child applies for financial aid, the college will require that a high percentage of the assets—usually about 35 percent—be used to pay for tuition. In contrast, colleges insist that parents spend only about 5.6 percent of their assets for their child's college costs. Therefore, if you want to be totally safe and able to have your child qualify for the maximum amount of financial aid available, keep all college funds in your name, and pay tuition bills out of your account.

If you maintain an account in your child's name, you should fund it with investments that produce little, if any, taxable income but, instead, provide long-term capital growth. Stocks of high-growth companies or aggressive-growth stock mutual funds are two examples of appropriate investments for your child's account. Another is municipal bonds or municipal bond funds, which pay tax-exempt interest.

STOCK MUTUAL FUNDS

Most people don't have the time or knowledge to invest in individual stocks. That's why they turn to stock mutual funds. A stock mutual fund is a pool of money that a fund manager invests in stocks to achieve a specific objective. The fund is sponsored by a mutual fund company, which may be an independent firm, such as Fidelity, T. Rowe Price, or Vanguard, or a division of a brokerage or insurance company, like Merrill Lynch, Salomon Smith Barney, or Kemper.

There are two kinds of funds. With load funds, you pay a commission to a salesperson, financial planner, or broker. No-load funds are sold directly by the mutual fund company, with no salesperson involved. You don't pay a commission—but you don't get the advice of a professional on which fund to buy. Both types, however, charge management fees, ranging from 0.2 percent to 2 percent, that are deducted from the value of the fund automatically.

Some major no-load fund companies include:

- American Century Investment, 800-345-3533
- Fidelity Group, 800-544-8888
- Gabelli Funds, 800-422-3544
- Janus, 800-525-8983
- Marisco Family of Funds, 800-860-8686
- T. Rowe Price, 800-225-5132
- Weitz Funds, 800-232-4161

ADVANTAGES OF MUTUAL FUNDS

Despite these fees, mutual funds have many advantages:

- A professional skilled in choosing stocks does all the work for you. Managers of funds devote all their time determining which stocks to buy and sell; you'd have to quit your job and take up investing full-time to do the same.
- A mutual fund gives you instant diversification, which helps protect you against the volatility of any one stock.
- A fund exists for every financial goal and risk tolerance level. There are funds designed for various degrees of growth and for varying levels of income, as well as funds that combine both growth and income objectives.
- You can get into and out of a mutual fund easily. All it takes is a phone call or Web site visit to your broker or the fund.
- You can easily switch from one fund to another within a fund family. Most mutual fund companies offer a broad array of mutual funds so that, as your needs change, you can simply switch from one fund to another.

TYPES OF FUNDS

There are many different categories of funds, with varying degrees of risk and potential for long-term reward. The riskier the investment, the greater the possibility for reaping big gains. Of course, there's also a bigger chance that you'll lose money. Here's a look at some of these categories, arranged in order of the level of risk.

High-Risk

Aggressive growth funds. These funds buy stocks of fast-growing companies or of other companies that have great capital gains potential. Or they might buy stocks in bankrupt or depressed companies, anticipating a rebound.

Foreign stock funds. They buy stocks of corporations based outside of the United States. In addition to the usual forces affecting stock prices, fluctuations in the value of the U.S. dollar against foreign currencies can dramatically affect the price of these funds' shares, particularly over the short term.

Sector funds. These funds buy stocks in just one industry or sector of the economy, such as oil, automotive, and gold-mining. Because these funds are undiversified, they soar or plummet based on the fate of the industry in which they invest.

Moderate-Risk

Growth funds. Growth funds invest in shares of well-known growth companies that usually have a long history of increasing earnings. Because the stock market fluctuates, growth funds rise and fall over time, though not as much as funds holding smaller, less proven stocks.

Index funds. These funds buy the stocks that make up a particular index to allow investors' returns to match the index. The most popular is the Standard & Poor's 500.

Low-Risk

Balanced funds. Balanced funds keep a fairly steady mix of high-yielding stocks and conservative bonds. This allows the funds to pay a high rate of current income and still participate in the long-term growth of stocks.

Utilities funds. These funds buy shares in electric, gas, telephone, and water utilities. Because these companies are regulated monopolies, they have steady earnings and pay high dividends, but they are subject to swings in interest rates.

SELECTING A FUND

There are hundreds of specific funds within a category. So, in addition to selecting the type of fund, you also have to choose which particular one you want. How do you choose?

Performance

Most important is to look at performance—those funds with solid, long-term records of achieving their objectives. It is also preferable if the fund has had the same manager for a long time, so you can be assured the fund's style will remain consistent.

The key to performance is total return. This combines all dividends and capital gains distributions with changes in a fund's price. It is a far better yardstick to use when comparing funds than just the change in a fund's price over a period of time. The listings for total return you will see from the ratings services and in the media normally show a fund's results thus far in the current year, over the past 52 weeks, and over the past 3, 5, and 10 years. They will also refer to the average annual return, which is the averaging of returns over longer periods of time. Any average return of more than 15 percent for at least 5 years is considered exemplary.

Several independent fund-monitoring organizations rank fund performance, most notably Lipper Analytical Services and Morningstar. Figure 3.2 shows you the Morningstar Web site. Results from both are published regularly in *The Wall Street Journal, USA Today,* and *Investor's Business Daily,* as well as other publications. Top performing funds are given four to five stars. For a look at some of these funds, see Figure 3.3. Remember: Before you run out and actually invest in a fund, you need to do a fair amount of research.

Style

You also need to be comfortable with the fund's style, or the methodology of selecting stocks that differentiates one fund from another. The two broadest kinds of stock-choosing styles are growth and value. Growth refers to selecting stocks with ever-rising earnings, while value means buying stocks temporarily out of favor that the manager expects will become popular again. In general, growth stocks shine when the economy is well into an economic recovery, while value stocks tend to outperform others when the economy is in recession or is just starting to emerge from a recession.

THE IMPORTANCE OF BALANCE

The higher the return you earn on your savings and investments, the less money you must set aside for your children's college tuition. Unfortunately, because no guarantees of high returns exist in the investment world without commensurate high risks, you should put together a balanced portfolio of high-, medium-, and low-risk investments to fund your children's college. In general, the longer you have until you need the money, the more risk you can take in search of high returns. As the tuition bills draw closer and closer, you should take less and less risk so that, ideally, all the money you need is sit-

Figure 3.2   Morningstar's Web Site

Source: Chicago-based Morningstar, Inc., is a leading provider of investment information, research, and analysis. For more information about Morningstar, visit <www.morningstar.com> or call 800-735-0700.

ting in your money market account on the day you write your first huge check to the institution of your child's choice.

What does that mean specifically? Figure 3.4 outlines a broad scenario you might follow. When your child is a baby, because you have a lot of time to go, you can take more risk and get the most growth you can. As a result, you can put all your money in stock funds, including a mix of blended, growth and income, growth, and international funds. By the time your child is ready to graduate, you need to be much more conservative. So, you'll invest most of your funds in safer bond and money market funds.

Figure 3.3   Top-Rated Stock Mutual Funds

Fund	Address	Web Site, Phone Number
American Funds Income Fund of America A	American Funds Group 333 S. Hope St. Los Angeles, CA 90071	www.americanfunds.com; 800-421-4120
Clipper	Clipper Funds 9601 Wilshire Blvd. Suite 800 Beverly Hills, CA 90210-5210	www.clipperfund.com 800-776-5033
Fidelity Low-Priced Stock	Fidelity Funds 82 Devonshire St. Boston, MA 02109-3605	www.fidelity.com; 800-526-0084
JP Morgan Mid Cap Value 1	J.P. Morgan Funds 522 Fifth Ave. 11th Floor New York, NY 10036	www.jpmorgan.com; 800-766-7722
Morgan Stanley Special Value A	Morgan Stanley Dean Witter Family of Funds Morgan Stanley Harborside Financial Center, Plaza 2 Jersey City, NJ 07311	www.deanwitter.com; 800-869-6397
Vanguard Capital Opportunity	Vanguard Group Vanguard Financial Center P.O. Box 2600 Valley Forge, PA 10482	www.vg.com; 800-662-7447

Figure 3.4   Allocation of Investments over Time

Age in Years	Allocation
0–3 years	100% Equity funds
4–6	90% Equity funds, 10% Fixed-income funds
7–9	80% Equity funds, 20% Fixed-income funds
10–12	60% Equity funds, 25% Fixed-income funds, 15% Money market funds
13–15	50% Equity funds, 30% Fixed-income funds, 20% Money market funds
16–18	40% Equity funds, 30% Fixed-income funds, 30% Money market funds
19+	25% Equity funds, 40% Fixed-income funds, 35% Money market funds

RESOURCES

Books

Business Week Guide to Mutual Funds, by Jeffrey M. Laderman (McGraw-Hill, P.O. Box 548, Blacklick, OH 43004; 800-634-3961; www.mcgraw-hill.com). Explains the different types of funds in an easy-to-read format. Recommends investment strategies for all ages and explains why some funds may work better than others. Explains how loads and high expenses can ruin investment returns.

But Which Mutual Funds?: How to Pick the Right Ones to Achieve Your Financial Dreams, by Steven T. Goldberg (Kiplinger Washington Editors, 1729 H St., Washington, DC 20006; 800-280-7165; www.kiplinger.com). Walks readers through the basics of mutual funds, helping decide how much they'll need to invest and for how long, and at what level of risk. Includes tables and worksheets.

Getting Started in Mutual Funds, by Alvin D. Hall (John Wiley & Sons, 1 Wiley Dr., Somerset, NJ 08875; 212-850-6000, 800-225-5945; www.wiley.com). Easy-to-follow commonsense guide for successful mutual fund investing. Suitable for novices; provides everything you need to know about mutual funds.

Mutual Funds for Dummies, by Eric Tyson and James C. Collins (Hungry Minds, 10475 Crosspoint Blvd., Indianapolis, IN 46256; 800-762-2974, 800-434-3422; www.hungryminds.com, www.dummies.com). Contains all new market data and analysis about the ever-changing world of mutual funds. Simplifies financial planning and points to the mutual fund investments best suited for you.

Software and Web Sites

CBS MarketWatch: SuperStar Funds. Features articles, news headlines, top fund performers, quotes, and charts, and a research directory. Includes links to fund families and a list of individual funds. <www.cbs.marketwatch.com/funds>

Charles Schwab Mutual Fund Marketplace. Includes information on more than 1,000 no-load mutual funds—all available without transaction fees. <www.schwab-online.com/mutual_funds.htm>

FundAlarm. Updated monthly. Offers information and commentary to help you decide when to sell a mutual fund. Includes data for 1,200 funds and a list of recent fund manager changes. <www.fundalarm.com>

Fund Spot. Links to mutual fund companies and investment sites. Includes a weekly list of links to the best mutual fund articles available on the Web. <www.fundspot.com/main.html>

ICI Mutual Fund Connection. Sponsored by the Investment Company Institute, this site offers information on mutual funds, closed-end funds, and unit investment trusts. Includes a mutual fund fact book, statistics, economic commentary, and retirement planning. Also includes full listing of member mutual funds and companies. <www.ici.org>

INVESTools. A large part of this comprehensive investing Web site is devoted to mutual funds. It offers access to the Morningstar ONDemand service, which allows you to screen thousands of mutual funds by their track records, Morningstar star rating, investment objective, and other measures. <www.investools.com>

InvestorGuide: Mutual Funds. Full explanations about mutual funds and how they work. Multiple links to other mutual fund sites, including Morningstar. <www .investorguide.com>

Quicken.com: Mutual Funds. Features articles, commentary, top funds, Morningstar profiles, a retirement planner, and links to related sites.

Trade Associations

Investment Company Institute (ICI) (1401 H St., N.W., Suite 1200, Washington, DC 20005; 202-326-5800; www.ici.org). The trade group for lobbying and public education on mutual fund issues. Will send you a free copy of the pamphlets, "A Guide to Mutual Funds" and "A Guide to Understanding Mutual Funds." They're available from their Web site, or write to the ICI at Publication Orders, 1401 H St., N.W., Washington, DC 20005-2148.

Mutual Fund Education Alliance (100 N.W. Englewood Rd., Suite 130, Kansas City, MO 64118; 816-454-9422; www.mfea.com). An educational group composed mostly of no-load mutual funds. Some of its members charge low loads, back-end loads, or 12b-1 fees. On their Web site, you'll find "A Guide to Mutual Funds" and "A Guide to Mutual Fund Investing."

National Investment Company Services Association (850 Boylston St., Suite 437, Chestnut Hill, MA 02167; 781-416-7200; www.nicsa.org). Trade group specializing in mutual fund service issues.

CHAPTER 4

Bonds and
Bond Funds

Bonds are one of the key investment vehicles available for saving for college. When you invest in a bond, you are loaning the issuer of that bond your money in return for a fixed rate of interest for a specific amount of time. Normally, you receive interest payments every six months, and when the bond matures, you receive your original principal, no matter how much the price of the bond fluctuated since it was issued.

In other words, bonds allow you to lock in a set rate of income for a long period of time. That can give your financing plan a rock-solid foundation. And, it can add a level of security to your planning that you won't get from stocks. At the same time, bonds are pretty complicated. There are many different types, with differing tax consequences. Before you invest in bonds, it's a good idea to understand the basics of how they work.

HOW BONDS HAVE CHANGED

Once upon a time, bonds were pretty simple. Interest rates remained remarkably stable at about 1 percent or 2 percent, because inflation was low. Few, if any, bonds defaulted, which happens when bond issuers fail to honor their pledge to pay interest or principal on time. Bond prices hardly budged.

But beginning in the mid-1970s, when the Arab oil embargo and soaring government budget deficits ignited inflation, all of that changed. Interest rates jumped from 4 percent to 5 percent in the early 1970s to more than 20 percent in the early 1980s, giving rise to tremendous volatility in the bond market. Even as rates fell during the 1980s and 1990s, bond *yields* remained higher than they had in the 1950s, and bond prices continued to jump around. On top of gyrating rates, the number of bond defaults increased dramatically, as many companies, and a few municipalities, were unable to handle the increased interest payments required from higher yielding bonds.

The bond market was also changed by an explosion in the variety of bond types. For decades, the major issuers of bonds had been the federal government and its agencies, state and local government and related agencies, foreign governments, and blue chip corporations. Beginning in the 1980s, billions of dollars' worth of junk bonds were issued by small and risky growth companies, or by raiders, who used the money to take over major corporations. Another new class of bond, called asset-backed securities, which back the promise to repay the bond with interest from assets such as mortgages, credit cards, and auto loans, was created and took in hundreds of billions of dollars.

Also, the bond market, which had formerly been the preserve of the rich, was democratized by the introduction of something new—the bond mutual fund. Like stock funds, bond funds allowed average people access to the huge and complicated world of investing for a small amount of money and reasonable fees. (More on these funds starting on page 35.)

BOND BASICS

When you buy bonds issued by a government agency or a company, you become a lender to that entity. This is very different from being a stockholder, which you become when you buy a company's stock. As a bondholder, you are entitled to receive the bond's stated interest rate when interest is due and your principal when the bond matures—nothing more. On the other hand, the yield you will receive from the bond will typically be higher than the stock dividend yield, because bondholders must be compensated for reduced purchasing power in the future because of inflation.

Bonds are normally quoted on a price scale of 0 to 200, with 100 being the price at which the bond was issued, or what is known as *par.* Because bonds are sold in minimum denominations of $1,000, a price of 100 means that the bond is trading at $1,000 per bond. If the bond's price rises to 110, your holdings are now worth $1,100.

INVESTING IN BONDS

When you consider investing in bonds, you should understand the one cardinal rule about the movement of bond prices: Bond prices move in the opposite direction from interest rates. It may sound counterintuitive, but it's true. Here's why:

Say you buy a bond yielding 10 percent at a price of 100 (the par price). If interest rates plummeted to 5 percent over several years, your 10 percent would become very valuable, indeed. It would soar—maybe to a dollar value of 150—because people would be willing to pay a big premium to get their hands on a 10 percent bond in an environment where bonds pay only 5 percent. Notice that as interest rates fell, your bond's value rose. Conversely, if interest rates rose to 15 percent instead, your 10 percent would not look very attractive because investors could now get 15 percent. So, the value of your bond would plummet to 50 or so. Figure 4.1 illustrates this point.

Bond prices move in such a seemingly perverse way because bonds are a fixed-rate instrument. The bond's rate is locked in at whatever level it was when the bond was first issued. So, the bond becomes more or less valuable as interest rates fall or rise. And, the longer the maturity of your bond, the more its price will react to the ups and downs of interest rates. A bond that locks in a high interest rate for 20 years is more valuable to an investor if interest rates have fallen than a bond that matures in a year or two.

If you buy individual bonds, purchase those that mature in the year your child starts college. This strategy is known as laddering, and it will ensure a hefty amount of principal when you need it. To carry this strategy even fur-

---

Figure 4.1   Relationship between Bond Prices and Interest Rates

When interest rates move up or down, the price of a bond usually moves in the opposite direction.

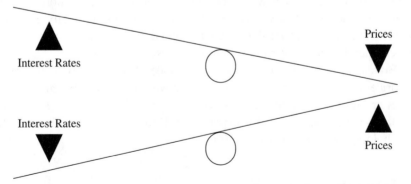

Short-term bonds (bonds that are close to maturity) are usually less affected by changes in interest rates than are long-term bonds.

ther, buy a series of bonds that mature in each of the four years that your child attends college. Make sure that the bonds you buy are not callable (or redeemable) before the date you need the money.

BOND RATINGS

Whether a bond is issued by a corporation or a municipal agency, investors evaluate it by the strength of its financial condition. The better its financial shape, the more confident investors are that their interest and principal will be repaid on time and, therefore, the lower the bond's interest rate will be. One major factor influencing investors' perceptions of the bond is the rating it receives from one of the three big bond-rating agencies: Standard & Poor's, Moody's, and Fitch. Analysts at these agencies, using detailed financial information and judgment based on years of experience, assign a rating to each bond issuer. The ratings scales of the three services appear in Figure 4.2.

Figure 4.2   Bond-Rating Services' Rating Systems

	Rating Service		
Explanation of Bond Rating	*Standard & Poor's*	*Moody's*	*Fitch*
Highest quality	AAA	Aaa	AAA
Very high quality	AA	Aa	AA
High quality	A	A	A
Medium quality	BBB	Baa	BBB
Predominantly speculative	BB	Ba	BB
Speculative, low grade	B	B	B
Poor to default	CCC	Caa	CCC
Highest speculation	CC	Ca	CC
Lowest quality, not paying interest	C	C	C
In default, in arrears, of questionable	D		DDD
value			DD
			D

Source: Reprinted by permission of Standard & Poor's Corporation, Moody's Investors Service, and Fitch Investors Service, Inc.

TYPES OF BONDS

There are many varieties of bonds. But, when it comes to college saving, several types are particularly worth noting. They all have varying benefits, of course, but also different tax implications.

Savings Bonds

Series EE savings bonds, though they do not have the growth potential of growth mutual funds, can provide a solid base for funding at least part of your child's college education. They are a type of Treasury bond, which is a type of security issued by the U.S. government with the backing of the full faith and credit of the government, and the interest they pay is free from state and local taxes.

One advantage to savings bonds is that you don't need a lot of money to invest in them. The minimum cost is just $25, and you can accumulate them through a payroll savings plan. The maximum you can invest per year is $15,000.

Savings bonds formerly had a guaranteed minimum rate, but that policy was discontinued in May of 1995. Yields on savings bonds also are not fixed. Bonds issued on May 1, 1997, or later, earn interest based on 90 percent of the average yields of five-year Treasury securities for the preceding six months. These bonds increase in value every month and interest is compounded semiannually. Therefore, if interest rates rise, savings bond returns will also rise, but if rates fall, yields will drop.

Under some circumstances, the interest is tax-exempt if you use the proceeds for college tuition. Specifically, if your modified adjusted gross income is between $57,600 and $72,600 for individuals, or between $86,400 and $116,400 for married couples filing jointly, at the time you redeem your savings bonds (this amount is adjusted slightly for inflation every year), the interest you earn from the bonds is either fully or partially tax-exempt if you use it for college tuition for either yourself, your spouse, or your children. The bonds must be redeemed in the same calendar year that tuition and fees are paid. Make sure to secure the bonds in the parent's name, not the child's name, if you want to take advantage of this tax break. This version of savings bonds is called an Education Bond, and it can apply to any bond purchased after December 31, 1989.

Another type of savings bond is called an I bond. What's the difference? I bonds are issued at face value, while EE bonds are issued at 50 percent of face value. So a $100 I bond costs $100, while a $100 EE bond costs $50. There's a $30,000 annual purchase limit for I's, versus a $15,000 limit for EEs. And, on I's, interest is calculated based on a combination of a fixed rate of return and a consumer price index inflation rate, adjusted semiannually.

For more information on how savings bonds can be used to finance college education, take a look at the Treasury's savings bond Web site at <www.savingsbonds.gov>. Not only can you purchase savings bonds online, but, as Figure 4.3 shows, you also can do such things as evaluate how the bonds' tax advantages will affect your savings using the site's Tax Advantages calculator.

Figure 4.3　Savings Bond Calculator

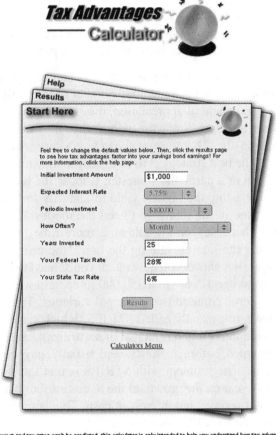

Source: www.savingsbonds.gov.

Zero-Coupon Bonds

Another way to make sure that a certain amount of principal will be available when you must pay tuition bills is to purchase zero-coupon bonds, or zeros, which are deeply discounted from their face value.

A zero-coupon bond gets its name from the fact that the bond is issued with a 0 percent coupon rate. Instead of making regular interest payments, a zero is issued at a deep discount from its face value of 100, or $5,000. The return on a zero comes from the gradual increase in the bond's price from the discount to face value, which it reaches at maturity.

The result:

- You know exactly how much money you will receive when the bond matures.
- You know exactly when you will receive that money.
- You do not have to worry about reinvesting the small amounts of interest regular full-coupon bonds pay.

There aren't many investments that can guarantee you a specific dollar amount of gain in a specified number of years. But, because zeros have a specific schedule of appreciation, they can. If, for example, you're the parent of a newborn, you know the month when his or her first college tuition payment will be due. Therefore, you can buy a zero maturing in 18 years.

The best strategy is to buy them so they mature when your child will start school or a particular semester. Choose the bond selling for the lowest price and boasting the highest yield to maturity for the date you want. The longer the time in the future you need the money, the fewer dollars you must pay now, because you are allowing more time for the zero to compound. The higher the interest rate on the bond, the faster it will appreciate over time. Figure 4.4 shows you how much you'll need to pay for your child, from newborn to age 18, to get a $50,000 lump sum when it's time to go to college.

Zeros come in two principal varieties: Treasuries and municipals. Treasury zeros, usually called STRIPS (which stands for separate trading of registered interest and principal of securities), have no risk of default, cannot be redeemed before maturity, and usually pay higher yields than municipal bonds. The problem with STRIPS is that the IRS expects you to pay taxes every year on the growth of the bonds attributable to interest even though you do not receive that interest in cash. This is more of a nuisance than a reason to avoid STRIPS, however.

If you buy a zero-coupon bond issued by a municipality, you can sidestep the tax problem altogether. Municipal bonds, issued by states, cities, counties, towns, villages, and taxing authorities of many types, have one notable feature: The interest they pay is totally free from federal taxes. In most

Figure 4.4   Zero-Coupon Bonds

Here's roughly how much you would have to invest to end up with $50,000 when your child is ready to start college, at a 3 percent, 5 percent, or 8 percent interest rate:

	Interest Rate: 3%	
Age	*Price Per Bond*	*Investment*
Newborn	$55.36	$29,179.00
1	60.28	30,138.50
2	62.10	31,049.50
3	63.98	31,988.00
4	65.91	32,955.00
5	67.90	33,951.00
6	69.95	34,977.00
7	72.07	36,034.50
8	74.25	37,123.50
9	76.50	38,245.50
10	78.80	39,401.50
11	81.19	40,592.50
12	83.64	41,819.50
13	86.17	43,083.50
14	88.77	44,385.50
15	91.45	45,727.00
16	94.22	47,109.00
17	97.07	48,533.00
18	99.99	49,996.00

	Interest Rate: 5%	
Age	*Price Per Bond*	*Investment*
Newborn	$40.93	$20,466.50
1	43.19	21,595.50
2	45.37	22,688.50
3	47.67	23,837.00
4	50.09	25,044.00
5	52.62	26,311.00
6	55.29	27,644.00
7	58.09	29,043.00

Figure 4.4   Zero-Coupon Bonds (continued)

8	61.03	30,513.00
9	64.12	32,058.50
10	67.36	33,681.00
11	70.77	35,386.50
12	74.36	37,178.00
13	78.12	39,060.00
14	82.08	41,037.50
15	86.23	43,115.00
16	90.60	45,297.50
17	95.18	47,590.00
18	99.99	49,993.00

	Interest Rate: 8%	
Age	*Price Per Bond*	*Investment*
Newborn	$24.20	$12,100.50
1	26.36	13,177.50
2	28.51	14,253.00
3	30.83	15,416.00
4	33.35	16,674.00
5	36.07	18,034.50
6	39.01	19,506.00
7	42.20	21,098.00
8	45.64	22,819.50
9	49.36	24,681.50
10	53.40	26,695.50
11	57.75	28,874.00
12	62.46	31,230.00
13	67.56	33,778.00
14	73.07	36,534.50
15	79.03	39,515.50
16	85.48	42,740.00
17	92.46	46,228.00
18	99.98	49,989.00

cases, bondholders who are also residents of the states issuing the bonds do not have to pay state or local taxes on the interest either. Because the bond's interest is tax-exempt, you never owe taxes on the growth of the bond. However, be careful to select a zero-coupon municipal that cannot be redeemed before maturity. You do not want your well-laid plans upset by an early return of your principal. You also can get a zero-coupon municipal that is insured so you don't have to worry about the issue defaulting.

BOND MUTUAL FUNDS

If the process of choosing individual bonds seems too complicated, bond mutual funds might be right for you. Bond funds buy either taxable government or corporate bonds or tax-free municipal bonds and pass the income on to shareholders. Bond funds offer the advantage of a diversified portfolio and the ease of continuously buying small amounts. But, while bonds within a portfolio might mature, the fund is constantly reinvesting the proceeds of matured or sold bonds back into more bonds. This means you have no guarantee that a bond fund will ever return to the price you purchased it at originally. So, you never know exactly what a fund will be worth until you sell it.

There are hundreds of funds available. Generally, two factors distinguish funds: the kinds of securities they buy and the average maturity of the bonds in their portfolios. In general, the longer the fund's portfolio maturity, the higher its yield, and the higher its risk. Figure 4.5 shows you the different kinds of bond funds that exist, listed according to their level of risk.

There also are two types of funds. Open-end funds continually offer new shares to the public as new money flows into the funds, and always trade at their net asset value, or the worth of their portfolios. But there are also closed-end bond funds, which issue a limited number of shares, trade on the various stock exchanges, and trade at a premium or discount to the value of their portfolios.

Fixed-income securities, or the mutual funds that invest in them, provide much more current income than stocks, but much less growth potential. If interest rates are very high—more than 10 percent—you might consider investing a more significant percentage of your money in bonds to build a college fund. But if bonds yield only 4 to 8 percent, invest a smaller amount of your assets in them while your child is young. By the time your child becomes a teenager, you can put more money in bonds, which have less risk of falling sharply in value than do stocks.

Figure 4.5   Types of Bond Funds

Low-Risk: Bond Type

Description

Government bond funds

Invest only in securities issued by the U.S. government. They are very safe, because there is no risk of default.

Municipal (muni) bond funds

Invest solely in tax-exempt bonds. There are three kinds of muni bond funds: national, which buy bonds from municipalities all over the country; state-specific, which are for residents of states who want to avoid federal and state taxation; and local, which buy bonds only from a locality that levies an income tax.

Short- and intermediate-term bond funds

They buy bonds with maturities of two to ten years. Because they fluctuate in price far less than long-term bonds, their prices remain relatively stable.

Moderate-Risk: Bond Type

Description

Convertible bond funds

They buy convertible debentures and convertible preferred stocks and provide their highest returns in a rising stock market.

High-grade corporate bond funds

They buy top-quality bonds issued by investment-grade corporations, with ratings of BBB or higher. Their yields are higher than government funds of similar maturities, but are still quite safe.

Mortgage-backed securities funds

They invest in mortgage-backed securities issued by certain quasi-governmental agencies, such as Freddie Mac. These securities are guaranteed against default, but not against price fluctuations.

High-Risk: Bond Type

Description

Global bond funds

They purchase bonds issued by governments and corporations from around the world. Currency fluctuations can create large swings in the value of fund shares, so they are risky.

High-yield junk bond funds

They buy bonds of corporations that are below investment grade. The companies backing these bonds are financially weaker than top-rated corporations, so the bonds pay higher yields to compensate investors for the increased risk of default.

Zero-coupon bond funds

They buy portfolios of zero-coupon bonds. Because zero-coupon bonds are the most volatile of all bonds, these funds fluctuate more dramatically than any other kind of bond fund when the bonds are outstanding. These funds mature at a particular year in the future.

RESOURCES

To learn more about bonds, read financial newspapers, such as *The Wall Street Journal* and *Barron's,* as well as personal finance magazines, such as *Money,* which feature articles about bonds regularly. For more in-depth information, consult the following books, newsletters, trade associations, and Web sites.

Books

All About Bonds and Bond Mutual Funds: The Easy Way to Get Started, by Esme Faerber (McGraw-Hill, P.O. Box 548, Blacklick, OH 43003; 800-634-3961; www.mcgraw-hill.com). Simple, comprehensive book about bonds and bond funds. Includes new material on bond mutual funds, tax-free municipal bonds, international bonds, and bond funds.

An Introduction to Bond Markets (The Reuters Financial Training Series) (John Wiley & Sons, 1 Wiley Dr., Somerset, NJ 08875-1272; 212-850-6000; 800-225-5945; www.wiley.com). Examines key debt market players, bond characteristics and valuation, credit agencies, ratings, and regulations.

Getting Started in Bonds, by Sharon Saltzgiver Wright (John Wiley & Sons, 1 Wiley Dr., Somerset, NJ 08875-1272; 212-850-6000; 800-225-5945; www.wiley .com). A guide for the novice bond investor. Covers basic concepts as well as explaining the broader factors that affect bond prices; well organized with solid fundamental bond information.

The Handbook of Fixed-Income Securities, by Frank Fabozzi (McGraw-Hill, P.O. Box 543, Blacklick, OH 43004; 800-634-3961; www.mcgraw-hill.com). A complete guide to the bond market, with great detail on every aspect of the subject.

Savings Bonds: When to Hold, When to Fold, and Everything In-Between, by Daniel J. Pederson (The Savings Bond Informer, P.O. Box 9249, Detroit, MI 48209; 800-927-1901; www.bondhelp.com). Offers a full understanding of savings bonds, tips on the best time to redeem your bonds, details on swapping EE bonds for HH bonds, and tax aspects of bonds.

Trade Associations

Bond Investors Association (P.O. Box 4427, 6175 N.W. 153rd St., Suite 221, Miami Lakes, FL 33014; 305-557-1832; 800-472-2680; www.biainc.com). A nonprofit group that educates the public about bonds and keeps statistics on defaulted bonds.

The Bond Market Association (40 Broad St., 12th Floor, New York, NY 10004-2373; 212-440-9400; www.bondmarkets.com and www.investinginbonds.com). The industry group representing brokerage firms, dealers, and banks that trade government, municipal, and mortgage-backed securities. Offers the following guides, among others, on its Web site, or they can be obtained as pamphlets or small books for a nominal charge: "Investor's Guide to Bond Basics," "Insured Municipal Bonds," "Municipal Bonds," and "Zero-Coupon Municipal Bonds."

Web Sites

The Bond Market Association. Offers a number of publications with extensive information on all types of bonds, both online and as brochures, which can be ordered online. <www.investinginbonds.com>

BondResources. Education about bonds, lots of expert opinion about bonds and the bond market, and a database of more than 20,000 types of bonds. The site also has links to brokers. <www.bondresources.com>

Bureau of Public Debt—Savings Bond Division. The complete source for information about savings bonds. The site explains all the rules affecting savings bonds, including how to buy and redeem them and how to calculate their value. It also features the Savings Bond Wizard, which calculates the current redemption value of your savings bond holdings. <www.savingsbonds.gov/>

CNN/Money. Research individual bond funds on this site and use their Portfolio Forecaster to see how they work with your portfolio. <www.cnnfn.com>

Moodys.com. Moody's maintains more than 68,000 ratings on 16,000 municipal bond issuers, including the general obligations of governments, revenue bonds, and other municipal instruments. <www.moodys.com>

Morningstar.com. This is probably the most comprehensive bond information site available. You can get bond news, bond analysis, descriptions of all the types of bonds available, and their performance. <www.morningstar.com>

CHAPTER 5

Savings Plans

Despite the hefty price of college tuition, today's parents saving for college have some benefits their parents didn't have just a few years ago. That's because a number of plans have recently come on the scene specifically designed to help you save for college. They all offer tax benefits, and a variety of other benefits as well.

Recently, the news has gotten even better. Thanks to the Economic Growth and Tax Relief Reconciliation Act of 2001, various changes in the law have vastly improved many of these plans. So, your choices are better than ever.

Of course, each one has its own upside and downside. Some, for example, might count as income and hurt your chances for getting financial aid. With savings plans, as with any part of the college-financing puzzle, there's always a balancing act.

COVERDELL EDUCATION SAVINGS ACCOUNT

The Coverdell Education Savings Account is a new type of account that was created as part of the Taxpayer Relief Act of 1997. (It used to be called the Education IRA, but the name was changed.) This account allows parents to save up to $2,000 per year per child under the age of 18 to help pay educational expenses, such as tuition, fees, books, and room and board; it applies to not just postsecondary institutions, but both private and religious secondary schools as well. That's a big change from the $500 allowed in the original plan. Consider this: If you invest $2,000 a year and earn an 8 percent return, you'll end up with about $58,000 tax-free in 15 years; if you only put in $500, you'll have about $15,000. You also can use the money for tuition at 771 foreign schools.

Advantages and Limitations

As with any investment, there are pros and cons to the Education Savings Account (ESA). Some of the advantages include:

- You can invest the money however you want. There are no restrictions on your options.
- The principal and all income and capital gains can be withdrawn completely tax-free to pay for educational expenses. Furthermore, no matter how much the account grows, you will not pay taxes on capital gains, as long as you use the money for educational expenses.

The money, however, is held in your child's name. That means your child can spend it all on a trip to Tahiti once he or she reaches the age of majority. In addition to the $2,000 cap on contributions, there are also restrictions. First is the matter of who is eligible. Only couples with joint adjusted gross incomes of $190,000 or less, and singles with incomes of $95,000 or less, qualify for the full Coverdell Education Savings Account. The $2,000 limit is phased out for couples with incomes between $190,000 and $220,000, and for singles with incomes between $95,000 and $110,000, after which no ESA is allowed. Also, if you do not use the assets in an ESA by the time your child is age 30, the account must be liquidated and taxes paid on the proceeds at regular income tax rates, unless you use the proceeds for another child. And, of course, withdrawals are tax-free only if you use the money for education expenses.

SECTION 529 COLLEGE SAVINGS PLANS

Section 529 plans, named after the section of the Internal Revenue Service code that authorized them, are increasingly popular. All 50 states and the District of Columbia are slated to have 529 savings plans in place by the end of 2002. There are two varieties. The older is called a prepaid tuition plan, through which participating state residents contribute a fixed amount of money for tuition to a state school, guaranteeing that the full tuition will be saved by the time a child enters college. The newer version is an investment program, similar to a 401(k) retirement plan.

COLLEGE SAVINGS PLANS

These state-sponsored education savings programs allow parents, relatives, and friends to invest in a fund for your children's college education.

The money can be used to pay for tuition, books, supplies, and room and board. Plus, contributions can be used to pay tuition at any accredited college or university, so you're not restricted to schools in the state sponsoring the plan. You also can invest in a plan not sponsored by the state you live in. And, you can use the money for tuition at 771 foreign schools. Some companies also let employees contribute to 529 plans through automatic payroll deductions. For now, they may be the best savings vehicle around for parents of college-bound children.

Investment Options

As a parent, you set up an account for your child with a brokerage firm or mutual fund company. That means you control the money, so you don't have to worry about whether your offspring will use it for that trip to Tahiti. Most states designate a particular investment company to offer the plan to that state's residents. But you're also perfectly free to invest in plans from other states. More than 40 financial services companies manage or distribute 529 plans, such as American Century, Fidelity, Merrill Lynch, Putnam, Salomon Smith Barney, Strong, TIAA-CREF, T. Rowe Price, and Vanguard.

The firm you choose invests the money in the account for you, but how the investments are made differs by state. In some states, the manager makes all investment decisions for you, while in others you have a choice of investment alternatives. Also, in some states, you choose between aggressive, moderate, or conservative tracks that stay the same throughout; in others, the investment manager will invest aggressively from the time your child is born to age 10 and then invest increasingly conservatively until the money is in a money market fund by the time it is needed for tuition bills. Most states include at least one such age-based option, and include at least one or two other non-age-based choices. The Utah Education Savings Plan, managed by Vanguard for the state of Utah, is one such plan. It often is viewed by analysts as one of the best, thanks in part to its age-based allocations, as well as its low fees and expenses. It offers two age-based options, both of which change their allocations as a child nears the age of 18. One, however, takes a more aggressive approach than the other. Figure 5.1 shows you how the allocation changes over time in both tracks.

While you are restricted in your investment options, it's not as limiting as it used to be. Plans average five options, compared to one a few years ago. And, in some cases, you can invest in certain mutual funds not offered by the plan's managers. For example, State Street Global Advisors, in the state of New Mexico, also allows funds from MFS, Janus, and Invesco. Merrill Lynch, the manager for the state of Maine, allows funds from AIM Capital Management, Franklin Advisors, and MFS. Also, if you think you made a mistake, the new law lets you change the investment track and the plan you chose once a year.

Figure 5.1   Allocation of 529 Plan Investments over Time

Here's how the Utah Educational Savings Plan Trust's two age-based options allocate funds as your child approaches the date of college enrollment:

Option 1

Age	Stocks	Bonds	PTIF*
0–3	95%	5%	
4–6	85%	15%	
7–9	75%	25%	
10–12	65%	35%	
13–15	50%	40%	10%
16+	25%	50%	25%
Enrolled			100%

*Public Treasurer's Investment Fund is invested in short-term money market funds.

Option 2

Age	Stocks	Bonds
0–3	100%	
4–6	100%	
7–9	100%	
10–12	95%	5%
13–15	85%	15%
16+	75%	25%
Enrolled	65%	35%

Source: Utah Educational Savings Plan Fact Book.

Tax Considerations

Here's the really good part: The money in the account grows tax-free. When you withdraw the funds, you owe no taxes at the federal level, and sometimes not at the state level. If your first child decides not to go to college, the assets can be transferred to a second child, or niece or nephew, and still retain the tax benefits. If you withdraw the money for noneducational purposes, however, you will be hit with a 10 percent penalty and have to pay income taxes on the money you take out.

Then there's the matter of tax deductions. Some states, such as Michigan, Missouri, and New York, sponsor plans that give tax deductions to state residents who invest in their plan. For example, New York's College Savings Program lets state residents deduct up to $5,000, or $10,000 for married couples filing jointly, from their state taxes. Colorado, New Mexico, and Illinois go even further: They give unlimited tax deductions to contributions. Experts tend to advise parents to invest in their state plan, if it offers a sizable tax deduction. If you want the deduction, but like the features of another state's option, you also can put money in more than one plan, or put money in your state plan and roll it over into another state's plan.

If you want to take advantage of your state's deduction, you may have to be assertive about it, however. Many plans are sold by brokers representing mutual fund companies, while others are sold directly to customers over toll-free lines and the Internet. Of course, brokers tend to be more eager to sell you the plans they represent. As a result, they may not tell you about an in-state plan that will give you a tax deduction. You should be careful, though, because some plans, such as Colorado's, are sold both by a broker and directly from the state. The difference is that, if you use a broker, you have to pay a fee; go direct, and you won't.

Contribution Limits

Unlike other college savings vehicles, you can contribute a lot of money to a Section 529 plan—a total maximum of as much as $269,000 or more in some states. Also, in some states, the plan matches part of your contribution. Michigan, for example, will match $1 for every $3 you contribute up to $200, if the plan is for a child six years old or younger and the family income is $80,000 or less. Note: If you give $55,000 in one year, you must file a form with the IRS saying that this is, in fact, a gift of $11,000 a year over the next five years for gift tax purposes.

If you have been investing money through a custodial account under UGMA (the Uniform Gifts to Minors Act), you can transfer those assets into a 529 plan. (That's as long as the state plan includes such a provision.) But, because the money in a custodial account is viewed as an irrevocable gift, it can't be shifted to another beneficiary. Furthermore, you will still face the Tahiti problem, because your child will control the money when he or she reaches the age of majority. Also, if you're looking for a tax deduction, it's usually the child who gets the deduction when shifting money from a custodial account into a 529 plan. One warning: To do such a transfer, you would have to liquidate the assets in your custodial account, because 529 plans do not accept securities. But that could mean paying taxes on capital gains. So, it's not a move you'd want to make without consulting an accountant.

State Variations

State plans vary widely in many other ways. Some states require a minimum amount of time before you can make a withdrawal, for example, while others offer only accounts that invest in *certificates of deposit*. And, fees and expenses also may vary widely. For the lowdown on all the plans in existence, see the Appendix. Remember: States are constantly altering their plans, so it's a good idea to double-check before making any final decisions. Another good resource is Savingforcollege.com, an award-winning site all about 529 plans that includes up-to-the-minute information about every plan and lets you compare them. Figure 5.2 shows you what it looks like.

Financial Aid Issues

Financial aid officers consider money in a 529 college savings plan to be part of the parents' assets for federal aid. That will reduce your need by up

---

Figure 5.2   Savingforcollege.com Web Site

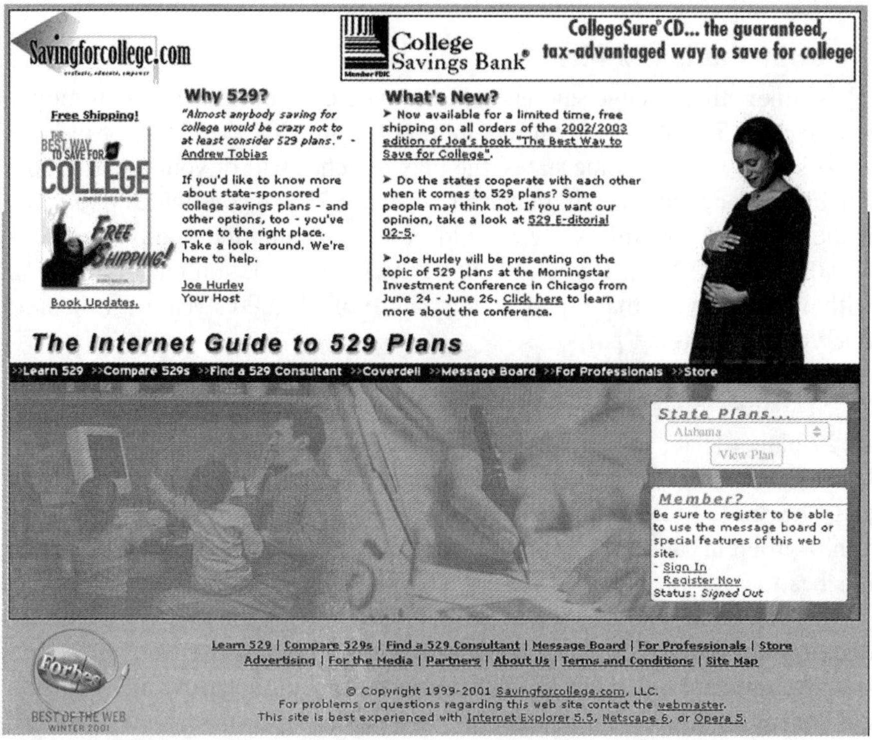

Source: Printed with permission of Savingforcollege.com LLC.

to 5.6 percent of whatever is in the account. But, once the money is withdrawn, untaxed earnings are assessed at the student's income, which can reduce an aid package substantially.

PREPAID TUITION PLANS

Prepaid tuition plans allow you to prepay college tuition bills years in advance. The idea is that you avoid increases in cost caused by inflation by paying tomorrow's tuition at today's prices. So, no matter what the cost of tuition, you are guaranteed to have enough in your account to cover it. For more information about these plans, see Figure 5.3. Or, for a detailed listing of all state prepaid tuition plans and the features of each plan, go to the Web site for the College Savings Plans Network of the National Association of State Treasurers at <www.collegesavings.org>.

Figure 5.3   Prepaid Tuition Programs

ALABAMA

Prepaid Affordable College Tuition Program

Contact: 800-252-7228; www.treasury.state.al.us

Open to nonresidents: Yes

State tax deduction: No

Restrictions: Beneficiary must be in the ninth grade or below at time of purchase; benefits must be used within ten years after college entrance date.

COLORADO

CollegeInvest/Prepaid Tuition Fund

Contact: 888-SAVE-NOW (728-3669) in-state; 800-478-5651 out-of-state; www.collegeinvest.org

Open to nonresidents: Yes

State tax deduction: Yes

Restrictions: Contract must be purchased three years before July 31 of the year you will start using benefits.

FLORIDA

Florida Prepaid College Program

Contact: 800-552-4723; www.floridaprepaidcollege.com

Open to nonresidents: No, beneficiary must be Florida resident.

State tax deduction: No, Florida does not have a state income tax.

Restrictions: Beneficiary must be in the eleventh grade or below when contract is purchased; benefits must be used within ten years after college entrance date.

Figure 5.3   Prepaid Tuition Programs (continued)

ILLINOIS

College Illinois!

Contact: 877-877-3724; www.collegeillinois.com

Open to nonresidents: No, account owner or beneficiary must be Illinois resident for 12 months prior to application.

State tax deduction: No

Restrictions: Benefits must be used within a ten-year period.

KENTUCKY

Kentucky's Affordable Prepaid Tuition

Contact: 888-919-KAPT (5278); www.getKAPT.com

Open to nonresidents: No, beneficiary must be Kentucky resident or intend to attend Kentucky institution.

State tax deduction: No

Restrictions: Must purchase contract at least two years before college enrollment date.

MARYLAND

Maryland Prepaid College Trust

Contact: 888-463-4723; www.collegesavingsmd.org

Open to nonresidents: No, account owner or beneficiary must be Maryland or District of Columbia resident.

State tax deduction: Up to $2,500 per year

Restrictions: Beneficiary must be in the ninth grade or below when contract is purchased; benefits must be used within ten years of high school graduation.

MASSACHUSETTS

Massachusetts U.Plan

Contact: 800-449-6332; www.mefa.org

Open to nonresidents: Yes

State tax deduction: No

Restrictions: Must be used at one of the participating schools.

MICHIGAN

Michigan Education Trust

Contact: 800-638-4543: www/treasury.state.mi.us/MET/metindex.htm

Open to nonresidents: No, beneficiary must be Michigan resident.

State tax deduction: Yes

Restrictions: Beneficiary must be in the eighth grade or below at time of purchase, tenth grade or below at time limited benefits or community college contract is purchased; benefits must be used within nine years after college enrollment date.

Figure 5.3 (continued)

MISSISSIPPI

Mississippi Prepaid Affordable College Tuition Program

Contact: 800-987-4550; www.treasury.state.ms.us

Open to nonresidents: No, account owner or beneficiary must be Mississippi resident.

State tax deduction: Yes

Restrictions: Beneficiary must be 18 years or younger at time of purchase; benefits must be used within ten years after college enrollment date.

NEVADA

Nevada Prepaid Tuition Program

Contact: 888-477-2667; www.nevadatreasurer.com/prepaid

Open to nonresidents: No, account owner or beneficiary must be Nevada resident or account owner must be alumnus of a Nevada college.

State tax deduction: No, Nevada does not have a state income tax.

Restrictions: Beneficiary must be in the ninth grade or below and 18 years or younger at time contract is purchased; benefits must begin no later than ten years after high school graduation or when beneficiary reaches age 18.

NEW MEXICO

The Education Plan's Prepaid Program

Contact: 800-499-7581 in-state, 877-337-5268 out-of-state; www.tepnm.com

Open to nonresidents: No, account owner or beneficiary must be New Mexico resident.

State tax deduction: Yes

Restrictions: Contract must be purchased at least five years before college enrollment date and used within ten years.

PENNSYLVANIA

Pennsylvania Tuition Account Program

Contact: 800-440-4000; www.patap.org

Open to nonresidents: No, account owner or beneficiary must be Pennsylvania resident.

State tax deduction: No

Restrictions: About a one-year wait after contribution is made before it can be withdrawn.

SOUTH CAROLINA

South Carolina Tuition Prepayment Program

Contact: 888-7SC-GRAD; www.scgrad.org

Open to nonresidents: No, beneficiary must be South Carolina resident for minimum of 12 months.

State tax deduction: Yes

Restrictions: Beneficiary must be in the tenth grade or below; benefits must be used by the time beneficiary is 30 years old, plus military service.

Figure 5.3   Prepaid Tuition Programs (continued)

TENNESSEE
Tennessee's BEST Prepaid Tuition Plan
Contact: 888-486-BEST; www.treasury.state.tn.us/best.htm
Open to nonresidents: No, account owner or beneficiary must be Tennessee resident.
State tax deduction: No
Restrictions: Benefits must be used within ten years of high school graduation; beneficiary must not have graduated high school at time of enrollment.

TEXAS
Texas Tomorrow Fund
Contact: 800-445-4723; www.texastomorrowfund.org
Open to nonresidents: No, beneficiary must be Texas resident for 12 months prior to application or nonresident child of Texas resident, who is account owner.
State tax deduction: No, Texas does not have a state income tax.
Restrictions: Benefits must be used within ten years of high school graduation; beneficiary must not have graduated high school at time of enrollment.

VIRGINIA
Virginia Prepaid Education Program
Contact: 888-567-0549; www.virginiacollegesavingsplan.com
Open to nonresidents: No, account owner, beneficiary, or parent of nonresident beneficiary must be Virginia resident.
State tax deduction: Yes
Restrictions: Beneficiary must be in the ninth grade or below at time of purchase; benefits must be used within ten years of high school graduation.

WASHINGTON
Guaranteed Education Tuition of Washington
Contact: 877-GET-TUIT (4388848); www.get.wa.gov
Open to nonresidents: No, beneficiary must be Washington resident.
State tax deduction: No, Washington does not have state income tax.
Restrictions: Units must be used within ten years after college enrollment date or first use of units, whichever is later.

WEST VIRGINIA
West Virginia Prepaid College Plan
Contact: 800-307-4701; www.wvtreasury.com/prepaid.htm
Open to nonresidents: No, account owner, beneficiary, or parent of nonresident beneficiary must be West Virginia resident.
State tax deduction: Yes
Restrictions: Beneficiary must be in ninth grade or below at time of enrollment; benefits must be used within ten years after college enrollment date.

Prepaid tuition plans allow you to choose one of two payment methods—a lump sum or a series of payments. In any case, your child is guaranteed up to four years at a state school when he or she reaches college age, no matter what the tuition at that time. As you might imagine, as a result, the price of college is deeply discounted. The younger your child is when you begin, the steeper the discount will be.

Prepaid tuition plans fall into two categories. In contract plans, you commit to buying a specified amount of tuition over a long-term schedule of payments—for example, in monthly installments or in one lump sum. In tuition unit plans, you buy as many units as you want, whenever you want.

Advantages

These plans can be a good deal if you are fairly sure that your children will want to attend college in your state. Plus, they may be a more reliable—or at least more stable—savings vehicle than the investment plans in a volatile stock market. That's particularly true because prepaid plans guarantee that contributions will match tuition inflation. The Colorado plan, for example, includes the provision that assets will match tuition increases or rise 4 percent, whichever is greater. That security—knowing that no matter what happens to costs, you will be able to cover the cost of tuition at a public school (and sometimes a private one)—is a major attraction for many parents.

Drawbacks

However, prepaid tuition plans have drawbacks. If your child decides not to attend an in-state school, each program has different refund policies. Some states will pay you the equivalent of a current state tuition. Others will give back only your initial investment, plus a low rate of interest (such as 5 percent in Florida). Some will refund only your initial investment without interest and also hit you with a cancellation fee. If your child chooses not to go to school or you have to withdraw from the plan because you can't meet the payment schedule, you may have to pay a substantial penalty—in many cases higher than the 10 percent of earnings that's standard on college savings plans.

There are other drawbacks as well. The IRS has ruled that you must pay federal income tax on the difference between your initial investment and the cost of tuition when your child enrolls. Also, these plans only cover tuition, not other expenses, as the investment plans do. And, they can lower the amount of financial aid a college will award you dollar for dollar—a real problem if you expect to be eligible for substantial need-based aid. Plus, unlike the savings plans, which let you enroll at any time during the year, you have to sign up during certain specified months.

COLLEGESURE CDS

CollegeSure CDs (certificates of deposit) are tied to increases in college costs, as opposed to the *prime rate*. That's the rate used by the Federal Reserve System when it makes loans to banks. The CDs, introduced in 1987 as a way of helping parents pay for increases in college costs, have a variable rate of return based on the cost of college inflation, determined by the expense budgets at colleges in the College Board's Independent College 500 Index. Every July 31, interest rates are reset at 1.5 percent below the annual inflation rate in college costs. The minimum deposit is $1,000; it's insured, up to $100,000, by the Federal Deposit Insurance Corp. Earned interest is taxable. For information, contact the College Savings Bank, 5 Vaughn Dr., Princeton, NJ 08540-6313; 800-888-2723; <www.collegesavings.com>.

UPROMISE AND BABYMINT

There's also new innovation in the area of college savings: two Web sites, Upromise and BabyMint. They use the idea of microinvesting—that is, putting very small amounts of money away over a long period toward a goal—to help you save for college. (For a better look at these Web sites, see Figure 5.4.) You register with these services for free, and when you purchase items from specific participating retailers and manufacturers, you get up to a 20 percent rebate on everyday purchases made through such retailers as Wal-Mart, Crate & Barrel, and the Gap, or when you buy brands such as Huggies, Kellogg's, and Keebler. You also can save with Upromise points when you buy or refinance your home. These rebates can be automatically tracked and deposited in your 529 plan or Coverdell account. Upromise savings can be deposited in plans sponsored by Fidelity and Salomon Smith Barney, while BabyMint rebates can be deposited in any 529 plan or Coverdell account.

HOW GRANDPARENTS CAN HELP

Grandparents can help save for college in a few ways—and they also can reduce their taxable estate by doing so. First, a grandparent can contribute up to $55,000 a year to a 529 savings plan, without having to pay a gift tax. Usually, the IRS taxes a gift of more than $11,000. If that $55,000 were to earn a somewhat conservative return of 6 percent, and the grandparents are in the top 38.6 percent income tax bracket, they would be spared paying $1,274 of income tax, figure accountants at Warren, Gorham & Lamont.

The IRS treats the gift as if it were made over a period of five years. For that reason, grandparents have to file a gift tax return, even if they aren't paying any taxes on the gift, as a way of officially saying that the money is being

Figure 5.4 Upromise and BabyMint Web Sites

Figure 5.4   Upromise and BabyMint Web Sites (continued)

Source: BabyMint.com.

treated as though it were being made in five installments. What if the grand-parent dies before the time is up? If he or she were to die after the second year, then he or she would have been allowed two $11,000 contributions, which leaves the other $33,000 to be included in the estate for tax purposes.

Because the grandparents are the owners, they have control. So, they can change the beneficiary or even withdraw the money if they need it. They will, however, have to pay both income tax and a 10 percent penalty.

Another possibility is for the grandparents to put money into an UTMA (Uniform Transfers to Minors Act) account. There is no limit to the amount that can be used, but they will have to pay a gift tax if they place more than $11,000 in each account. Or, they can just pay part of the tuition themselves. In that case, they won't have to pay a gift tax on any of the money.

INVESTMENTS TO AVOID

Several forms of savings and investments are frequently touted as being ideal for college savings but truly are inappropriate. A few examples include cash value life insurance, annuities, limited partnerships, unit investment trusts, and highly speculative devices, such as options or futures. All of these are designed to achieve other financial goals, such as insuring a life or providing retirement income, and therefore are inefficient and costly ways to pay for your children's college education.

RESOURCES

Books

The Best Way to Save for College: A Complete Guide to 529 Plans, by Joseph F. Hurley (BonaCom Publications, 171 Sully's Trail, Suite 201, Pittsford, NY 14534, 800-400-9113; www.savingforcollege.com). Comprehensive look at 529 plans, including tax rules, planning strategies, and impact on college financial aid. Also includes comparisons to alternatives, such as the ESA, savings bonds, and mutual funds, and describes the features of each state's plan.

Company

College Savings Bank (5 Vaughn Dr., Princeton, NJ 08540-6313; 800-888-2723; www.collegesavings.com). Sells the CollegeSure CD, designed to let parents prepay college education costs, either in a lump sum or in smaller amounts over time. The CD pays a variable rate indexed to the change in college costs.

Web Sites

College Savings Plans Network. This network is designed to administer college savings plans. College savings plans allow participants to save money in a special college savings account on behalf of a designated beneficiary's qualified higher education expenses. Contributions can vary, depending on the individual's savings goals. The plans offer a variable rate of return, although some programs guarantee a minimum rate of return. The College Savings Plans Network is an affiliate to the National Association of State Treasurers. <www.collegesavings.org>

BabyMint.com. When you shop at participating retail partners, you earn money for college on every purchase. BabyMint then tracks your savings and transfers them to your child's college fund. <www.babymint.com>

Fidelity. On Fidelity's College Planning section, you will find a concise explanation of Section 529 college savings plans, along with comparisons of those plans with Custodian, Brokerage, ESA, and prepaid tuition plans. <www.personal100.fidelity.com/planning/college/parents/chartparents.html>

Saving forcollege.com. This site provides a lot of information about Section 529 college savings plans. Includes details of all the state government college financing plans. Just select your state and the information comes up. <www.savingforcollege.com>

Upromise.com. When you buy from participating retailers, you earn money that goes into a 529 account. You also earn money for savings when you finance a home or book a vacation from participating vendors. <www.upromise.com>

CHAPTER 6

Federal and State Grants

E ven if you have saved diligently and amassed a large college fund, it's unlikely you'll have enough to foot the entire bill. That means you will need to apply for financial aid to cover at least part of your children's college costs. Many grants, loans, scholarships, and other programs exist, some offering better opportunities than others.

About one-quarter of all grant money comes from federal and state governments. Figure 6.1 shows you more of a breakdown. It's worth taking a good look at what the government has to offer before you investigate other sources.

When it comes to need-based grants from the federal government, however, you have to be realistic. It's unlikely that you'll be able to qualify for one large enough to meet most of your tuition. There just isn't enough grant money for everyone who wants it. And, if you're a middle-income family, your chances will be even worse: You're not poor enough to qualify for a government grant, not rich enough to pay the full fare without any help. So, your best bet is to put most of your effort into other options.

DIFFERENCES BETWEEN STUDENT AID PACKAGES

Most student aid packages include a mix of options. But, the variety is so wide that it can be quite confusing. So, before you do anything more, you need to understand the difference between each choice:

Figure 6.1   Estimated Student Aid by Source, 2000–2001 (in Billions)

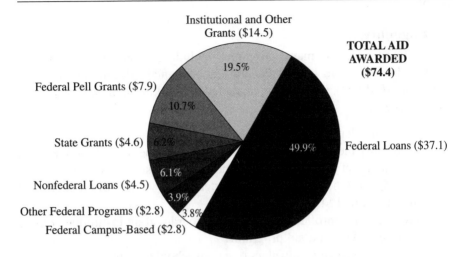

Institutional and Other
Grants ($14.5)

19.5%

TOTAL AID
AWARDED
($74.4)

Federal Pell Grants ($7.9)

10.7%

State Grants ($4.6)   6.2%

49.9%   Federal Loans ($37.1)

6.1%

Nonfederal Loans ($4.5)

3.9%

Other Federal Programs ($2.8)   3.8%

Federal Campus-Based ($2.8)

- Grants are money awarded to you that you don't have to pay back. They're usually awarded on the basis of need and are available from state and federal governments, colleges, and a host of private organizations.
- Scholarships are also awards you don't need to repay, but they're given out on the basis of other factors, such as academic achievement, and may, or may not, also include a need-based component. They are available from state and federal governments, colleges, and private organizations.
- Work-study options let students finance part of their education through their own earnings. They're funded by the federal government, as well as state governments and private companies.
- Loans are money you have to pay back with interest. You get them from the federal government and various private sources.

FEDERAL GRANT PROGRAMS

Unfortunately, the level of federal funding hasn't kept up with the increase in college costs. What's more, the proportion of need-based federal aid has decreased since the mid-1980s. While it accounted for 80 percent of all federal aid ten years ago, it now accounts for around 60 percent. Still, the federal government provides the largest single source of financial aid. So, it's the place to start.

Eligibility

To be eligible for many programs, including a federal Pell grant, a Stafford loan, a PLUS loan, a Federal Supplemental Educational Opportunity Grant (FSEOG), work-study, and a federal Perkins loan, you must meet certain criteria:

- You must demonstrate financial need.
- You must meet attendance requirements. Some schools require that you attend at least six semester hours of courses per semester or the equivalent, others want full-time attendance, while still others need a minimum of 12 hours per semester.
- You must be enrolled in an eligible program at an institution eligible to receive financial aid programs.
- You must have the equivalent of a high school diploma or General Education Development (GED) certificate.
- You must have a valid Social Security number.
- You must sign a statement on the Free Application for Federal Student Aid (FAFSA) form that you will use the money for educational purposes and that you are not in default on a federal student loan.
- In most cases, you must be a U.S. citizen, although some state programs may require that you be a state resident. Federal aid programs also may give money to refugees or people seeking political asylum.

Pell Grants

The Pell grant is the largest need-based grant program. It's given primarily to students in low-income families with less than $35,000 in income. Grants range in size from about $400 to $3,000 per year, with the higher amount reserved for the families earning the least.

To apply, you'll have to fill out a FAFSA form. To determine whether your child is eligible for a Pell grant, calculate your expected family contribution (EFC) using the standard formula reproduced on the application. If your EFC is low enough, your child might receive a grant. To calculate the amount of your Pell grants, subtract your EFC from the maximum authorized Pell grant. The size of the grant will depend somewhat on the cost of tuition at a school, whether your child will be a full-time or part-time student, and whether he or she will attend school for a full academic year.

Your child should apply for a Pell grant even if he or she knows there's no chance of getting one. This is because colleges normally won't consider a student for another grant unless he or she already has been rejected for a Pell. For more information about the Pell grant application process, call 800-4-FED-AID (800-433-3243), or go to <www.ed.gov>.

Federal Supplemental Educational Opportunity Grant (FSEOG) Program

FSEOGs are funded by the federal government and administered through college financial aid offices. The grants to undergraduates range from $100 to $4,000 per year, with larger amounts of money going to lower-income students. Generally, $1,000 to $1,500 is considered a good award. The priority is to those receiving Pell grants. FSEOG funds are limited—schools receive a specific amount of money and dole it out until it's used up—so it is important to submit an application as early as possible.

If you're turned down for an FSEOG, you can obtain an additional un-subsidized federal Stafford or Direct loan—$4,000 for each of your first two years of school and $5,000 for the last two. For more information about the FSEOG, call 800-4-FED-AID, or go to <www.ed.gov>.

STATE AID

States offer a wide array of grants, as well as scholarships, loans, and work-study opportunities. State grants increased by 90 percent over the past decade, according to the College Board. What's more, it's usually easier to win state aid than it is to get money from the federal government. That's because of the way they determine your need. The federal government includes both your adjusted gross income and your assets. States, on the other hand, generally look at just adjusted gross income. And, that, of course, is good news for middle-income families who aren't eligible to receive aid from the federal government.

Students in certain parts of the country also can benefit from a program called the Western Undergraduate Exchange. A number of states, including Alaska, Arizona, Colorado, Hawaii, Idaho, Montana, Nevada, North Dakota, Oregon, South Dakota, Utah, Washington, and Wyoming, allow students to pay a tuition rate of 150 percent of an institution's regular residential tuition rate. But it's tricky. Not all universities participate, and not all departments within a school participate. Check with each school you're considering to find out what their arrangements are.

Eligibility Requirements

Eligibility criteria vary. To be eligible for some grants, your child must meet a certain academic threshold, such as a B average; then your family's financial status is considered. Other grants are made solely on academic accomplishment, no matter what your family's level of need. There are also many kinds of other stipulations. In most cases, you need to have resided in the state for one year, although that may vary even from school to school within a state. You also have to present such things as a driver's license, vehicle registration, voting card, and state tax return.

Generally, you must attend a school in the state. However, a few states have reciprocal arrangements with other states that let you use the money for tuition in those states. But, it's complicated. While Arkansas, Massachusetts, Nebraska, and Ohio, for example, have reciprocity, it depends on the institution whether such arrangements are accepted.

States also vary in the forms you need to fill out. Some require the FAFSA form; others need a supplemental form that is processed by the state's financial aid office.

Need versus Non-Need

Most states provide student grants and scholarships, such as Alaska's Gear-Up scholarship, based on a combination of merit and financial need to legal residents of the state. The Gear-Up grant requires that parents submit recent income tax filings and gives $7,000 a year to full-time students, and $3,500 to part-timers, for up to four years.

The majority of state aid goes to need-based aid, although, recently, there's been a move among some states to increase the amount of non-need-based aid, as you can see from Figure 6.2. Non-need-based state aid has increased 336 percent since the early 1990s, while need-based aid has grown just 88 percent, according to the National Association of State Student Grant and Aid Programs. Also, some states are a lot more generous in the amount of total aid they award. Five states, including California, Illinois, New Jersey, New York, and Pennsylvania, awarded half of all need-based grants in 1999.

State-Administered Federal Programs

Some federally funded programs are administered by the states, including the following:

- State Student Incentive Grants. States decide whether to give these grants, which are partially funded by the federal government, to full-time or part-time students.

Figure 6.2 Proportion of State Aid That Is Need-Based

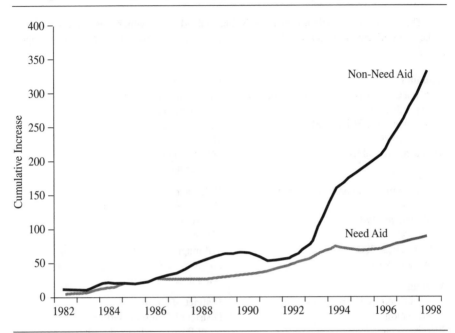

- Robert C. Byrd Honors Scholarship Program. It provides $1,500 for the first year of college to ten students from each Congressional district.
- Paul Douglas Teacher Scholarship Program. States can award a maximum of $5,000 a year for four years to students who graduate in the top 10 percent of their class. The recipient is obligated to teach for two years.

How to Apply

The rules regarding grants and scholarships often change. Your child's high school guidance counselor should know the details of grants available in your state. Or, call your state's office of higher education or state financial aid office. They oversee state aid, serve as central clearinghouses, and should have the most up-to-date information. For contact information, Figure 6.3 lists state financial aid agencies.

Figure 6.3   State Financial Aid Agencies

The following list includes each state's financial aid office, which acts as a central clearinghouse of information, and can direct you to what is available in your state and how to apply for it.

Alabama
Alabama Commission on Higher Education
P.O. Box 302000
Montgomery, AL 36130-2000
334-242-1998
www.ache.state.al/us

Alaska
Alaska Commission on Postsecondary
    Education
3030 Vintage Blvd.
Juneau, AK 99801
907-465-2962, 800-441-2962
www.state.ak.us

Arizona
Arizona Commission on Postsecondary
    Education
2020 N. Central Ave.
Phoenix, AZ 85004
602-229-2591
www.arizonapsa.org

Arkansas
Arkansas Department of Higher Education
114 E. Capitol
Little Rock, AR 72201
501-371-2000, 800-54-STUDY (78839)
www.arkansashighered.com

California
California Student Aid Commission
P.O. Box 416026
Rancho Cordova, CA 95741
916-526-8002
www.csac.ca.gov

Colorado
Colorado Commission on Higher Education
1300 Broadway
Denver, CO 80203
303-866-2723
www.state.co.us

Connecticut
Connecticut Department of Higher
    Education
61 Woodland
Hartford, CT 06105
860-947-1833
www.ctdhe.org

Delaware
Delaware Higher Education
    Commission
820 N. French St.
Wilmington, DE 19801
302-577-3240
www.doe.state.de.us

District of Columbia
District of Columbia Office
    of Postsecondary Education
2100 Martin Luther King Jr. Ave.
Washington, DC 20020
202-727-6436

Florida
Florida Department of Education
Office of Student Financial Assistance
325 W. Gaines St.
Tallahassee, FL 32399
850-487-0649
www.firn.edu

Georgia
Georgia Student Finance Commission
2082 E. Exchange Pl.
Tucker, GA 30084
770-414-3200; 800-776-6878
www.gsfc.org

Hawaii
Hawaii State Postsecondary Education
    Commission
2444 Dole St.
Honolulu, HI 96822

Figure 6.3 (continued)

808-956-8213
www.hern.hawaii.edu

Idaho
Idaho State Board of Education
P.O. Box 83720
Boise, ID 83720
208-334-2270
www.sde.stateid.us

Illinois
Illinois Student Assistance Commission
1755 Lake Cook Rd.
Deerfield, IL 60015
847-948-8500, 800-899-4722
www.isac-online.org

Indiana
Indiana State Student Assistance
    Commission
150 W. Market St.
Indianapolis, IN 46204
317-232-2350
www.in.gov

Iowa
Iowa College Student Aid Commission
200 Tenth St.
Des Moines, IA 50309
515-281-3501, 800-383-4222
www.state.ia.us

Kansas
Kansas Board of Regents
Curtis State Office Building
1000 S.W. Jackson St.
Topeka, KS 66602
785-296-3421
www.kansasregents.org

Kentucky
Kentucky Higher Education Assistance
    Authority
1050 U.S. 127 S.
Frankfort, KY 40601
502-696-7496, 800-928-8926
www.kheaa.com

Louisiana
Louisiana Student Financial Assistance
    Commission
P.O. Box 91202
Baton Rouge, LA 70821
225-922-1012, 800-259-5626
www.osfa.state.la

Maine
Maine Finance Authority
5 Community Dr.
Augusta, ME 04332
207-626-3263, 800-228-3734
www.famemaine.com

Maryland
Maryland Higher Education Commission
16 Frances St.
Annapolis, MD 21401
410-974-2971
www.mhec.state.md.us

Massachusetts
Massachusetts Board of Higher Education
One Ashburton Place
Room 1401
Boston, MA 02108
617-994-6950
www.bhe.mass.edu

Michigan
Michigan Higher Education Assistance
    Authority
Office of Scholarships and Grants
P.O. Box 30462
Lansing, MI 48909
517-373-3394, 888-447-2687
www.michigan.gov

Minnesota
Minnesota Higher Education Services Office
1450 Energy Park Dr.
St. Paul, MN 55108
651-642-0533, 800-657-3866
www.mheso.state.mn.us

Figure 6.3   State Financial Aid Agencies (continued)

Mississippi
Mississippi Office of Student Financial Aid
3825 Ridgewood Rd.
Jackson, MS 39211
601-982-6663, 800-327-2980
www.ihl.state.ms.us

Missouri
Missouri Department of Higher Education
3515 Amazonas Dr.
Jefferson City, MO 65109
573-751-2361, 800-473-5767
www.cbhe.state.mo.us

Montana
Montana University System
2500 Broadway
Helena, MT 59620
406-444-6570
www.montana.edu

Nebraska
Nebraska Coordinating Commission for
   Postsecondary Education
P.O. Box 95005
Lincoln, NE 68509
402-471-2847
www.ccpe.state.us

Nevada
Nevada Office of Financial Aid
University of Nevada-Reno
1664 N. Virginia St.
Reno, NV 89557
775-784-1100
www.unr.edu

New Hampshire
New Hampshire Postsecondary Education
   Commission
2 Industrial Park Dr.
Concord, NH 03301
603-271-2555
www.state.nh.us

New Jersey
New Jersey Higher Education Assistance
   Authority
4 Quakerbridge Plaza
Trenton, NJ 08625
609-588-3226, 800-792-8670
www.hesaa.org

New Mexico
New Mexico Commission on Higher
   Education
1068 Cerrillos Rd.
Santa Fe, NM 87501
505-827-7383, 800-279-9777
www.nmche.org

New York
New York State Higher Education Services
   Corporation
99 Washington Ave.
Albany, NY 12255
518-473-7087, 888-697-4372
www.hesc.com

North Carolina
North Carolina State Education Assistance
   Authority
P.O. Box 13663
Research Triangle Park
Chapel Hill, NC 27709
919-549-8614, 800-700-1775
www.ncscaa.edu

North Dakota
North Dakota Student Financial Assistance
   Program
600 E. Boulevard Ave.
Bismarck, ND 58505
701-328-4114
www.ndus.edu

Ohio
Ohio Student Aid Commission
P.O. Box 182452
Columbus, OH 43218

Figure 6.3   (continued)

614-466-7420, 888-833-1133
www.regents.state.oh.us

Oklahoma
Oklahoma State Regents for Higher
    Education
655 Research Pkwy.
Oklahoma City, OK 73101
405-225-9100
www.okhighered.org

Oregon
Oregon State Scholarship Commission
1500 Valley River Dr.
Eugene, OR 97401
541-687-7400
www.osac.state.or.us

Pennsylvania
Pennsylvania Higher Education Assistance
    Agency
1200 N. Seventh St.
Harrisburg, PA 17102
717-720-2800, 800-654-5988
www.pheaa.org

Rhode Island
Rhode Island Higher Education Assistance
    Authority
560 Jefferson Blvd.
Warwick, RI 02886
401-736-1100, 800-922-9855
www.riheaa.org

South Carolina
South Carolina Higher Education Tuition
    Grants Commission
101 Business Park Blvd.
Columbia, SC 29203
803-896-1120
www.sctuitiongrants.com

South Dakota
South Dakota Board of Regents
306 E. Capitol Ave.
Suite 200

Pierre, SD 57501
605-773-3455
www.ris.sdbor.edu

Tennessee
Tennessee Higher Education Commission
404 James Robertson Pkwy.
Nashville, TN 37243
615-741-3605
www.state.tn.us

Texas
Texas Higher Education Coordinating Board
P.O. Box 12788, Capitol Station
Austin, TX 78711
512-427-6101; 800-242-3062
www.thecb.state.tx.us

Utah
Utah State Board of Regents
355 W. North Temple
Salt Lake City, UT 84180
801-321-7100, 800-418-8757
www.utahsbr.edu

Vermont
Vermont Student Assistance Corporation
Champlain Mill
P.O. Box 2000
Winooski, VT 05404
802-655-9602
www.vsac.org

Virginia
Virginia State Council of Higher Education
James Monroe Building
101 N. Fourteenth St.
Richmond, VA 23219
804-225-2137
www.schev.edu

Washington
Washington State Higher Education
    Coordinating Board
917 Lakeridge Way, S.W.
Olympia, WA 98504

Figure 6.3   State Financial Aid Agencies (continued)

360-753-7800
www.hecb.gov

West Virginia
West Virginia College and University
    System
1018 Kanawha Blvd., E.
Charleston, WV 25301
304-558-2101
www.hepc.wvnet.edu

Wisconsin
Wisconsin Higher Educational Aids Board
131 W. Wilson St.
Madison, WI 53707

608-267-2206
www.heab.state.wi.us

Wyoming
Wyoming Community College
    Commission
2020 Carey Ave.
Cheyenne, WY 82002
307-777-7763
www.commission.wcc.edu

RESOURCES

Books

Discounts and Deals at the Nation's 360 Best Colleges: The Parent Soup Financial Aid and College Guide, by Bruce G. Hammond (Western Publishing Co., P.O. Box 1228, North Platte, NE 69103; 800-951-6700; www.wespub.com). Combines financial aid information with a detailed guide to the nation's best colleges. Reveals which colleges offer the best need-based aid, which give the biggest merit scholarships, and how to qualify for scholarships and discounts.

Don't Miss Out: The Ambitious Student's Guide to Financial Aid, by Anna and Robert Leider (Octameron Press, P.O. Box 2748, Alexandria, VA 22301; 703-836-5480; www.octameron.com). Detailed descriptions of qualifications for financial aid. Also lists many sources of government and private aid. Contains complete tables and worksheets for family contribution under federal methodology.

The Financial Aid Book: The Insider's Guide to Private Scholarships, Grants, and Fellowships, by Student Financial Services (Perpetual Press, P.O. Box 30414, Lansing, MI 48909-7914; 800-444-4226). Lists and details some 3,000 graduate and undergraduate scholarships, grants, fellowships, and loans for study in the United States, and contains listings for study abroad. Helps direct readers to suitable listings for their situation.

The Government Financial Aid Book: The Insider's Guide to State and Federal Government Grants and Loans, by Student Financial Services (Perpetual Press, P.O.

Box 30414, Lansing, MI 48909-7914; 800-444-4226; www.readersndex.com). A variety of federal and state financial aid programs exist to help students pay for college, but, if the proper procedures are not followed when applying for them, applications can be disqualified. This book simplifies the application process by helping the reader understand each program and by providing detailed instructions and tips for completing forms. Internet instructions to access the latest federal aid policies are included.

Loans and Grants from Uncle Sam: Am I Eligible and for How Much? (Octameron Press, P.O. Box 2748, Alexandria, VA 22301; 703-836-5480; www.octameron .com). Describes the major federal loan and grant programs, such as Stafford, Perkins, PLUS, and Direct loans. Details loan limits, interest rates, repayment plans, deferments, and consolidation options. Helps you increase your eligibility and find the best lenders. Worksheets help you assess your eligibility and estimate the size of your award.

Peterson's Insider's Guide to Paying for College: Find Out How to Get More Money for College, by Don M. Betterton (Peterson's Publishing, Princeton Pike Corporate Center, 2000 Lennox Dr., P.O. Box 67005, Lawrenceville, NJ 08648; 800-643-5506; www.petersons.com). Takes each type of student and sets them up with as many financial aid avenues as possible.

Company Specializing in College Financing

The College Board (45 Columbus Ave., New York, NY 10023-6992; 212-713-8000; www.collegeboard.org). Publishes many books on financing college. The three most popular are *College Costs & Financial Aid Handbook; Meeting College Costs: What You Need to Know Before Your Child and Your Money Leave Home;* and the *College Board Scholarship Handbook.* Another book, designed for adult students, is *Financing Your College Degree.*

Web Sites

Federal Student Financial Assistance Program. On this Department of Education Web site, students can apply for financial aid online. They can even electronically sign the application forms on completion. All the worksheets can be downloaded from the Web site. <www.fafsa.ed.gov>

FinAid. A public service site that provides information about college loans, scholarships, and grants. Assists you with financial aid applications, demystifies the paperwork, and provides forms and instructions. Includes calculators to help determine how much money you will need and what your loan payments will be. Has advice on college admissions and jobs. <www.finaid.org>

CHAPTER 7

Scholarships and Private Money

Lf you can't get a grant, you may be able to win a scholarship. It would be awarded to you on the basis of merit and a variety of other factors. Need may, or may not, play a factor.

Thousands of groups, from government agencies and foundations to civic associations, religious organizations, and colleges, offer such scholarships. Some are given by companies to their employees' children, others by the local chamber of commerce. An assortment of trade groups offer scholarships to students wanting to pursue careers in their industry. In fact, according to some estimates, the number of scholarships has tripled over the past five years.

Applying for a scholarship is a very competitive process, however. Scholarship committees have limited funds and many applicants. Identifying the right programs and applying as soon as possible are of vital importance.

DIFFERENT TYPES OF SCHOLARSHIP FUNDS

Scholarship funds tend to have very specific requirements. Depending on the fund, they may be interested in your academic record, specific extracurricular activities, religious or ethnic background, career aspirations, or a combination of any of these factors. They may require recommendations, an original essay, and/or a copy of your transcript. Many scholarships cover only one year, but are renewable.

The broader scholarships are national in scope and give out more money. The National Merit Scholarship Program Awards are a case in point. Sponsored by colleges, universities, and businesses, they awarded $45 million worth of scholarships to high academic achievers in 2001.

National Merit scholarships are also highly competitive. The three winners of The American Legion National High School Oratorical Contest Awards competed against 54 candidates in 2001 to receive $14,000 to $18,000 each. Others, such as the Slovenian Women's Union Scholarship—which gives $1,000 to four full-time freshmen who are, or whose parents are, members or participants of the Slovenian Women's Union of America—have narrower applicant guidelines and offer smaller awards. Figure 7.1 gives you a more extensive look at some of the scholarships available.

WHO OFFERS SCHOLARSHIPS?

Scholarships are available from a slew of sources, including the following:

Employers and Corporations

Hundreds of companies, from Mattel to Alcoa, offer scholarships to employees or their dependents and relatives. Many others don't limit the awards only to the people who work for the company or their relatives. For example, Siemens provides the Siemens Awards for Advanced Placement—24 $3,000 to $8,000 awards—to students who excel in the sciences and math.

Professional Associations and Unions

If your child knows what he or she wants to do after graduation, then it's worth checking out the professional association that matches his or her interests. Many associations give money to students who want to pursue occupations in their fields. The Hawaii Dental Association, for example, gives ten awards of $1,050 each to students interested in dentistry, dental hygiene, or dental laboratory technology, or in working as a dental assistant. The Air Traffic Controllers Association offers no less than three different scholarship programs. Other professional organizations that give scholarships include The Actuarial Education and Research Fund, Women Grocers of America, the American Chemical Society, and the American Electroplaters and Surface Finishers Society.

Many unions also offer scholarships to members' children. For information, contact your union local or get in touch with the union's main headquarters.

Colleges

Most institutions offer several kinds of grants, which may or may not be based on financial need. Many merit scholarships are awarded purely on

---

Figure 7.1   A Sample of Scholarships

This list is meant to provide a feel for the kinds of national scholarships that are available. Keep in mind that there are many more that are locally or state-oriented as well. Also, remember that the specifics change frequently. Check with the fund before applying.

Association of Former Agents of the U.S. Secret Service
Former Agents of the U.S. Secret Service Scholarship
Intended use: For full-time sophomore, junior, senior, master's, or postgraduate study at an accredited 2-year, 4-year, or graduate institution in the United States
Eligibility: Applicant must be U.S. citizen.
Basis for selection: Major/career interest in criminal justice/law enforcement. Applicant must demonstrate financial need, high academic achievement, depth of character, leadership, patriotism, seriousness of purpose, and service orientation.
Amount of award: $1,000–$3,000
Number of awards: 5
Application deadline: May 1
Contact: Scholarship Coordinator, P.O. Box 848, Annandale, VA 22003-0848

BMI Foundation Inc.
BMI Student Composer Awards
Intended use: For undergraduate study at accredited 4-year institution
Eligibility: Applicant must be no older than 25, a U.S. citizen, permanent resident, or an international student from or a citizen of a Western Hemisphere country.
Basis for selection: Competition/talent/interest in music performance/composition, based on composition of classical concert music. Major/career interest in music. Applicant must demonstrate seriousness of purpose.
Amount of award: $500–$5,000
Number of awards: NA
Application deadline: February 12
Contact: Ralph N. Jackson, BMI, 320 W. 57th St., New York, NY 10019;
    <www.bmi.com/bmifoundation/studentcomp.asp>

Boy Scouts of America
National Eagle Scout Scholarship
Intended use: For undergraduate study at accredited 2-year or 4-year institution
Eligibility: Applicant or parent must be member/participant of Boy Scouts of America, Eagle Scouts. Applicant must be male, high school senior. Applicant must be U.S. citizen or permanent resident.
Basis for selection: Applicant must demonstrate financial need, high academic achievement, and leadership.
Amount of award: $3,000–$48,000
Number of awards: NA
Application deadline: February 28
Contact: Boy Scouts of America, 1325 W. Walnut Hill Ln., Irving, TX 75015-2079; 972-580-2032; <www.bsa.scouting.org>

Figure 7.1   (continued)

Broadcast Education Association

Alexander M. Tanger Scholarship

Intended use: For full-time junior, senior, or graduate study at accredited 4-year or graduate institution in the United States

Eligibility: NA

Basis for selection: Major/career interest in radio/television/film; communications; journalism; film/video or computer/information sciences. Applicant must demonstrate high academic achievement, depth of character, and seriousness of purpose.

Amount of award: $2,500

Number of awards: 2

Application deadline: September 15

Contact: Broadcast Education Association, 1771 N St., N.W., Washington, DC 20036-2891; 202-429-5354; <www.beaweb.org>

Coca-Cola Scholars Foundation

Coca-Cola Scholars Program

Intended use: For full-time undergraduate study at accredited 2-year or 4-year institution in the United States

Eligibility: Applicant must be high school senior and U.S. citizen or permanent resident.

Basis for selection: Applicant must demonstrate high academic achievement, depth of character, leadership, seriousness of purpose, and service orientation.

Amount of award: $4,000–$20,000

Number of awards: 250

Application deadline: October 31

Contact: Coca-Cola Scholars Foundation, P.O. Box 442, Atlanta, GA 30301-0442; 800-306-COKE

Congressional Hispanic Caucus Institute

CHCI Scholarship Award

Intended use: For full-time undergraduate or graduate study at accredited 2-year or 4-year institution in the United States

Eligibility: Applicant must be Mexican American, Hispanic American, or Puerto Rican. Must be U.S. citizen or permanent resident.

Basis for selection: Applicant must demonstrate financial need, depth of character, leadership, and service orientation.

Amount of award: $2,000–$5,000

Number of awards: 40

Application deadline: April 1

Contact: Congressional Hispanic Caucus Institute, 504 C St., N.E., Washington, DC 20002; 202-546-2143; <www.chci.org>

Discover Financial Services, Inc. & The American Association of School Administrators

Discover Card Tribute Award Scholarship Program

Intended use: For undergraduate study at accredited vocational, 2-year, or 4-year institution

Eligibility: Applicant must be high school junior. Must be U.S. citizen or permanent resident.

Figure 7.1   A Sample of Scholarships (continued)

Basis for selection: Applicant must demonstrate depth of character, seriousness of purpose, and service orientation.
Amount of award: $2,500–$25,000
Number of awards: 468
Application deadline: January 1
Contact: Discover Card Tribute Awards, AASA, P.O. Box 9338, Arlington, VA 22219; <www.aasa.org/discover.htm>, <www.discovercard.com/tribute.htm>

Karla Scherer Foundation
Karla Scherer Foundation Scholarship
Intended use: For full-time undergraduate, master's, or doctoral study at accredited 4-year or graduate institution in the United States
Eligibility: Applicant must be female.
Basis for selection: Major/career interest in finance/banking, economics, business, international or business/management/administration. Applicant must demonstrate financial need, high seriousness of purpose, and service orientation.
Amount of award: NA
Number of awards: 25
Application deadline: March 1
Contact: The Karla Scherer Foundation, 737 N. Michigan Ave., Suite 2330, Chicago, IL 60611; <www.comnet.org/kscheref>

National Institutes of Health
National Institutes of Health Undergraduate Scholarship Program
Intended use: For full-time undergraduate study at accredited 4-year institution in the United States
Eligibility: Applicant must be U.S. citizen or permanent resident.
Basis for selection: Major/career interest in biology, chemistry, medical specialties/research, or life sciences. Applicant must demonstrate financial need and high academic achievement.
Amount of award: $20,000
Number of awards: NA
Application deadline: March 31
Contact: NIH Office of Loan Repayment and Scholarships, 2 Center Dr., MSC 0230, Bethesda, MD 20892-0230; <www.ugsp.info.nih.gov>

National Merit Scholarship Corporation
Achievement Scholarship Awards
Intended use: For full-time undergraduate study in the United States
Eligibility: Applicant must be African-American. Must be U.S. citizen or permanent resident.
Basis for selection: Applicant must demonstrate high academic achievement and leadership.
Amount of award: $2,500,000—total amount awarded
Application deadline: NA
Contact: National Achievement Scholarship Program, 1560 Sherman Ave, Suite 200, Evanston, IL 60201-4897; <www.nationalmerit.org>

Figure 7.1   (continued)

Merit Scholarship Program Awards
Intended use: For full-time undergraduate study in the United States
Eligibility: Applicant must be high school junior. Must be U.S. citizen or permanent resident.
Basis for selection: Applicant must demonstrate high academic achievement and leadership.
Amount of award: $45,000,000—total amount awarded
Number of awards: 9,600
Application deadline: NA
Contact: National Merit Scholarship Program, 1560 Sherman Ave., Suite 200, Evanston, IL
   60201-4897; <www.nationalmerit.org>

National Urban League
American Chemical Society Minority Scholars Program
Intended use: For full-time undergraduate study at accredited 2-year or 4-year institution in
   the United States
Eligibility: Applicant must be African-American, Mexican American, Hispanic American, or
   Puerto Rican. Must be U.S. citizen or permanent resident.
Basis for selection: Major/career interest in chemistry, biochemistry, or engineering.
   Applicant must demonstrate financial need, high academic achievement, and seriousness
   of purpose.
Amount of award: $2,500
Number of awards: 75
Application deadline: February 15
Contact: National Urban League Scholarship Program, 120 Wall St., New York, NY 10005;
   888-839-0467; <www.nul.org>

Oak Ridge Institute for Science and Education
ORISE Energy Research Undergraduate Laboratory Fellowship
Intended use: For full-time undergraduate study at designated 4-year institution in the United
   States
Eligibility: Applicant must be U.S. citizen or permanent resident.
Basis for selection: Major/career interest in computer information sciences, engineering,
   environmental science, mathematics, general science, or health sciences.
Amount of award: $3,500–$5,600
Number of awards: NA
Application deadline: NA
Contact: Oak Ridge Institute for Science and Education, P.O. Box 117, Oak Ridge, TN
   37831-0117; 865-576-3192; <www.orau.org>

Society of Automotive Engineers
Society of Automotive Engineers (SAE) Engineering Scholarships
Intended use: For full-time freshman study at designated 4-year institution in the United
   States
Eligibility: Applicant must be high school senior. Must be U.S. citizen.
Basis for selection: Major/career interest in engineering. Applicant must demonstrate high
   academic achievement, depth of character, and leadership.

Figure 7.1   A Sample of Scholarships (continued)

Amount of award: Full tuition
Number of awards: 53
Application deadline: December 1
Contact: Society of Automotive Engineers, SAE Educational relations, 400 Commonwealth
    Dr., Warrendale, PA 15096-0001; 724-772-4047; <www.sae.org/students/engschlr.htm>

Women's Sports Foundation
Linda Riddle/SGMA Endowed Scholarship
Intended use: For full-time freshman study at accredited 2-year or 4-year institution
Eligibility: Applicant must be female, high school senior. Must be U.S. citizen or permanent
    resident.
Basis for selection: Major/career interest in athletic training or sports/sports administration.
    Applicant must demonstrate financial need, high academic achievement, and leadership.
Amount of award: $250–$10,000
Number of awards: 466
Application deadline: December 8
Contact: Women's Sports Foundation, Eisenhower Park, Nassau County, NY 11554; 800-
    227-3988; <www.womenssportsfoundation.org>

superlative high school academic achievement and high SAT scores. Some colleges give cash grants, while others offer tuition discounts. Colleges also award grants to athletes, musicians, and others with special skills that the schools particularly are interested in cultivating. The criteria and application procedures vary widely. The money for college aid usually comes from tuition revenues and private donations. Not surprisingly, private schools often provide more in aid than public institutions.

States

More states are awarding money that is not based on need to residents. Some scholarships, like Indiana's Minority Teacher Scholarship Program, are aimed at encouraging students to enter teaching, occupational therapy, and other professions deemed critical or in which there is a shortage of qualified workers. It provides money to African-American and Hispanic state residents enrolled in a teacher certification program, on condition that recipients teach in an accredited elementary or secondary school in Indiana after graduation. Others are more general. For example, the Governor's Scholarship Program in Georgia gives awards to top-performing high school students attending college full-time in Georgia. The scholarship covers tuition, with a maximum of $1,575 per academic year.

Two states, Oregon and Vermont, administer private scholarship funds. Oregon, for example, administers 250 funds, totaling $8.5 million, spanning everything from the Oregon Dungeness Association Scholarship, for dependents of employees in the fishing industry, to the Ford Opportunity Program, for single parents going to college for the first time. It manages the scholarships, takes applications, and decides who gets the money. For more information about state-sponsored scholarships, contact the state agencies listed in Chapter 6.

Minority and Women's Advocacy Groups

Many private and government organizations give scholarships to minorities and women. Some of the most notable include the Bureau of Indian Affairs, which awards scholarships to Native Americans, ranging from $500 to $2,500. The National Urban League also sponsors a number of scholarships. Freddie Mac awards $5,000 per year for the first two years of college to African Americans from low- and moderate-income families in urban communities, and the Gillette/National Urban League Minority Intern Scholarship, a $10,000 award given over two years, is awarded to Alaskan natives, Asian Americans, Mexican Americans, Hispanic Americans, Puerto Ricans, or Native Americans. The Gillette award, like many scholarships aimed at minorities or women, focuses on those interested in certain industries and professions; in this case, it's engineering, banking, manufacturing, and human resources. The Women's Western Golf Foundation Scholarship is for female athletes; the National Association of Women in Construction Scholarship is aimed at encouraging women in construction and construction management.

That's Not All

Those aren't the only groups that award scholarships. Religious groups, as well as organizations interested in helping people with disabilities, are also possibilities. And many civic, federal, and community groups, such as the Knights of Columbus, Rotarians, Elks, and Kiwanis, have their own scholarship funds that they award to local students or sons and daughters of members.

How to Find Scholarships

To locate private grants or scholarships for which your child may be eligible, there are a host of scholarship search software programs. Ask your child's guidance counselor or stop in at the high school career center to see what software they have available. Also, the Internet has many scholarship search information sites. There are a lot of these free sites that offer extensive databases of scholarships. You fill in specifics about your child's background—for example, grade point average and special interests—and the service provides a list of scholarships that match your child's profile. See Figure 7.2 for a look at the Web sites of two such services. You also can consult some of the books listed in the Resources section at the end of this chapter.

Figure 7.2   Online Scholarship Search Services

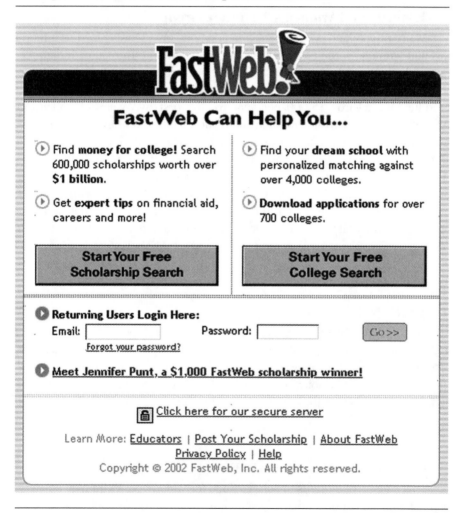

Source: FastWeb.com.

Figure 7.2   Online Scholarship Search Services (continued)

Edit Profile | FAQ | Publications | Search | Contact

A one stop resource for financial aid

Scholarship Resource Network Express contains a database of over **8,000 programs** with a distribution level of over **150,000 awards** for undergraduate and postgraduate students worth a total of more than **$35 million!** This database also includes student loan forgiveness programs for those who have graduated from college and need alternatives for repayment.

Click Here To Begin Your Free Scholarship Search

[Home | Financial Aid | Scholarships | SRN Product | Loan Forgiveness | Loan Consolidation]

Source: SRNExpress.com.

You may want to consult a scholarship search service that will send you, for a fee, a printout of grants and scholarships that your child may be eligible to receive. You must be careful about claims made by many commercial scholarship search services. The Federal Trade Commission has launched Project $cholar$cam to alert consumers about potential fraud in this arena and how to avoid it. Here are the six promises services may make that are warning signs to tell you the service is not legitimate:

1. "Scholarships are guaranteed or your money back." No one can legitimately guarantee you will receive a scholarship or grant, and refunds may be difficult to get.
2. "You can't get this information anywhere else." There are a multitude of books and Web sites with just about every scholarship in existence.
3. "Please give me your credit card number so I can hold this scholarship for you." Because no one can guarantee you will get a scholarship, it is dangerous to give your credit card number over the phone.
4. "We'll do all the work for you." Services may be able to identify potential scholarships, but you or your child has to write the essay and fill out the application to win the money.
5. "This scholarship will cost you some money." Your child will win a grant because of his or her qualifications, not because you pay for it.

6. "You've been selected by a national foundation to receive this scholarship." It is highly unlikely that a foundation has selected your child if he or she did not apply in the first place.

How to Win a Scholarship

It takes a lot of planning and preparation to win an award, so here are some tips to allow you to do as good a job as possible:

- Don't wait until senior year. If your child starts early, you get a good idea of what scholarship programs are looking for and how they evaluate applicants.
- Take a careful inventory of interests and skills. You'll be better prepared to determine which scholarships your child might be eligible for.
- Establish exact criteria before going ahead with the application. To make the best impression, you need to know, for example, whether they're particularly interested in volunteer work your child may have done or the fact that he or she joined a lot of clubs.
- Tailor the application. Once you understand the criteria, shape your responses to meet them.

How Scholarships Affect Financial Aid

Some colleges subtract the value of an outside scholarship from need-based grants they would otherwise have awarded. The award is considered a source of income, and parents must declare all sources of income when applying for loans. How does the school find out? When students win a scholarship, they are required to let the school's financial aid office know. If you're considering keeping it to yourself, don't do it. By law, you have to report outside scholarships if you're applying for aid. Your child could lose all of his or her financial assistance if you fail to notify them.

Policies about how private scholarships affect aid awards vary widely. Sometimes, schools simply take the amount of the scholarship and apply it to the student's grants. Others take half the amount of the scholarship and subtract that from any loans and grants.

Recently, however, some top-of-the-line schools have started changing their policy. Now, scholarships replace student loans and work-study first. Whatever scholarship money is left over will replace a need-based grant.

It's a good idea to ask the financial aid officer what the school's policy is. Even if your school doesn't take this more liberal approach, scholarships may still be worth trying for. That's particularly true if your child won't qualify for much financial aid. At the very least, it can reduce the amount you must borrow.

RESOURCES

Books

The A's and B's of Academic Scholarships, by Anna Leider and Ann Schimke (Octameron Press, P.O. Box 2748, Alexandria, VA 22301; 703-836-5480; www .thinktuition.com). Lists 100,000 merit scholarships as they exist at more than 1,200 U.S. colleges. The reader gets all the information required in a tabular guide, including award name, amount, eligibility criteria, renewal options, and application deadlines. Scholarships range from $300 to $30,000.

The College Blue Book: Scholarships, Fellowships, Grants, and Loans (The Gale Group, 27500 Drake, Farmington Hills, MI 48331-3535; 800-877-4253; www .gale.com). Lists thousands of scholarships, many of which go unclaimed because they are not well-known.

Dan Cassidy's Worldwide Graduate Scholarship Directory, by Dan Cassidy (Career Press, P.O. Box 687, Franklin Lakes, NJ 07417; 201-848-0310; www.careerpress .com). Lists thousands of grants, scholarships, loans, fellowships, and internships from colleges, foundations, corporations, trust funds, associations, and private philanthropists for every major field of study in graduate school.

The Financial Aid Book: The Insider's Guide to Private Scholarships, Grants, and Fellowships, by Student Financial Services (Perpetual Press, P.O. Box 30414, Lansing, MI 48909; 800-444-4226; www.readersndex.com). Lists and details some 3,000 graduate and undergraduate scholarships, grants, fellowships, and loans for study in the United States, and contains listings for study abroad. Helps direct readers to suitable listings for their situation.

Free Money for College, by Laurie Blum (Facts On File, 11 Penn Plaza, 15th Floor, New York, NY 10001; 800-322-8755; www.factsonfile.com). Lists some 1,000 grants and scholarships available for undergraduate study, organized into five sections: state listings, area of study listings, grants for women, grants for ethnic students, and grants for handicapped students.

How to Go to College Almost for Free, by Benjamin R. Kaplan (Waggle Dancer Books, P.O. Box 860, Gleneden Beach, OR 97388; 800-574-2354; www.waggledancer .com). Takes a detailed look at the entire process of applying for scholarships. Includes strategy tips on finding hidden judging criteria to specific guidance on extracurricular activity lists, essays, recommendation letters, and interviews.

The College Money Handbook (Peterson's Publishing, Princeton Pike Corporate Center, 2000 Lennox Dr., P.O. Box 67005, Lawrenceville, NJ 08648; 800-338-3282; www.petersons.com). A huge book detailing all government and private aid programs and explaining how to obtain financial aid at 1,600 undergraduate colleges. Ranks colleges by their net costs for freshman year based on the average financial aid package. Also covers the most frequently asked questions about financial aid.

The Scholarship Advisor: Hundreds of Thousands of Scholarships Worth Over $1 Billion, by Christopher Vuturo (Princeton Review, 2315 Broadway, New York, NY 10024; 800-2-REVIEW [800-273-8439]; www.beta2.review.com). The author qualified for $885,000 in scholarships and shares his wisdom to find and research scholarships, write inquiry letters and essays, fill out applications, and conduct successful interviews.

The Scholarship Book, by Daniel Cassidy (Prentice-Hall Publishing, Order Dept., P.O. Box 11071, Des Moines, IA 50336; 800-282-0693; www.phdirect.com). The ultimate listing of private sector scholarships, loans, and grants assembled by the founder of the National Scholarship Research Service.

Scholarships, Grants & Prizes (Peterson's Publishing, Princeton Pike Corporate Center, 2000 Lennox Dr., P.O. Box 67005, Lawrenceville, NJ 08648; 800-338-3282; www. petersons.com). Extensive listings of scholarships, including a CD-ROM with search capabilities. The listings are broken down into ten categories, including academic field-career goals, civic affiliation, employment experience, impairment, military service, nationality-ethnicity, religious affiliation, state of residence, special talents, and special interests.

Winning Money for College, by Alan Deutschman (Peterson's Publishing, Princeton Pike Corporate Center, 2000 Lennox Dr., P.O. Box 67005, Lawrenceville, NJ 08648; 800-338-3282; www. petersons.com). A complete guide to scholarship money. Describes contests and scholarships for specific professions, from arts to sciences.

Winning Scholarships for College: An Insider's Guide, by Marianne Ragins (Owl Books, Henry Holt and Company, 115 W. 18th St., New York, NY 10011; 212-886-9200; www.henryholt.com). Tells the reader how to track down scholarship money; how to perfect skills in test taking, essay writing, and interviewing; and how to fill out applications.

Web Sites

CollegeClub. A general student site with lots of information and help for students, including a scholarship search engine and a loan finder. <www.collegeclub.com>

FastWeb. This site allows you to conduct a personalized search of potential loans and scholarships you or your child may qualify for. You fill in a detailed form about you or your child, and the site searches its vast database for financing options, with the details about each program. For more information, call 800-327-8932. <www.fastweb.com>

FinAid. A public service site that provides information about college loans, scholarships, and grants. Assists you with financial aid applications, demystifies the paperwork, and provides forms and instructions. Includes calculators to help determine how much money you will need and what loan payments will be. Has advice on college admissions and jobs. <www.finaid.org>

National Scholarship Research Service. The world's largest and oldest private sector scholarship database. Students also can compare available loans and apply on-line for a student loan. <www.fastaid.com>

Project $cholar$cam. The Federal Trade Commission's Web site about commercial scholarship search service scams. <www.ftc.gov/bcp/conline/pubs/scholarship/index.html>

RSP Funding Focus. Reference Service Press (RSP) provides a one-stop information resource for scholarships, fellowships, loans, grants, awards, and internships. The site features a financial aid library, a listing of state financial aid agencies, and a mailing list you can get on that provides a free electronic newsletter filled with the latest information about financial aid programs. You also can contact RSP at 5000 Windplay Dr., Suite 4, Eldorado Hills, CA 95762; 916-939-9620. RSP also publishes 19 books, including *Financial Aid for the Disabled and Their Families* and *High School Senior's Guide to Merit and Other No-Need Funding.* <www.rspfunding.com>

ScholarshipExperts.com. For an annual fee starting at $29.95, you get access to a database of 2 million scholarships. <www.scholarshipexperts.com>

Scholarship Resource Network Express. A search engine and database of private scholarships designed to assist students in identifying sources for undergraduate through postgraduate study. <www.srnexpress.com>

Scholarships.com. Provides a database of 600,000 scholarships, grants, fellowships, and internships. <www.scholarships.com>

CHAPTER 8

Work and the Military

O ne other way to help foot the education bill or reduce costs is for students to work. Through government-subsidized programs that provide work to eligible students, or school-sponsored programs at participating colleges and universities, students can help finance some or all of their tuition. Some of these programs are only for those who can demonstrate financial need, while others are open to anyone.

While participation in some of these work programs can add a year or so to the length of a college education, there are lots of benefits to compensate. Students not only get invaluable real-world experience, but, they also stand a good chance of being hired at the company they're working for after graduation.

Another option is the U.S. Armed Forces. There are many opportunities to get financial help from military programs aimed at enlisted personnel, veterans, and family members. From the Air Force and the Army to the Coast Guard and Navy, scholarships and tuition aid for qualified applicants abound.

FEDERAL WORK-STUDY

The federal work-study program allows your child to work a certain number of hours each week to earn a college grant and at least the minimum wage at on- and off-campus work. It is awarded according to financial need, along with other financial aid, and administered by the college financial aid office, which sets the work schedule. The government subsidizes 50 percent of wages for jobs in the private sector, and 70 percent for on-campus work.

The work-study program encourages community service work and work related to the recipient's course of study. Typically, your child works on campus in the cafeteria, library, or gym. In some cases, your child works for a local business in a field related to his or her course of study. Other jobs are offered at local, state, or federal public agencies, as well as at private nonprofits.

Your child will be paid by the hour. He or she cannot work more hours than the office approves and cannot earn more money than the work-study award. He or she will be paid directly by the school at least once a month. The total award depends on when you apply, your financial need, and the funding level at the school you are attending. Priority is given to those who hand in the paperwork by June 1. The actual hiring and placement occur in August and September.

COOPERATIVE EDUCATION

Co-op education provides a way to combine traditional classroom work with on-the-job experience. Usually, the job is tied to the student's area of interest. Students also often get course credit for the work they do, although they may not earn as much as they would at places where they don't get credit. Unlike work-study programs, co-op programs are not need-based.

The scheduling of work and school is flexible. Some students opt for parallel study and work, in which they attend school in the morning and work in the afternoon, or vice versa. The other option is to alternate semesters—one at work, then one at school. The one downside is that it can take co-op students five years to graduate, instead of four. But, there's a big upside: It's not uncommon for students to find jobs at their co-op employers after they graduate. About 40 percent of students at co-op assignments work at those places after they earn their degree, according to the U.S Department of Education.

The largest employer of co-op students is the federal government. It sponsors thousands of students, who take jobs in the Treasury Department, the Department of Health and Human Services, and many other agencies. But hundreds of private employers also offer co-op education and opportunities. Some examples include Fidelity, Merrill Lynch, and General Motors.

More than 1,000 schools offer co-op opportunities. In some schools, such as Northeastern University, 90 percent of the students are in a co-op program; in others, the participation is much lower. Figure 8.1 provides a partial list of co-op programs.

Figure 8.1   Co-op Programs and Participating Employers

This list includes some of the colleges offering co-op opportunities and the participating employers.

School, Web Address	Employers
American University, www.american.edu	State Dept., Discovery Communications, Sotheby's, the National Institutes of Health, CNN, Fannie Mae
Drexel University, www.drexel.edu	GlaxoSmithKline, Unisys Corp., Merck & Co., Philadelphia Water Department, Lockheed Martin, E.I. duPont de Nemours & Co., Rohm and Haas
Florida Institute of Technology, www.fit.edu	Fort Lauderdale Executive Airport, IBM, U.S. Army Corps of Engineers
Northeastern University, www.neu.edu	Alcatel, American International Group, The Boston Consulting Group, GE Capital, General Motors, PricewaterhouseCoopers
Rochester Institute of Technology, www.rit.edu/co-op-careers	Eastman Kodak, Xerox, IBM, Bausch & Lomb, Lockheed Martin, Pratt & Whitney, Central Intelligence Agency
University of Cincinnati, www.uc.edu	Abercrombie & Fitch, Dow Chemical Co., Elkus/Manfredi Architects, General Electric, Hasbro Toys, Walt Disney Imagineering

To learn more about federal co-op education, contact the employment divisions of federal agencies directly or the Federal Job Information Center in Atlanta, Chicago, Dallas, Philadelphia, San Francisco, or Washington, D.C.

AMERICORPS

The National Community Service Trust Act of 1993 established the Americorps program, through which students can finance some or all of their college education in return for agreeing to perform specified community service. Americorps volunteers receive a living stipend of about $7,500 a year and get the opportunity to accrue educational awards of $4,725 a year, which can be used to pay tuition costs or repay student loans. Applicants must be U.S. citizens who are at least 17 years old and who have graduated from high school. Americorps volunteers typically work in underprivileged areas of American cities and rural districts in four fields: education, public safety, human services, and the environment.

DEFERRED ENROLLMENT

Your child also may be able to apply to college and then put off actually enrolling for a year or two, using that time to work and save money. Find out whether the schools your child is interested in have a regular deferred enrollment policy. In many cases, once your child starts attending college, he or she may be more mature and motivated, thanks to that year or two of work.

THE MILITARY

The U.S. Armed Forces provide a number of avenues for helping pay for college. In some cases, they involve educational programs. In others, they take the form of financial assistance or ways to reduce costs.

Military Academies

Your child's entire college tuition, plus a monthly allowance, will be paid if he or she attends one of the military academies, such as West Point for the U.S. Army, Annapolis for the U.S. Navy, or the Air Force Academy. These are four-year colleges that offer bachelor's degrees. Your child must then serve in that branch of the military for a specified number of years after graduation. To get into these academies, however, your child must be nominated by your congressional representative or senator. So, you may have to do some networking first.

Your child should apply to the academies during his or her junior year in high school. You can't apply en masse, however. Separate applications must be made to each school.

If your child enrolls, then decides it was a mistake, what then? You'll still be ahead of the game. In that case, in the eyes of financial aid officers, your child will become an independent student. The result is, he or she will qualify for the maximum amount of aid, because neither his or her pay as a cadet nor his or her parents' income is counted.

For more information, you can contact the following:

- The Air Force: Director of Admissions, HQ USAFNRRS, U.S. Air Force Academy, 2304 Cadet Dr., Suite 200, Colorado Springs, CO 80840-5025; 719-333-1110
- The Army: Director of Admissions, West Point, 600 Thayer Rd., West Point, NY 10996-1797; 845-938-4041
- The Coast Guard: Director of Admissions, U.S. Coast Guard Academy, 15 Mohegan Ave., New London, CT 06320-4195; 860-444-8501
- The Navy: Candidate Guidance Office, U.S. Naval Academy, 117 Decatur Rd., Annapolis, MD 21402-5018; 410-293-4361

Reserve Officers Training Corps (ROTC)

If your child would rather combine military training with education at a public or private university, he or she can apply to an ROTC program. The U.S. Army and Air Force run their own ROTC programs, while the U.S. Navy and Marines operate a combined program. All ROTC programs offer both two-year and four-year terms. Tuition, fees, and books are paid for; you also get a monthly allowance. (You have to pay income taxes, however, because it's considered income.)

To enroll in the ROTC, your child must be a high school graduate and be physically and academically qualified. Applicants must take the ACT or SAT and also be interviewed. He or she also must be between the ages of 17 and 21 and a U.S. citizen. Some ROTC scholarships are available for students who decide to join in their sophomore or junior year. Once accepted, your child will be required to study ROTC courses during the year and take part in summer sessions. After graduation and at least two years in the reserves, your child must serve at least four years of active duty in the service for which he or she was trained.

ROTC programs also offer various specialty training courses, such as for doctors, nurses, and engineers. These programs can give your child a solid, marketable skill, making it easier to get a job once your child completes his or her military career. For more details, contact a military recruiter or the school's ROTC representative, or contact the sources provided in the Resources section at the end of this chapter.

Veterans Programs

Another option is to join the Armed Forces before you go to college and take advantage of the Montgomery GI Bill when you leave. This bill applies to anyone who entered active duty for the first time after June 30, 1985. It provides financial aid to those who attend school after serving in the military for 36 months. The amount currently is $650 a month. To receive maximum benefits, recipients must serve at least three years on continuous active duty, or two years' active duty and four years in the Selected Reserve or National Guard. The bill covers attendance at not just four-year colleges and universities, but also business, technical, and vocational schools, on-the-job training programs, and, in certain cases, flight training programs.

Active members of the military also can qualify for educational benefits. The government will pay for 75 percent of classes—up to $3,500 a year—taken by people in the Air Force, Army, and Navy. Participants must, however, take classes only during off-duty hours. In addition, there are benefits for members of the military reserves and the National Guard. They can receive $9,400 toward educational costs and $22,000 in pay, in return for six years of part-time duty. Figure 8.2 contains the VA Education Benefits Appli-

Figure 8.2   VA Education Benefits Application

OMB Approved No. 2900-0154
Respondent Burden: 35 Minutes

Department of Veterans Affairs	APPLICATION FOR VA EDUCATION BENEFITS

PART I - APPLICANT

NOTE: PLEASE TYPE OR PRINT CLEARLY IN BLACK INK OR NO. 2 PENCIL.

1. EDUCATION BENEFIT BEING APPLIED FOR:

☐ A. MONTGOMERY GI BILL - ACTIVE DUTY EDUCATIONAL ASSISTANCE PROGRAM (Chapter 30, Title 38 U.S.C.) *(See Part I Instructions)*

☐ B. VEAP/NON-CONTRIBUTORY VEAP (Post-Vietnam Era Educational Assistance Program) (Chapter 32, Title 38 U.S.C.) (Section 903, Public Law 96-342) *(See Part I Instructions)*

☐ C. Montgomery GI Bill - Selected Reserve Educational Assistance Program (Chapter 1606 Title 10 U.S.C.) *(See Part I Instructions)*

☐ D. UNSURE WHICH EDUCATION BENEFIT APPLIES TO ME *(Explain why you think you are eligible in Item 18, Remarks)*

2. NAME OF APPLICANT *(First, Middle Initial, Last)*	3. SEX ☐MALE ☐FEMALE	4. DATE OF BIRTH *(Month, Day, Year)*

5. MAILING ADDRESS *(Number and street or rural route, city or P.O., State and 9 DIGIT ZIP Code)*

6. VA FILE NUMBER OR SOCIAL SECURITY NUMBER	7. TELEPHONE NUMBER *(Including Area Code)*	
	A. DAY ( )	B. EVENING ( )

8. DIRECT DEPOSIT INFORMATION - Please attach a voided personal check, or provide the following information
(Caution: Direct Deposit may not be available for VEAP or Chapter 1606. See Item 8 of Instructions)

A. TYPE OF ACCOUNT *(Check the type of account, if you do not have an account check the box)*
☐ CHECKING   OR   ☐ SAVINGS   ☐ I DO NOT HAVE AN ACCOUNT

B. NAME OF FINANCIAL INSTITUTION	C. ACCOUNT NUMBER (OR ATTACH VOIDED CHECK)	D. ROUTING OR TRANSIT NUMBER (OR ATTACH VOIDED CHECK)

9. PLEASE PROVIDE THE NAME, ADDRESS AND PHONE NUMBER OF SOMEONE WHO WILL ALWAYS KNOW WHERE YOU CAN BE REACHED

10. HAVE YOU PREVIOUSLY APPLIED FOR DEPARTMENT OF VETERANS AFFAIRS BENEFITS? *(If "Yes," list each benefit claimed. See Item 10 of Instructions)*

☐ YES ☐ NO

11. HAVE YOU ALREADY RECEIVED AN INFORMATION PAMPHLET EXPLAINING EDUCATION BENEFITS? *(See Item 11 of Instructions)*

☐ YES ☐ NO

12. PROGRAM OF EDUCATION OR TRAINING

A. SHOW THE NAME AND ADDRESS OF YOUR SCHOOL OR TRAINING ESTABLISHMENT *(If known)*

B. THE DATE YOU STARTED OR WILL START TRAINING *(If known)*

C. IF YOU KNOW YOUR EDUCATION OR CAREER GOAL *(Please specify)*

D. EDUCATION OR TRAINING WILL BE BY:
☐ SCHOOL ATTENDANCE   ☐ APPRENTICESHIP OR ON-THE-JOB TRAINING

☐ CORRESPONDENCE   ☐ VOCATIONAL FLIGHT TRAINING

VA FORM JUL 2000 **22-1990**	EXISTING STOCKS OF VA FORM 22-1990, APR 1999, WILL BE USED.	PAGE 1 OF 3

Figure 8.2   VA Education Benefits Application (continued)

13. ACTIVE DUTY SERVICE INFORMATION

NOTE: If you are on active duty but in a Terminal leave status (on leave continuously between the date that you last performed military duties until the date of your discharge from active duty), check YES in Items 13A and 13B.

A. ARE YOU NOW ON ACTIVE DUTY?

☐ YES ☐ NO

B. ARE YOU NOW ON TERMINAL LEAVE JUST BEFORE DISCHARGE?

☐ YES ☐ NO

C. ARE YOU ATTACHING A COPY OF YOUR DISCHARGE PAPER? *(If "NO," complete Items 13D through 13F and see Instructions for these Items)*

☐ YES ☐ NO

D. DATE ENTERED ACTIVE DUTY	E. DATE SEPARATED FROM ACTIVE DUTY	F. BRANCH OF SERVICE

14. CIVILIAN AND MILITARY EDUCATION
(Complete Item 14A or 14B. Leave both blank if you did not graduate from high school and did not complete the requirements for a certificate)

A. DATE YOU GRADUATED FROM HIGH SCHOOL	B. DATE YOU COMPLETED THE REQUIREMENT FOR A HIGH SCHOOL EQUIVALENCY CERTIFICATE

C. BELOW PLEASE SHOW ALL TRAINING AFTER HIGH SCHOOL, INCLUDING ALL APPRENTICESHIP OR ON-THE-JOB TRAINING *(See Item 14C of Instructions)*

NAME AND LOCATION OF COLLEGE OR OTHER TRAINING PROVIDER *(Include City and State)*	DATES OF TRAINING FROM	DATES OF TRAINING TO	HOURS *(Semester, Quarter, or Clock)*	DEGREE, DIPLOMA, OR CERTIFICATE RECEIVED	MAJOR FIELD OR COURSE OF STUDY

D. WHAT FAA FLIGHT CERTIFICATES DO YOU HOLD?

15. NON-MILITARY OCCUPATION

	PRINCIPAL OCCUPATION	NUMBER OF MONTHS IN THAT OCCUPATION	LICENSE OR RATING
A. BEFORE ENTERING MILITARY SERVICE			
B. AFTER LEAVING MILITARY SERVICE			

PAGE 2 OF 3

Figure 8.2   (continued)

16. ENTITLEMENT TO OTHER TYPES OF GOVERNMENT EDUCATIONAL ASSISTANCE *(See Instructions for Item*

NOTE: If you check "Yes," to any of these questions, provide full details in Item 18, REMARKS.

A. IF YOU ARE ON ACTIVE DUTY OR IN THE SELECTED RESERVE, ARE YOU RECEIVING OR DO YOU EXPECT TO RECEIVE NON-VA EDUCATIONAL BENEFITS (SUCH AS TUITION ASSISTANCE) FROM THE ARMED FORCES OR THE PUBLIC HEALTH SERVICE FOR THE SAME PERIOD WHEN YOU EXPECT TO RECEIVE VA EDUCATIONAL ASSISTANCE?	☐ YES ☐ NO
B. IF YOU ARE PARTICIPATING IN AN ROTC SCHOLARSHIP PROGRAM, DOES THAT PROGRAM PAY FOR YOUR TUITION, FEES, BOOKS AND SUPPLIES UNDER SECTION 2107, TITLE 10 U.S. CODE?	☐ YES ☐ NO
C. IF YOU PARTICIPATED IN, OR ARE CURRENTLY PARTICIPATING IN, AN ROTC SCHOLARSHIP PROGRAM AND RECEIVED OR WILL RECEIVE AN OFFICER'S COMMISSION UPON COMPLETION OF THAT PROGRAM, SHOW THE DATE OF YOUR COMMISSION	Month Day Year
D. IF YOU ARE A FEDERAL GOVERNMENT EMPLOYEE, DO YOU EXPECT TO RECEIVE EDUCATIONAL BENEFITS UNDER THE GOVERNMENT EMPLOYEES' TRAINING ACT FOR THE SAME TIME PERIOD WHEN YOU EXPECT TO RECEIVE VA EDUCATIONAL ASSISTANCE?	☐ YES ☐ NO

17. MARITAL AND DEPENDENCY STATUS *(See Instruction for Item 17)*

NOTE: **ONLY MONTGOMERY GI BILL VETERANS** with military service (or delayed entry) before **January 1, 1977 need** to provide the following information:

A. ARE YOU CURRENTLY MARRIED?	☐ YES ☐ NO
B. DO YOU HAVE ANY CHILDREN WHO ARE:	
(1) UNDER AGE 18? OR	☐ YES ☐ NO
(2) OVER 18 BUT UNDER AGE 23 AND ATTENDING SCHOOL?	☐ YES ☐ NO
(3) OF ANY AGE PERMANENTLY HELPLESS FOR MENTAL OR PHYSICAL REASONS	☐ YES ☐ NO
C. IS EITHER YOUR FATHER OR MOTHER DEPENDENT UPON YOU FOR SUPPORT?	☐ YES ☐ NO

18. REMARKS *(If more space is needed, please attach separate sheet)*

19. CERTIFICATION AND SIGNATURE OF APPLICANT

I CERTIFY THAT all statements in my application are true and complete to the best of my knowledge and belief.

PENALTY: Willfully false statement as to a material fact in a claim for education benefits is a punishable offense and may result in the forfeiture of these or other benefits and in criminal penalties.

19A. SIGNATURE OF APPLICANT (DO NOT PRINT)	19B. DATE SIGNED
SIGN HERE IN INK ▶	

PART II - CERTIFICATION FOR PERSONS ON ACTIVE DUTY

I CERTIFY THAT this individual is a member of the branch of the Armed Forces shown below and has consulted with me regarding his/her education program.

20A. SIGNATURE, TITLE AND BRANCH OF SERVICE OF ARMED FORCES EDUCATION SERVICE OFFICER	20B. DATE SIGNED

PAGE 3 OF 3

Source: Department of Veterans Affairs.

cation. For more information, contact the Regional Veterans Administration Office closest to you. For the address, see Figure 8.3.

Assistance for Dependents

Federal and state governments provide benefits to spouses and children of veterans. They're generally for families of veterans who died while in the service, were prisoners of war, or were missing in action. Federal aid is paid at the rate of $427 a month for up to 45 months. State benefits vary. Some don't include fees and books, for example, or exclude spouses.

Figure 8.3   Regional VA Offices

Eastern Region
(Includes Connecticut, Delaware, Maine, Massachusetts, New Hampshire, New Jersey, New
    York, Ohio, Pennsylvania, Rhode Island, Vermont, West Virginia)
VA Regional Office
P.O. Box 4616
Buffalo, NY 14240-4616
800-827-1000

Southern Region
(Includes Alabama, Arkansas, District of Columbia, Florida, Georgia, Louisiana, Maryland,
    Mississippi, North Carolina, Puerto Rico, South Carolina, Tennessee, Virginia)
VA Regional Office
P.O. Box 54346
Atlanta, GA 30308-0346
800-827-1000

Central Region
(Includes Colorado, Illinois, Indiana, Iowa, Kansas, Kentucky, Michigan, Minnesota,
    Missouri, Montana, Nebraska, North Dakota, South Dakota, Wisconsin, Wyoming)
VA Regional Office
P.O. Box 66830
St. Louis, MO 63103
800-827-1000

Western Region
(Includes Alaska, Arizona, California, Hawaii, Idaho, New Mexico, Nevada, Oklahoma,
    Oregon, Philippines, Texas, Utah, Washington)
VA Regional Office
P.O. Box 8888
Muskogee, OK 74402-8888
800-827-1000

Loan Repayment

If your child enlists in the U.S. Army, he or she may be eligible to receive repayment assistance from its Loan Repayment Program. For a four-year enlistment in a selected skill in the active Army, up to $65,000 in repayment assistance may be available. For an enlistment in the Army Reserve, up to $20,000 may be available. Members of the National Guard also are eligible for loans.

Financial Aid Programs

There also are many scholarships aimed at military personnel, veterans, dependents, and spouses. Some are targeted at specific groups, such as children of prisoners of war or members of a particular infantry division; others are broader. For a sampling of some of these, see Figure 8.4.

Figure 8.4   Military Scholarships

Here's a look at some of the many military financial assistance scholarship programs available.

Air Force Aid Society
Air Force Aid Society Education Grant
Who it's for: Children and spouses of qualified Air Force personnel or veterans
Amount of award: $1,500
Number of awards: 5,000
Contact: Air Force Aid Society, Education Assistance Department, 1745 Jefferson Davis
   Hwy., Suite 202, Arlington, VA 22202; 800-429-9475; <www.afas.org>

Airmen Memorial Foundation
Chief Master Sergeants of the Air Force Scholarship
Who it's for: Children of qualified Air Force, Air National Guard, or Air Force Reserves
   personnel or veterans
Amount of award: $500–$3,000
Number of awards: 35
Contact: Airmen Foundation Scholarships, P.O. Box 50, Temple Hills, MD 20757-0050;
   800-638-0594

Army Emergency Relief
MF James Ursano Scholarship Fund
Who it's for: Children of Army personnel or veterans
Amount of award: $700–$1,800
Number of awards: 1,600
Contact: Army Emergency Relief, 200 Stovall St., Alexandria, VA 22332-0600;

Figure 8.4   Military Scholarships (continued)

Marine Corps Scholarship Foundation
Marine Corps Scholarship
Who it's for: High school seniors who are children of qualified Marine personnel or veterans
Amount of award: $500–$2,500
Number of awards: 1,080
Contact: Marine Corps Scholarship Foundation, P.O. Box 3008, Princeton, NJ 08543-3008;
    609-921-3534; <www.marine-scholars.org>

Navy-Marine Corps Relief Society
Vice Admiral E.P. Travers Scholarship
Who it's for: Active Navy or Marine personnel or children or spouses of active personnel or
    veterans
Amount of award: $2,000
Number of awards: NA
Contact: Navy-Marine Corps Relief Society, 801 N. Randolph St., Suite 1228, Arlington, VA
    22203-1978; 703-696-4960

Navy Supply Corps Foundation
Navy Supply Corps Foundation Scholarship
Who it's for: Children of qualified active Navy personnel or veterans
Amount of award: $1,000–$10,000
Number of awards: NA
Contact: Navy Supply Corps Foundation, Navy Supply Corps School, 1425 Prince Ave.,
    Athens, GA 3006-2205; <www.usncf.com>

Non-Commissioned Officers Association
Non-Commissioned Officers Association Scholarship for Children of Members
Who it's for: Qualified members of the Non-Commissioned Officers Association or their
    children
Amount of award: $900–$1,000
Number of awards: 25
Contact: Non-Commissioned Officers Association, P.O. Box 33610, San Antonio, TX 78265;
    210-653-6161

Society of Daughters of the United States Army
Society of Daughters of United States Army Scholarship Program
Who it's for: Female children or grandchildren of qualified Army active personnel or
    veterans
Amount of award: $1,000
Number of awards: NA
Contact: Society of Daughter of the United States Army, Janet B. Otto, Chairman, 7717
    Rockledge CT, Springfield, VA 22152-3854

Source: *The College Board Scholarship Handbook 2002.* © 2001 by College Entrance Examination Board. Reprinted
with permission. All rights reserved. <www.collegeboard.com>

RESOURCES

Books

America's Top Internships, by Mark Oldman and Samer Hamadeh (Princeton Review, 2315 Broadway, New York, NY 10024; 800-2-REVIEW [738439]; www.beta2.review.com). Includes in-depth, candid reviews of the internship and its daily responsibilities, feedback from actual interns, and advice on how to land the internship of your choice. Also includes more than 20,000 internship opportunities.

Directory of Cooperative Education Programs (Greenwood Publishing, 88 Post Rd., W., Westport, CT 06881; 203-226-3571; www.greenwood.com). Directory of co-op programs.

Earn & Learn: An Introduction to Cooperative Education, by Joseph Re (Octameron Press, P.O. Box 2748, Alexandria, VA 22301; 703-836-5480; www.octameron.com). Describes how cooperative education programs work, allowing you to combine off-campus work with on-campus schooling. Also discusses distance learning in which you attend college via modem or correspondence, so you can earn college credits where you live.

Need a Lift? (American Legion, P.O. Box 1055, Indianapolis, IN 46206; 317-630-1200, 888-453-4466; www.legion.org). The American Legion's annual guide to financial aid for veterans and their families. Send $3 to Need A Lift, P.O. Box 1050, Indianapolis, IN 46206.

Government Agency

Corporation for National Service (1201 New York Ave., N.W., Washington, DC 20525; 1-800-94-ACORPS [226777]; www.cns.gov). The agency that oversees the Americorps program.

Web Sites

Americorps. Official site for the government service program. <www.cns.gov/americorps/index.html>

Multimedia Learning Center. Helps you find the right work-study spot. <www.mmlc.nwu.edu/jobs/>

National Commission for Cooperative Education. The site for this co-op education association has information for students, parents, and employers. <www.co-op.edu>

Veterans Administration. The site has information about VA programs, plus on-line applications. <www.va.gov>

ROTC Information

Air Force ROTC (HQ/RROO, 551 E. Maxwell Blvd., Maxwell Air Force Base, AL 36112-6106; 205-953-2091, 800-522-0033, ext. 2091; www.afoats.af.mil), or see a local recruiter. Offers the following free brochures: "Air Force ROTC and Your Future," "Air Force ROTC: An Opportunity to Succeed," "ROTC Scholarships for Medical and Nursing Students," and "Science and Engineering."

Army ROTC (GoldQUEST Center, P.O. Box 3279, Warminster, PA 18974-0128; National Headquarters at Fort Monroe, VA 23651-5238; 800-USA-ROTC; www .tradoc.army.mil/rotc/index.html), or see a local recruiter. Offers the following explanatory brochures: "Army Nursing," "The Army ROTC Two-Year Program," "The Facts about Army ROTC," "The Path of Leadership: Your Future as an Army Officer," "ROTC Prior Service," and "ROTC Science and Engineering."

Navy and Marine Corps ROTC (250 Dallas St., Naval Air Station, Pensacola, FL 32508-5220; 904-452-4960, 800-NAV-ROTC [800-628-7682]; www.cnet.navy .mil), or see a local recruiter. Will send a free brochure titled "The Navy-Marine Corps ROTC College Scholarships Bulletin."

CHAPTER 9

The Lowdown on Loans

I f the combination of savings, grants, scholarships, and work-study programs falls short of tuition costs, your child can apply for one of the many loans intended to finance college costs. Three main sources of loans exist: the federal or state government; colleges; and commercial enterprises, such as banks or firms that specialize in college loans. The majority of student aid, in fact, comes in the form of loans. More than 60 percent of bachelor of arts recipients graduate with some federal student loan debt, according to the American Council on Education.

Of course, the big downside to loans is that you have to pay them back. Typically, there will be late charges if your payment is late. Worse, if you default, there could be serious consequences for your ability to take out future loans and your credit rating. The bottom line: Taking out a loan to finance college is a serious commitment that will probably take many years to repay, so help your child to shop diligently for the best deal.

There's also a really attractive upside. If you meet the eligibility qualifications, you can deduct a portion of the interest on student loans. That's also true for people who don't itemize deductions on their income tax returns. While loans aren't free, they do come with some nice extras.

GOVERNMENT LOANS

Several types of local and federal government loans exist. For reasonable —and sometimes rock-bottom—interest rates and flexible repayment schedules, it's hard to beat them. Some are aimed at families with a very low income, while others are targeted at middle-class parents or are not need-based at all. In fact, according to the American Council on Education, 44.3 percent of students from families with incomes of $100,000 or more graduated with a student loan in 1999–2000, compared to 8.2 percent in 1992–1993.

Federal Perkins Loans

Federal Perkins loans, named after former Kentucky Representative Carl Perkins, used to be called National Direct Student Loans, and charge a low-interest rate of 5 percent. They are designed for undergraduate and graduate students with exceptional need—meaning that their families earn $30,000 or less annually. Exceptional need is determined by the school's financial aid officer. Students usually can borrow up to $4,000 for each year of undergraduate study—depending on when they apply, their financial need, and the funding level at the school—up to a maximum of $15,000. Graduate students usually can borrow up to $5,000 a year, with total debt—including loans for undergraduate study—of no more than $30,000.

The college or university granting Perkins loans acts as the lender, using money provided by the federal government. The loans are made through a school's financial aid office. The school either will pay the student directly or apply the loan to school charges. Students receive the loan in at least two payments during the academic year. When it's time to start repaying, your child will be responsible for monthly payments; the size will depend on how much has been borrowed and how long the repayment period will be.

Aside from the low interest rate, Perkins loans have a few other extremely attractive features. If your child is attending school at least half time, there is a grace period of nine months after graduating, leaving school, or dropping below half-time status before he or she must begin repayment. Also, there is as long as ten years to repay the loan, which reduces the monthly payment considerably from shorter-term student loan programs. (Periods of deferment and forbearance, however, do not count as part of this ten-year period.) In addition, certain professions, such as teachers in underprivileged areas, nurses, medical technicians, and law-enforcement officers, can cancel either all or part of their loan repayments.

Stafford Loans

Once known as Guaranteed Student Loans, Stafford loans were renamed for former Vermont Senator Robert Stafford. They are available to all students, without regard to financial status, and are made directly to students, as part of a financial-aid package. Stafford loans come in two versions, which differ mostly according to where the money comes from. If you receive a Federal Family Education Loan (FFEL), the funds come from a bank, credit union, or other participating lender, with the government guaranteeing the loan. That means it will pay if the student defaults. If, on the other hand, you receive a Federal Direct Student Loan (FDSL), the money comes directly from the federal government. How is it decided which one a student will get? If the school participates in the FDSL program, you get that one. If not, you get a government-guaranteed loan from a participating lender.

Limits. The two types of Stafford loans are very similar, and the amount you're allowed to borrow each year is the same. Currently, first-year students enrolled in a program of study that is at least a full academic year can borrow up to $2,625. For those who have completed their first year of study and the remainder of their program is at least one full academic year, a total of $3,500 can be borrowed. Students can borrow up to $5,500 if they have completed two years of study and the remainder of their program is at least one full academic year. Independent undergraduate students or dependent students whose parents can't get a loan from Parent Loans to Undergraduate Students (PLUS, discussed later in this chapter) can borrow up to $6,625, if they're first-year students, and $7,500, if they've completed their first year of study and have at least one full academic year to go. For those who have completed two years of study with at least one year to go, the limit is raised to $10,500.

Your child is not guaranteed to get the maximum, because you can't borrow more than the cost of attendance, minus both the amount of any Pell Grant you're eligible for and other financial aid received. Otherwise, all undergraduate loans (for dependent students) combined cannot exceed $23,000, and the maximum total for independent undergraduates is $46,000. Graduate students who are still dependents can assume loans for up to $18,500 a year, up to a maximum of $138,500, which includes any money borrowed as an undergraduate. For independent graduate students, the maximum rises to $18,500 per year with a lifetime cap of $138,500, including undergraduate loans. For students attending school part-time, lower lending limits are imposed.

Interest rate. Once a year, on June 30, the interest rate on Stafford loans is fixed at 3.1 percent more than the yield on a 91-day Treasury bill. By law, however, the rate cannot rise above 8.5 percent. If your child demonstrates financial need, the government will pay the interest on the loan while your child attends school, as well as for a six-month grace period after graduation. If borrowing is not based on need, an unsubsidized Stafford loan accrues interest while your child attends school, though he or she does not have to begin repaying the loan until after graduation. The minimum annual repayment amount on a Stafford loan is $600, and your child can repay the loan in five to ten years.

Subsidies. Both types of loans may be subsidized or unsubsidized. With subsidized loans, the government pays the interest during the entire time a student is attending college, six months after graduation, and any time during which the student takes a deferral. Only students who demonstrate need can qualify, however. If students don't qualify for the subsidized loan, they get the unsubsidized variety. In that case, interest starts accruing as soon as they take out the loan. No matter what, your child will have a six-month grace period before making payments. It is important that your child applies as soon as he or she is accepted by a school, because the application procedure and processing can take several months. But, as Figure 9.1 shows, the amount of unsubsidized Stafford loans made available over the past ten years has been growing at a much larger rate than the subsidized variety.

Fees. Lenders of subsidized Stafford funds often charge a 5 percent loan origination fee as well as an insurance fee of up to 3 percent, which are deducted from the loan proceeds. For unsubsidized Stafford loans, the combined origination and insurance fee may total 6.5 percent. Not all lenders charge the same fees, however; it pays to shop around.

Parent Loans to Undergraduate Students (PLUS)

PLUS loans are made to parents and, as a result, are not considered to be part of a financial aid package. Like the Stafford loan, they come in two vari-

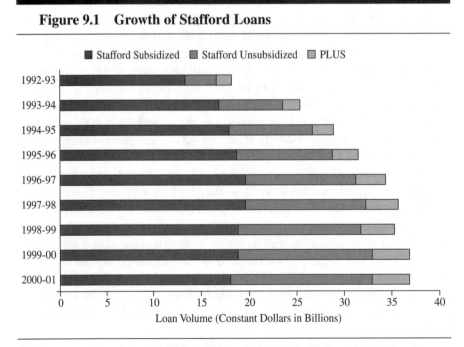

Figure 9.1   Growth of Stafford Loans

■ Stafford Subsidized   ■ Stafford Unsubsidized   □ PLUS

Loan Volume (Constant Dollars in Billions)

Source: "Figure 4. Growth of Stafford and PLUS Loan Volume, 1992–1993 to 2000–2001." *Trends in Student Aid 2001:* 9.
© 2001 by College Entrance Examination Board. Reprinted with permission. All rights reserved. <www.collegeboard.com>

eties: the Direct Loan Program, through which parents borrow directly from the government, and the FFEL Program, through which parents take out a loan from a private lender. In either case, they allow parents to borrow an unlimited amount to finance college. PLUS loans and other financial aid, however, cannot exceed the student's cost of attending school. If your child's cost of attendance is $15,000 and he or she is eligible for $10,000 in financial aid, parents can borrow $5,000. The interest rate of PLUS loans is set at 3.1 percent more than the one-year Treasury bill rate and is adjusted annually in June. It also cannot exceed 9 percent. Repayment of these loans must begin within 60 days of receiving the loan proceeds, and the loans can be repaid in five to ten years.

The loan money will be sent directly to the school, although no one payment can exceed half the loan amount. The school will then apply the money to tuition, fees, and room and board. If there's any money left, it must be applied to education expenses.

To be eligible to receive a PLUS loan, parents generally have to pass a credit check. You can't be turned down for having no credit history, but you can be denied for having a bad one. Even if you fail, however, you may still be able to get a loan if it is endorsed by a creditworthy friend, relative, or associate, who promises to back the loan in case of a default. In addition, parents and students must meet other general eligibility requirements for federal student aid.

State Loan Programs

In addition to federal aid, many states offer their own loan programs. Usually, these programs are designed for state residents; however, in some cases, even out-of-state students can qualify. The terms, interest rates, repayment schedules, and amounts of loans vary widely from state to state. A number of states offer special incentive programs to train teachers, doctors, nurses, and other professionals in short supply. Maine, for example, offers the Educators for Maine Forgiveness Loan, for students who become teachers, librarians, or guidance counselors. Students receive up to $3,000 a year, for a total of $12,000 for four years. For every year they teach, they get a forgiveness for one year of their loan. Other states offer programs aimed at veterans or those enlisted in the state's National Guard.

COLLEGE LOANS

Most colleges, seeking to fill the gaps created by limited federal and state programs, offer their own loan programs. Rules vary widely, as some loans are designed for parents, others for students, and still others for both parents and students. Interest rates—usually tied to some index of Treasury securities—also range from very low to quite high, and repayment terms can be strict or lenient. Ask a school's financial aid officer about specific programs, preferably when your child applies to the school, but certainly once he or she is accepted.

COMMERCIAL LOANS

In addition to the loans made by banks through government programs and as personal loans based on creditworthiness, several commercial lenders specialize in college lending. These programs allow your child to repay the principal on a loan after he or she has graduated, though he or she must pay interest while still in school. Following are some of the major players in this market.

College Board

The College Board's CollegeCredit program offers the ExtraCredit Loan to cover the full cost of your child's education. The minimum loan is $2,000. The loan's rate floats at 4½ percentage points over the 91-day Treasury bill rate, adjusted quarterly. There is a 3 percent loan fee, and your child has 15 years to repay. Another loan that is part of the CollegeCredit program is called the ExtraTime Loan, which is designed to pay for a single year of education expenses. It has similar features to the ExtraCredit Loan, except that you have the option of monthly payments of interest only while a student is enrolled, or monthly payments of principal and interest after the education is complete. For more information on these loans, call the College Board's College Answer Service line at 800-831-5626, or go to <www.collegeboard.com>.

ConSern Loans for Education

ConSern Loans for Education lend up to $25,000 each year per child at the 30- or 90-day commercial paper rate plus 4.6 percentage points, adjusted monthly. ConSern charges a 4½ percent origination fee and allows your child to repay a loan over a period of 15 years. These loans are designed for employees of companies that have adopted the ConSern program. For more information on how to qualify, call ConSern at 800-767-5626; for a company to join this program, call 800-207-9416, ext. 1415.

The Education Resources Institute (TERI)

A nonprofit group, known as TERI, offers loans based on creditworthiness, not income limitations or needs. Loans are guaranteed and administered by TERI, and the funds come from participating lending banks. TERI lends a minimum of $2,000 up to the cost of education, minus financial aid, per year per child, at the prime rate plus 1½ to 2 percentage points, adjusted monthly with no cap. That's a lower rate than those offered by traditional banks. Their loans do not require collateral, but they do charge a guarantee fee of between 5 and 10 percent of the loan amount. Your child can repay over a period as long as 25 years. TERI also offers the Professional Education Plan (PEP) for graduate students. While loans are made to parents or to students, students generally need someone to co-sign. For more information, call TERI at 800-255-8374, or go to <www.teri.org>.

Key Education Resources

One of the country's largest education lenders, Key Education Resources provides federal and private financing options, payment plans, and counseling from prep school through graduate school. Besides the traditional federal Stafford loans and PLUS loans, Key offers private supplemental loans, such as the Key Alternative Loan, which allows undergraduates enrolled full-time to share the cost of their education. Key also offers the AchieverLoan to parents, with three different ways to finance college or prep school tuition. This loan charges 4½ percentage points over the 91-day Treasury bill rate, adjusted quarterly. Fees range from 3 percent to 5 percent of the loan amount, depending on the repayment method. The Key CareerLoan is designed for adult students attending college part-time. Key also offers the Monthly Payment Plan, an interest-free budget plan administered through the school that allows families to make equal monthly payments to meet annual expenses. Key also offers several programs tailored to graduate students in specific fields of study, such as law, business, medicine, and dentistry. For more information, call Key at 800-KEY-LEND (800-539-5363), or go to <www.keybank.com/educate.htm>.

Nellie Mae

Formerly known as the New England Education Loan Marketing Association, Nellie Mae offers the EXCEL and SHARE programs for undergraduate or graduate study, in addition to making Stafford and PLUS loans. They're given regardless of financial need, as long as you're deemed creditworthy. That means you have had no major credit problems for two years and your debt payments are not greater than 40 percent of your gross monthly income.

Nellie Mae will lend from $2,000 up to the cost of education, minus the amount of other financial aid received by the student. One-year renewable loans charge the prime rate, plus ½ percent for the first year and plus 1 percent in subsequent years, and are adjusted monthly. You can repay both principal and interest on the loan or interest only for up to four years while the student is still enrolled in school. These loans charge a guarantee fee of 7 percent. Your child can repay the loan over as many as 20 years. Nellie Mae also offers a loan consolidation program, allowing you to consolidate several student loans into one manageable payment. For more information, call 800-634-9308, or visit the Nellie Mae Web site at <www.nelliemae.org>.

Sallie Mae

Sallie Mae, which makes a secondary market in student loans and helps students consolidate their existing loans, buys and services federally insured educational loans made by lenders. Sallie Mae has introduced several programs to reward borrowers who make on-time payments on their Stafford loans by reducing their interest rates. Great Rewards enables Stafford loan borrowers who make their first 48 scheduled monthly payments on time to receive an interest rate reduction of two full percentage points for the remaining term of the loan. SMART REWARDS is a similar program for SMART LOAN (consolidation) borrowers who make their first 48 scheduled payments on time. They are rewarded with an interest rate reduction of one full percentage point for the remaining repayment term. The Great Returns Program helps heavily indebted Stafford borrowers who make their first 24 scheduled payments on time to receive an account credit equivalent to federal origination fees of up to 3 percent (less $250). The SMART LOAN program (800-448-3533) helps students consolidate their loans into one loan on advantageous terms.

Another Sallie Mae program is called Direct Repay, which allows you to repay your student loans through an automatic debit on your checking or savings account and earns you a quarter-point interest rate reduction on your loan as long as you make payments through the plan. For more details on these programs, call the Sallie Mae Service Center at 800-524-9100 or the College Answer Service at 888-888-3460. You also can get more details on these programs at Sallie Mae's Web site at <www.salliemae.com>.

WHERE TO FIND LENDERS

You can ask your state's higher education office for lenders that make specific types of loans. See Chapter 3 for the list of state financial aid agencies. Your school also undoubtedly will provide a list of recommended lenders deemed reliable and trustworthy, and who offer competitive rates. But the lenders also may offer other services, such as flexible payment options, budgeting calculators, and debt counseling. So, it's worth taking the time to find out exactly what they offer.

You also can use the Web to find loans. There are many sites you can use to look for lenders, as well as figure out what your loan payments might be. For example, with eStudentLoan (www.estudentloan.com), students or parents can compare student loans and apply online. Ultimately, the site will provide a list of lenders based on your state, intended college or university, and other factors. For a look at their home page, see Figure 9.2. By using the Internet Student Loans Company site (www.istudentloan.com/loan.htm),

Figure 9.2   eStudentLoan Web Site

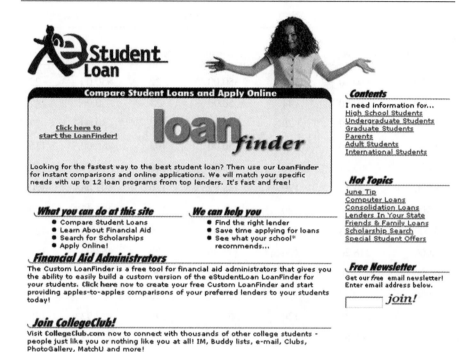

Source: eStudentLoan.

you can apply for a private loan online, as well as a federal undergraduate Stafford loan or a federal PLUS loan.

REPAYMENT

If your child takes out a loan, repayment requires a major commitment after graduation. Make sure he or she understands what's involved as soon as possible. For an idea of what the obligation might involve, look at Figure 9.3, which gives you an estimate of how much it would take to pay back a Stafford loan of various amounts at different time periods and interest rates.

TAX DEDUCTIONS AND CREDITS

There are a variety of tax deductions and tax credits available to help you to finance your child's education, and get the most out of whatever loans you take out. (Tax deductions, of course, are used to reduce your taxable income,

Figure 9.3   Repayment Schedule for Stafford Loans

| Balance at | 5% | | 6% | | 7% | |
Repayment	Payment	Month	Payment	Month	Payment	Month
$ 1,000	$50.00	21	$50.00	22	$50.00	22
2,000	50.00	44	50.00	23	50.00	47
3,000	50.00	70	50.00	72	50.00	77
4,000	50.00	98	50.00	103	50.00	115
6,000	63.64	120	66.41	120	72.80	120
8,000	84.85	120	88.82	120	97.06	120
10,000	106.07	120	111.02	120	121.33	120
20,000	212.13	120	222.04	120	242.66	120
30,000	318.20	120	333.06	120	363.98	120
40,000	424.26	120	555.10	120	485.31	120
50,000	530.33	120	555.10	120	606.64	120
60,000	636.39	120	666.12	120	727.97	120
100,000	1,060.66	120	1,110.21	120	1,121.28	120

Source: © 2002 Sallie Mae Inc. Courtesy of Sallie Mae.

while tax credits are applied to your federal income tax and reduce the amount you owe in taxes.) They do have income limits, however, so make sure you qualify.

HOPE Scholarship Tax Credit

HOPE, which stands for Helping Outstanding Pupils Educationally, is an annual tax credit that covers 100 percent of the first $1,000 in payments for tuition and fees, 50 percent of the second $1,000, and that can be taken in the first two years of school. The maximum is $1,500 a year. The credit does not cover room and board or other expenses.

You're eligible for the credit if you're a married couple filing jointly with an adjusted gross income of $80,000 a year, or if you're an individual, $40,000 a year. The credit you can take decreases until you reach $100,000 for couples or $50,000 for singles. At that point, you can't take the credit at all. Students also must take at least half the full-time load for their major for a minimum of one academic period. Starting in 2002, the limits will be indexed for inflation, although the amount of the credit will not be.

Students also are ineligible if they have a felony conviction arising from possessing or distributing a controlled substance. But, there's also a big plus: If you have two or more children in the first two years of school at the same time, you can take more than one tax credit in the same year.

Lifetime Learning Tax Credit

The Lifetime Learning Tax Credit provides tax credits for students in their third year of college and after, including graduate school or adult education classes. There's also no limit on the number of years this credit can be used. Starting in 2002, the credit equals 20 percent of the first $10,000 a year in tuition and fees. The same income limits that apply to the HOPE Scholarship are also true for the Lifetime Credit. Beginning in 2002, the limits will be indexed for inflation, although the amount of the credit will not be.

You only can take one credit per taxpayer, however, while you're allowed a HOPE Scholarship for more than one tuition. But, you can double dip: You're allowed to take a Lifetime Credit and multiple HOPE Scholarships at the same time.

Tax Deductions

If you make too much to qualify for a HOPE Scholarship or Lifetime Learning Credit, you may be eligible for a tax deduction. Starting in 2002, parents who meet the income restrictions can write off up to $3,000 of higher education expenses; in 2004 and 2005, the amount increases to $4,000. That's true even if you don't itemize when you file your taxes. The limits are an adjusted gross income of less than $130,000 for married couples filing jointly, or $65,000 for individuals. In 2004 and 2005, there's a $2,000 deduction for joint filers making less than $160,000, or singles making $80,000.

You can get a tax deduction for interest paid on student loans. Again, you're eligible even if you don't itemize deductions. The maximum deduction is $2,500 a year, as long as your adjusted gross income is less than $100,000 for joint filers, with a partial deduction if it's less than $130,000, or $50,000 for singles, with a partial deduction if it's no more than $65,000. (These limits will be adjusted to increases in inflation.) Better yet, if you qualify, you can take a $2,500 deduction for both a PLUS loan and a Stafford loan.

There's one caveat, however: Parents cannot take a deduction if they're repaying a loan that their child is responsible for. That's because, to be eligible for the deduction, you have to be the one legally responsible for the loan and you can't be a dependent.

RESOURCES

Books

The College Blue Book: Scholarships, Fellowships, Grants, and Loans (The Gale Group, 25700 Drake, Farmington Hills, MI 48331-3535; 800-877-4253; www .macmillan.com). Lists thousands of loans, fellowships, and scholarships.

Funding a College Education: Finding the Right School for Your Child and the Right Fit for Your Budget, by Alice Drum and Richard Kneedler (Harvard Business School Publishing, 300 N. Beacon St., 4th Floor, Watertown, MA 02472; 800-988-0886; www.hbsp.harvard.edu). Targeted to parents, this book explains how to negotiate the maze of available education choices and financial aid options. Provides worksheets to help assess family resources and explain the different types of colleges with the different types of aid, loans, and scholarships.

The Government Financial Aid Book: The Insider's Guide to State and Federal Government Grants and Loans, by Student Financial Services (Perpetual Press, P.O. Box 30414, Lansing, MI 48909-7914; 800-444-4226; www.readersndex.com). A variety of federal and state financial aid programs exist to help students pay for college, but if the proper procedures are not followed when applying for them, the application can be disqualified. This book simplifies the application process by helping the reader to understand each program, and by providing detailed instructions and tips for completing forms. Internet instructions to access the latest federal aid policies are included.

Loans and Grants from Uncle Sam: Am I Eligible and for How Much? (Octameron Press, P.O. Box 2748, Alexandria, VA 22301; 703-836-5480; www.octameron .com). Describes the major federal loan and grant programs, such as Stafford, Perkins, and PLUS loans. Details loan limits, interest rates, repayment plans, deferments, and consolidation options. Helps you increase your eligibility and find the best lenders. Worksheets help you assess your eligibility and estimate the size of your award.

Take Control of Your Student Loan Debt, by Robin Leonard and Shae Irving (Nolo.com, 950 Parker St., Berkeley, CA 94710; 800-992-6656; www.nolo.com). Presents simple, effective ways for you to get out of student loan debt. Explains repayment options, how to postpone repayment, how to avoid or get out of default, how to handle collection efforts, and when to choose bankruptcy.

Companies Specializing in College Financing

The College Board (45 Columbus Ave., New York, NY 10023-6992; 212-713-8000; www.collegeboard.org). Publishes many books on financing college. The three most popular are *College Costs & Financial Aid Handbook; Meeting College Costs: What You Need to Know before Your Child and Your Money Leave Home;* and the *College Board Scholarship Handbook.* Another book, designed for adult students, is *Financing Your College Degree.* Also sponsors a loan program called CollegeCredit (call 703-707-8999 for more information). The Board's College Scholarship Service also administers the CSS/Financial Aid PROFILE program, used by many colleges to help determine a student's need for financial aid.

ConSern (205 Van Buren St., Suite 200, Herndon, VA 20170; 703-709-5626; www.consern.com). Sponsors the ConSern Loans for Education program, through which about 5,000 employers offer education loans to their employees at advantageous rates. Loan proceeds can be used for either undergraduate or graduate study.

The Education Resources Institute (330 Stuart St., Suite 500, Boston, MA 02116-9123; 781-426-0681, 800-255-8374; www.teri.org). A nonprofit group known as TERI. Offers loans based on creditworthiness, not income limitations or needs. Loans are guaranteed and administered by TERI, and the funds come from participating lending banks. Will send the following free brochures describing these loan programs: "Taxing Matters: College Aid, Tax Policy & Equal Opportunity," "The Next Step: Student Aid for Student Success," "Do Grants Matter? Student Grant Aid & College Affordability," "The Tuition Puzzle: Putting the Pieces Together," and "Student Loan Debt: Problems & Prospect."

Key Education Resources (745 Atlantic Ave., Suite 300, Boston, MA 02111-2735; 617-348-0010, 800-KEY-LEND [800-539-5363]; www.keybank.com/educate.htm). Key is one of America's largest education lenders. They provide federal and private financing options, payment plans, and counseling from prep school through graduate school.

Nellie Mae (Nellie Mae Inc., 50 Braintree Hill Office Park, Suite 300, Braintree, MA 02184; 800-634-9308, 781-849-1325; www.nelliemae.com). Formerly known as the New England Education Loan Marketing Association, Nellie Mae offers the EXCEL and SHARE student loan programs for undergraduate or graduate study, and a loan consolidation program. Nellie Mae offers two free brochures explaining the college financing process, including "Get Ready for College," which is designed for parents with children in elementary or junior high school, and "Steps to Success," which is aimed at those with high-school-age children.

USA Group Funds (P.O. Box 7039, Indianapolis, IN 46207-7039, 30 S. Meridian St., Indianapolis, IN 46204-3503; 317-849-6510, 800-LOAN-USA [800-562-6872]; www.usagroup.com). Does not lend directly to students but guarantees education loans made by lending institutions. Will send a free copy of its "Education Loan Guide," which describes federal loan programs, such as the Stafford and PLUS programs. USA Group offers a loan consolidation service with no fee, allowing borrowers to consolidate several student loans into one and extending the repayment terms. On their Web site, they offer "In Your Interest: A Common-Sense Guide to Repayment Strategies for Federal Education Loans," which explains different repayment strategies, such as ten-year level repayment, long-term level repayment, graduated repayment, income-sensitive repayment, and income-contingent repayment, as well as how loan consolidation works. The USA Group's Web site offers calculators to help you figure how much different repayment plans will cost you.

Sallie Mae (formerly the Student Loan Marketing Association) (11600 Sallie Mae Dr., Reston, VA 20193; 703-810-3000; www.salliemae.com). Makes a secondary market in student loans and helps students consolidate their existing loans. For information on these programs or other college financing questions, call Sallie Mae's College Answer Line at 800-239-4269.

Government Agencies

United States Department of Education (Federal Student Aid Program, 400 Maryland Ave., S.W., Washington, DC 20202; 800-433-3243; www.ed.gov). Oversees all federal aid programs. Will send brochures titled "Looking for Student Aid," "Funding Your Education," and "The Student Guide: Financial Aid from the U.S. Department of Education," which explains Pell grants, FSEOGs, college work-study programs, Perkins loans, Stafford loans, and PLUS and SLS loans. For information on the Education Department's direct loan origination and consolidation program, call the Federal Direct Student Loan Origination Center at 800-557-7392 or 800-557-7394. If you already have an existing loan and have a question about it, you can call the Direct Loan Servicing Center at 800-848-0979.

Web Sites

CollegeClub. A general student site with lots of information and help for students, including a scholarship search engine and a loan finder. <www.collegeclub.com>

College Express. This site presents information on hundreds of private colleges and universities. It also has an extensive section on the financial aid process, including the best ways to apply for federal and college-based aid, and how to negotiate a lower tuition cost from the school. <www.collegexpress.com>

Embark.com. This site offers an admission service to colleges, graduate schools, business schools, and law schools. It also offers online degrees and certificates. Helps prepare for standardized tests and offers student loans, credit cards, and online banking for students. <www.embark.com>

eStudent Loan. Students or parents can compare student loans and apply online. The site first asks you to select the type of student that you or your child is; for example, an undergraduate or a graduate student. The site then will give you a list of lenders based on your state, intended college or university, and other factors. <www.estudentloan.com>

FinAid. A public service site that provides information about college loans, scholarships, and grants. Assists you with financial aid applications, demystifies the paperwork, and provides forms and instructions. Includes calculators to help determine how much money you will need and what loan payments will be. Has advice on college admissions and jobs. <www.finaid.org>

Internet Student Loans Company. On this site, you can learn about the various types of student loans available. You also can apply for a private loan online, and the site claims that they will have the loan approved or otherwise in five minutes. You also can apply online for a federal undergraduate Stafford loan or a federal PLUS loan. <http://istudentloan.com/loan.htm>

Internal Revenue Service. The IRS site includes examples of how tax credits can help you. <www.irs.ustreas.gov>

Key Education Resources. This Web site for one of the country's largest education lenders features KeyScape, a software program that allows you to calculate your estimated family contribution and project a typical budget for repaying loans once you have graduated, among other features. You also can apply for a loan online. <www.keybank.com/educate.htm>

RSP Funding Focus. Reference Service Press provides a one-stop information resource for scholarships, fellowships, loans, grants, awards, and internships. The site features a financial aid library, a listing of state financial aid agencies, and a mailing list you can get on that provides a free electronic newsletter filled with the latest information about financial aid programs. You also can contact RSP at 5000 Windplay Dr., Suite 4, Eldorado Hills, CA 95762; 916-939-9620. RSP also publishes 19 books, including *Financial Aid for the Disabled and Families* and *High School Senior's Guide to Merit and Other No-Need Funding.* <www.rspfunding.com>

Studentmarket.com. This site offers a good student loan education section; you can apply online for prequalification and an information kit. You also can apply online for a student Discover, American Express, or CapitalOne credit card. The site has a number of offers for students for long distance telephone rates, software, computers, clothing, and jobs. <www.studentmarket.com>

CHAPTER 10

Applying for
Financial Aid

The process of applying for financial aid can be daunting. You must fill out several confusing forms and provide a detailed profile of your financial situation to colleges, federal agencies, banks, and other lenders. And, you must do so in as timely a manner as possible.

To receive financial aid, a student must prove his or her family needs the money. To determine how much is needed, a standard needs analysis examines what the parents can afford to pay and what the student can contribute. Financial aid is designed to supplement, not replace, a family's contribution to college costs. Therefore, lenders expect a family to pay as much as possible. The amount the family is expected to pay is called the Expected Family Contribution (EFC). Basically, the amount of financial aid you qualify for should equal the cost of college minus your EFC.

Don't assume you make too much money for your child to qualify for financial aid. And, don't assume you can't afford to send him or her to a top school, even an Ivy League school. Why? At a more expensive private school, your EFC will pay a smaller portion of college costs than at a less expensive public school. Thus, the financial aid office may award you a heftier aid package to make up the difference. Plus, that private college will probably have a bigger endowment. Sometimes, families actually get more aid money from well-endowed, costly private institutions than from public schools.

Understanding what goes into the financial aid process—and increasing your child's chances of winning any—involves understanding a number of areas: the types of aid and the criteria used to determine need, financial planning steps to take well before you apply, what to do once your child gets an awards letter, and, of course, how to fill out the form. (That last part will be covered in the next chapter.)

FEDERAL AID

Schools determine whether your child is eligible to receive federal aid based on your responses on a form called the Free Application for Federal Student Aid (FAFSA). For a peek at it, skip ahead to Figure 11.6 in the next chapter. The school probably also will need it when determining whether to give other aid, such as state aid, as well.

In fact, even if you're positive your child won't be eligible for federal aid, you still should fill out the form. Before most schools can consider providing their own loans or other grants, they will require that you complete the FAFSA and that your child has been denied federal or state aid. So, if you don't hand in the form, he or she might lose out on potential aid from additional sources.

How to Get the Form

You can get the FAFSA form any number of ways. If you want to do it the old-fashioned way, and send in a paper copy, you can get one in English or Spanish from your local library or high school. Or, write to the Federal Student Aid Information Center, P.O. Box 84, Washington, DC 20044. Another option is to apply on the Web using FAFSA On the Web, at <www.fafsa.ed.gov>. You complete the form online and submit your data over the Internet. Or, your child might be able to apply at the school he or she plans to attend. Fill out a paper FAFSA and bring it to the school, which will then enter the information into a computer and transmit it electronically. For more information, go online to <www.ed.gov/studentaid/apply.html>. There's also the Department of Education's FAFSA Express software, which you can download from their Web site at <www.fafsa.ed.gov>. If you have access to a personal computer with the Windows operating system and a modem, you also can order the software on disk by calling 800-801-0576.

If you apply over the Internet, you must use your personal identification number (PIN). The PIN is a number you get from the Department of Education that serves as your overall identifying code. Each parent, as well as the student, gets one. To get a PIN, go to <www.pin.ed.gov>. Increasingly, more and more students are applying over the Web. It's possible, in fact, that sometime in the not too far distant future, paper FAFSAs will be a thing of the past.

How the EFC Is Computed

Your EFC is calculated by processors at the U.S. Department of Education, using a formula established by the U.S. Congress called the Federal Methodology (FM). It takes into account a number of factors. First is income for the previous calendar year, including such sources as dividends, wages, Social Security, and welfare benefits. You're not expected to use all that money to pay for college, however, because financial aid officers will figure the most significant portion of income is needed for your daily living expenses—everything from the mortgage to doctors' bills. After those expenses are subtracted from your income, the difference is the amount you're supposed to use to contribute to college costs (although you're not expected to use the entire remainder for college).

The second consideration is assets—your child's and yours. This includes such elements as the value of a business, savings, stocks, mutual funds, and bonds. Again, you're expected to contribute part, not all, of these assets to college costs. If you have more than one child in college, that's also taken into account. Divorced parents report the income and assets of the custodial parent.

After the numbers have been analyzed, you'll get a response in the form of a Student Aid Report (SAR). It should take a few weeks, if you've mailed in a paper copy, or 10 to 14 days, if you've submitted an electronic version. The report will provide a summary of the data on your FAFSA. At the top of the document, to the right, you'll find your EFC.

NONFEDERAL AID

After government aid is awarded, schools divvy up their own aid, including grants, scholarships, and loans. Public schools generally stick to the federal formula. But, when it comes to doling out their own money, private colleges often use something called the Institutional Methodology (IM). In addition, many private colleges use their own formulas when calculating aid.

IM versus FM

The Institutional Methodology includes a variety of information not required on the FAFSA and also has different criteria. In some respects, it's tougher. For example:

- It asks how much equity you have in your home.
- It asks how much another child has in such assets as a custodial account.

- Losses from a business or investments don't reduce your income.
- If you have more than one child in college, you're expected to contribute 60 percent of your EFC for each child in school, while the federal rules require you contribute half.
- It requires that the first $2,250 of a student's income be rolled into the family contribution.

On the other hand, it's more generous in some ways:

- It places more weight on such factors as medical expenses and secondary school tuition.
- Students are expected to contribute 25 percent of their assets, as opposed to the 35 percent for the FM.
- You have to contribute 46 percent of income after taxes and allowances over $34,381, compared to 47 percent of available income over $23,000 in the federal formula.

Unfortunately, it all means you'll have to fill out more forms—something called the CSS/Financial Aid PROFILE. In addition, you may have to turn in the school's own form. The PROFILE is available from the College Scholarship Service at <www.collegeboard.com>, or by calling 800-778-6888. Figure 10.1 shows you what the profile looks like.

Gapping and Merit Awards

There are also a few other factors that affect the aid that private schools award. First, the bad news: A practice known as gapping, whereby schools award 80 percent to 90 percent of a student's need, expecting you to fund the rest on your own, has become more widespread in recent years.

The good news, though, is that there has been an increase in the awarding of non-need-based awards, which, in effect, lowers the cost of tuition. Southern New Hampshire University in Manchester, New Hampshire, is a case in point. It awards many of its 1,500 undergraduates one of three types of merit-based scholarships: a $5,000 award for students with a 3.0 grade point average (GPA) and a minimum 900 SAT score; a $7,000 scholarship for those with a 3.5 GPA and at least 1,000 on the SATs; and $9,000 for a GPA of at least 3.5, 1100 SAT score, and a strong extracurricular background.

Schools often use these awards to attract students who might not otherwise be interested in attending. The top schools don't do this—they don't need to—but most others do. Check with the school's financial aid office to see what the practice is at the school your child is interested in.

Figure 10.1   The PROFILE Basic Application Form

The College Board   **CSS/ FINANCIAL AID PROFILE**   3093701-5   **2002–2003**
www.collegeboard.com   **Basic Application 1**

Section A — Student's Information

1. Student's name
Last   First   M.I.

2. Student's permanent mailing address
(Mail will be sent to this address. See instructions.)
Number, street, and apartment number
City   State   Zip

For students outside the U.S. and Puerto Rico only
Postal Code
Country

3. Student's home telephone number
Area Code

4. Title (optional)   1 ○ Mr.   2 ○ Miss, Ms., or Mrs.

5. Student's date of birth
Month   Day   Year   1 9

6. Student's social security number

7. What will be the student's year in school during 2002–2003?
(Fill in only one oval.)

1 ○ 1st year (never previously attended college)
2 ○ 1st year (previously attended college)
3 ○ 2nd year
4 ○ 3rd year
5 ○ 4th year
6 ○ 5th year or more undergraduate
7 ○ first-year graduate/professional (beyond a bachelor's degree)
8 ○ second-year graduate/professional
9 ○ third-year graduate/professional
10 ○ fourth-year or more graduate/professional

8. What is the student's current marital status? (Fill in only one oval.)
1 ○ unmarried (single, divorced, widowed)   2 ○ married/remarried
3 ○ separated

9. Is the student an orphan, or a ward of the court, or was the student a ward of the court until age 18? Yes ○ 1   No ○ 2

10. Does the student have legal dependents (other than a spouse) that fit the definition in the instructions? Yes ○ 1

11. How many people are in the student's (and spouse's) household? Always include the student (and spouse). List their names and give information about them in Section M. See instructions.

12. Of the number in 11, how many will be college students enrolled at least half-time between July 1, 2002, and June 30, 2003? Include yourself.

13. What is the student's state of legal residence?

14. What is the student's citizenship status?
1 ○ U.S. citizen (Skip to Question 15.)
2 ○ Eligible noncitizen—see instructions (Skip to Question 15.)
3 ○ Neither of the above (Answer "b" and "c" below.)

b. **Country of citizenship?**

c. **Visa classification?**
1 ○ F1   2 ○ F2   3 ○ J1   4 ○ J2   5 ○ G   6 ○ Other

Section B — Student's 2001 Income & Benefits
If married, include spouse's information in Sections B, C, D, E, and M.

15. The following 2001 U.S. income tax return figures are (Fill in only one oval.)
1 ○ Will file IRS Form 1040EZ, 1040A, or Telefile. Go to 16.
2 ○ estimated with IRS Form 1040. Go to 16.
3 ○ from a completed IRS Form 1040EZ, 1040A, or Telefile. Go to 16.
4 ○ from a completed IRS Form 1040. Go to 16.
5 ○ a tax return will not be filed. Skip to 20.

Tax Filers Only

16. 2001 total number of exemptions (IRS Form 1040, line 6d or 1040A, line 6d or 1040EZ or telefile — see instructions.)

17. 2001 Adjusted Gross Income from IRS Form 1040, line 33 or 1040A, line 19 or 1040EZ, line 4 or Telefile, line I $ .00

18. a. 2001 U.S. income tax paid (IRS Form 1040, line 52 or 1040A, line 34 or 1040EZ, line 11 or Telefile, line K) $ .00

b. **2001 Education Credits—Hope and Lifetime Learning** (IRS Form 1040, line 46 or 1040A, line 29) $ .00

19. 2001 itemized deductions (IRS Form 1040, Schedule A, line 28) $ .00

20. 2001 income earned from work by student (See instructions.) $ .00

21. 2001 income earned from work by student's spouse $ .00

22. 2001 dividend and interest income $ .00

23. 2001 untaxed income and benefits (Give total amount for year.)
a. **Social security benefits** (untaxed portion only) $ .00
b. **Welfare benefits including TANF** (See instructions.) $ .00
c. **Child support received for all children** $ .00
d. **Earned Income Credit** (IRS Form 1040, line 61a or 1040A, line 39a or 1040EZ, line 9a or Telefile, line L) $ .00
e. **Other – write total from instruction worksheet, page 3** $ .00

24. 2001 earnings from Federal Work-Study or other need-based work programs plus any grant, fellowship, and scholarship aid required to be reported on your U.S. income tax return (See instructions.) $ .00

Page 1

Figure 10.1 (continued)

Section C — Student's Assets — Include trust accounts only in Section D.

			What is it worth today?	What is owed on it?
25. Cash, savings, and checking accounts (as of today)	$_____.00	**29.** Other real estate	$_____.00	$_____.00
26. Total value of non-education IRA, Keogh, 401(k), 403(b), etc. accounts as of December 31, 2001	$_____.00	**30.** Business and farm	$_____.00	$_____.00

27. Investments (Including Uniform Gifts to Minors—see instructions.) What is it worth today? $_____.00 What is owed on it? $_____.00

31. If a farm is included in 30, is the student living on the farm? Yes ○ 1 No ○ 2

28. Home (Renters write in "0.") $_____.00 $_____.00

32. If student owns home, give a. year purchased |__|__|__| b. purchase price $_____.00

Section D — Student's Trust Information

33. a. Total value of all trust(s) $_____.00

b. Is any income or part of the principal currently available? Yes ○ 1 No ○ 2

c. Who established the trust(s)? 1 ○ Student's parents 2 ○ Other

Section E — Student's 2001 Expenses

34. 2001 child support paid because of divorce or separation $_____.00

35. 2001 medical and dental expenses not covered by insurance (See instructions) $_____.00

Section F — Student's Expected Summer/School-Year Resources for 2002–2003

36. a. Is the student a veteran of the U.S. Armed Forces? Yes ○ 1 No ○ 2

b. If yes, write in student's veterans benefits (July 1, 2002 – June 30, 2003) Amount per month $_____.00 Number of months |__|__|

37. Student's (and spouse's) resources (Don't enter monthly amounts.) Summer 2002 (3 months) School Year 2002–2003 (9 months)

	Summer	School Year
a. Student's wages, salaries, tips, etc.	$_____.00	$_____.00
b. Spouse's wages, salaries, tips, etc.	$_____.00	$_____.00
c. Other taxable income	$_____.00	$_____.00
d. Untaxed income and benefits	$_____.00	$_____.00

e. Grants, scholarships, fellowships, etc. from sources other than the colleges or universities to which the student is applying (List sources in Section Q.) $_____.00

f. Tuition benefits from the parents' and/or the student's or spouse's employer $_____.00

g. Amount the student's parent(s) think they will be able to pay for the student's 2002–2003 college expenses $_____.00

h. Amounts expected from other relatives, spouse's parents, and all other sources (List sources in Section Q.) $_____.00

Complete the worksheet on page 5 of the instructions, which will tell you whether or not parents' information is required.

Section G — Parents' Household Information — See page 5 of the instruction booklet.

38. How many people are in your parents' household? Always include the student and parents. List their names and give information about them in Section J. (See instructions.) |__|__|

39. Of the number in 38, how many will be college students enrolled at least half-time between July 1, 2002, and June 30, 2003? Do not include the parents. Include the student. |__|

40. How many parents will be in college at least half-time in 2002–2003? (Fill in only one oval.)
1 ○ Neither parent 2 ○ One parent 3 ○ Both parents

41. What is the current marital status of your parents? (Fill in only one oval.)
1 ○ single 3 ○ separated 5 ○ widowed
2 ○ married/remarried 4 ○ divorced

42. What is your parents' state of legal residence? |__|__|

Section H — Parents' Expenses

		2001	Expected 2002
43. Child support paid because of divorce or separation	**43.**	$_____.00	$_____.00
44. Repayment of parents' educational loans (See instructions.)	**44.**	$_____.00	$_____.00
45. Medical and dental expenses not covered by insurance (See instructions.)	**45.**	$_____.00	$_____.00
46. Total elementary, junior high, and high school tuition paid for dependent children			
a. Amount paid (Don't include tuition paid for the student.)	**46.**	$_____.00	$_____.00
b. For how many dependent children? (Don't include the student.)		|__|	|__|

Page 2

Figure 10.1 The PROFILE Basic Application Form (continued)

Section I — Parents' Assets – If parents own all or part of a business or farm, write in its name and the percent of ownership in Section Q.

47. Cash, savings, and checking accounts (as of today) $ _____ .00

48. Total value of assets (see instructions) held in:
   a. names of the student's brothers and sisters who are under age 19 and not college students $ _____ .00
   b. state-sponsored prepaid tuition plans for the student's brothers and sisters $ _____ .00
   c. state-sponsored prepaid tuition plans for the student $ _____ .00

	What is it worth today?	What is owed on it?
49. Investments	$ _____ .00	$ _____ .00

50. a. Home (Renters write in "0." Skip to 50d.) $ _____ .00 $ _____ .00
   b. Year purchased _____   c. Home purchase price $ _____ .00

d. Monthly home mortgage or rental payment (If none, explain in Section Q.) $ _____ .00

	What is it worth today?	What is owed on it?
51. Business	$ _____ .00	$ _____ .00
52. a. Farm	$ _____ .00	$ _____ .00

   b. Does family live on the farm? Yes ○ 1 No ○ 2

53. a. Other real estate $ _____ .00 $ _____ .00
   b. Year purchased _____   c. Purchase price $ _____ .00

Section J — Parents' 2000 Income & Benefits

54. 2000 Adjusted Gross Income (IRS Form 1040, line 33 or 1040A, line 19 or 1040EZ, line 4 or Telefile, line I) $ _____ .00
55. 2000 U.S. income tax paid (IRS Form 1040, line 51 or 1040A, line 33 or 1040EZ, line 10 or Telefile, line K) $ _____ .00
56. 2000 itemized deductions (IRS Form 1040, Schedule A, line 28) $ _____ .00
57. 2000 untaxed income and benefits (Include the same types of income and benefits that are listed in 65a – k.) $ _____ .00

Section K — Parents' 2001 Income & Benefits

58. The following 2001 U.S. income tax return figures are (Fill in only one oval.)
   1 ○ estimated. Will file IRS Form 1040EZ, 1040A, or Telefile. Go to 59.
   2 ○ estimated. Will file IRS Form 1040. Go to 59.
   3 ○ from a completed IRS Form 1040EZ, 1040A, or Telefile. Go to 59.
   4 ○ from a completed IRS Form 1040. Go to 59.
   5 ○ a tax return will not be filed. Skip to 63.

59. 2001 total number of exemptions (IRS Form 1040, line 6d or 1040A, line 6d or 1040EZ or Telefile—see instructions) 59. ☐☐

60. 2001 Adjusted Gross Income (IRS Form 1040, line 33 or 1040A, line 19 or 1040EZ, line 4 or Telefile, line I) 60. $ _____ .00

Breakdown of income in 60
   a. Wages, salaries, tips (IRS Form 1040, line 7 or 1040A, line 7 or 1040EZ, line 1) 60. a. $ _____ .00
   b. Interest income (IRS Form 1040, line 8a or 1040A, line 8a or 1040EZ, line 2 or Telefile, line C) b. $ _____ .00
   c. Dividend income (IRS Form 1040, line 9 or 1040A, line 9) c. $ _____ .00
   d. Net income (or loss) from business, farm, rents, royalties, partnerships, estates, trusts, etc. (IRS Form 1040, lines 12, 17, and 18—enter the amount in parentheses). d. $ _____ .00
   e. Other taxable income such as alimony received, capital gains (or losses), pensions, annuities, etc. (IRS Form 1040, lines 10, 11, 13, 14, 15b, 16b, 19, 20b, and 21 or 1040A, lines 10, 11b, 12b, 13, and 14b or 1040EZ, line 3 or Telefile, line D) e. $ _____ .00
   f. Adjustments to income (IRS Form 1040, line 32 or 1040A, line 18—see instructions) f. $ _____ .00

61. a. 2001 U.S. income tax paid (IRS Form 1040, line 52 or 1040A, line 34 or 1040EZ, line 11 or Telefile, line K) 61. a. $ _____ .00
   b. 2001 Education Credits – Hope and Lifetime Learning (IRS Form 1040, line 46 and 1040A, line 29) b. $ _____ .00

62. 2001 itemized deductions (IRS Form 1040, Schedule A, line 28) 62. $ _____ .00
63. 2001 income earned from work by father/stepfather 63. $ _____ .00
64. 2001 income earned from work by mother/stepmother 64. $ _____ .00

65. 2001 untaxed income and benefits (Give total amount for the year. Do not give monthly amounts.)
   a. Social security benefits received (untaxed portion only) $ _____ .00
   b. Welfare benefits, including TANF (See instructions.) $ _____ .00
   c. Child support received for all children $ _____ .00
   d. Deductible IRA and/or SEP, SIMPLE, or Keogh payments (See instructions.) $ _____ .00
   e. Payments to tax-deferred pension and savings plans (See instructions.) $ _____ .00
   f. Amounts withheld from wages for dependent care and medical spending accounts $ _____ .00
   g. Earned Income Credit (IRS Form 1040, line 61a or 1040A, line 39a or 1040EZ, line 9a or Telefile, line L) $ _____ .00
   h. Housing, food, and other living allowances received by military, clergy, and others (See instructions.) $ _____ .00
   i. Tax-exempt interest income (IRS Form 1040, line 8b or 1040A, line 8b) $ _____ .00
   j. Foreign income exclusion (IRS Form 2555, line 43 or Form 2555EZ, line 18) $ _____ .00
   k. Other – write total from worksheet, page 7 $ _____ .00

Section L — Parents' 2002 Expected Income & Benefits
(If the expected total income and benefits will differ from the 2001 total income and benefits by $3,000 or more, explain in Section Q.)

66. 2002 income earned from work by father $ _____ .00
67. 2002 income earned from work by mother $ _____ .00
68. 2002 other taxable income $ _____ .00
69. 2002 untaxed income and benefits (See 65a – k.) $ _____ .00

Tax Filers Only

Page 3

Figure 10.1 (continued)

Section M — Family Member Listing — Give information for all family members entered in question 11 or 38. List up to seven family members in addition to the student. **Failure to complete all columns could reduce your aid eligibility.** Leave shaded sections blank.

70.

Full name of family member (If more lines are needed, use Section Q.)	Use codes from below	Age (Required-use whole numbers)	Claimed by parents as tax exemption in 2001? Yes? No?	Name of school or college	Year in school	Scholarships and grants	Parents' contribution	Attend college at least one term full-time half-time	College or university Type	Name
1 You — the student applicant			○ ○			$	$			
2			○ ○			$	$	1○ 2○		
3			○ ○			$	$	1○ 2○		
4			○ ○			$	$	1○ 2○		
5			○ ○			$	$	1○ 2○		
6			○ ○			$	$	2○		
7			○ ○			$	$	1○		
8			○ ○			$	$	1○		

Write in the correct code from the right. 1 = Student's parent, 2 = Student's stepparent, 3 = Student's brother or sister, 4 = Student's husband or wife, 5 = Student's child/stepchild 6 = Student's grandparent, 7 = Student's stepbrother or stepsister, 8 = Other. Write in the correct code from the instructions on page 8.

Section N — Parents' Information (to be answered by the parent(s) completing this form)

71. Fill in one: ○ Father ○ Stepfather ○ Legal guardian ○ Other (Explain in Q.)

a. Name _____ Age |__|__|

b. Fill in if: ○ Self-employed ○ Unemployed – Date: _____

c. Occupation _____

d. Employer _____ No. years

e. Work telephone |__|__|__|-|__|__|__|-|__|__|__|__|

f. Retirement plans: ○ Social security ○ Union/employer ○ Civil service/state ○ IRA/Keogh/tax-deferred ○ Military ○ Other

72. Fill in one: ○ Mother ○ Stepmother ○ Legal guardian ○ Other (Explain in Q.)

a. Name _____ Age |__|__|

b. Fill in if: ○ Self-employed ○ Unemployed – Date: _____

c. Occupation _____

d. Employer _____ No. years

e. Work telephone |__|__|__|-|__|__|__|-|__|__|__|__|

f. Retirement plans: ○ Social security ○ Union/employer ○ Civil service/state ○ IRA/Keogh/tax-deferred ○ Military ○ Other

Section O — Information About Noncustodial Parent (to be answered by the parent who completes this form if the student's biological or adoptive parents are divorced, separated, or were never married to each other)

73. a. Who last claimed the student as a tax exemption?

b. How much does the noncustodial parent plan to contribute to the student's education for the 2002–2003 school year? $ _____ .00

Section P — Student's Schools & Programs

74. Schools and programs to receive PROFILE information (See instructions.)
*Housing Plans: 1 = On campus 3 = With parents 2 = Off campus 4 = With relatives

CSS Code No. | Housing Plans*
1 |__|__|__|__|__| |__|
2 |__|__|__|__|__| |__|

75. What will be the student's 2002–2003 financial aid status?
1 ○ First-time applicant, entering student ○ Renewal applicant, continuing student 3 ○ First-time applicant, continuing student (including transfer student)

76. Fee and type of payment
○ $21 for 1 CSS® Code Number
○ $38 for 2 CSS Code Numbers
Enclose a check or money order for either $21 or $38. Make payable to The College Board. Write the number from the top of page 1 on your payment.

A check or money order must be included with this form. If you fail to do so, the form will be returned unprocessed.

CSS Use Only	
	W
	B
	G
	S

Section Q — Explanations/Special Circumstances — Use this space to explain any unusual expenses such as high medical or dental expenses, educational and other debts, child care, elder care, or special circumstances. Also, give information for any outside scholarships you have been awarded. **If more space is needed, use sheets of paper and send them directly to your schools and programs.** Please print.

Certification: All the information on this form is true and complete to the best of my knowledge. I agree to pay all appropriate fees and, if asked, to give proof of the information that I have given on this form. I realize that this proof may include a copy of my U.S., state, or local income tax returns. I certify that all information is correct at this time, and that I will send timely notice to my schools/programs of any significant change in family income or assets, financial situation, college plans of other children, or the receipt of other scholarships or grants.

1 Student's signature
2 Student's spouse's signature
3 Father's (stepfather's) signature
4 Mother's (stepmother's) signature

Date completed: |__|__| |__|__| Year
Month Day 1 ○ 2001 2 ○ 2002

Page 4

30937015

SAMPLE

PLANNING, PLANNING, PLANNING

It's important to start planning for the financial aid process well before you actually apply. That way, you can maximize the amount of aid your child is eligible for. And, you avoid taking steps that could result in a higher EFC. We're not suggesting you should take actions to hide your income or deceive the financial aid office. But, it's also not a bad idea to avoid steps that could actually hurt your child's chances of getting aid.

Deadlines

For starters, don't delay turning in the form. Although you shouldn't apply before January 1, check the deadline and try to turn it in as close to that date as possible, because many schools consider applications for financial aid based on a first-come, first-served basis. Also, don't wait to apply for financial aid until your child has been accepted at a school. If you do, there may not be any money left over for you by the time you apply. Schools understand that you need to know how much aid you're likely to get from them before your child can decide which college to accept.

If your child has previously attended a postsecondary institution, your financial aid also may be delayed if you don't send a Financial Aid Transcript (FAT) to the college's financial aid office. You will have to send one even if your child did not receive financial aid. The FAT is a record of money your child received (or a record of the fact that he or she never received money), and has no relationship to the academic transcript.

Other Steps

That's not all you might do. Schools ask you to report income from the previous calendar year, although they ask to see a snapshot of your assets as of the day you send in the form. That means, if you intend on selling a lot of stock to fund tuition, you may want to do so during your child's sophomore year in high school. If you wait, the profits will be reported as additional income on your FAFSA and could affect your EFC. Remember: If you sell any securities during the first three years your child attends college, it may hurt his or her chances of getting aid for the year after you make the transaction.

You also may consider filing a separate tax return for another child's investment income. In that case, the money won't be included in your own income for tax purposes, and so it won't play a part in determining your EFC. Also, reconsider withdrawing money from your IRA. If you're aged 59½ and over, you can use those funds to pay for college tuition without paying a 10 percent penalty. But, again, that money will be considered part of your income and could result in a bigger EFC. Keep in mind that even small changes in income can have a big effect on what financial aid offices expect you to pay.

To reduce the amount of income you report, you also can step up spending on big-ticket expenses. Don't throw your money away on nonessentials. But, for example, if you need a new car, buy it during your child's junior year.

There are also potential steps you can take regarding assets. Financial aid officers expect to take 35 percent of the money held in accounts that are in your child's name, under the Federal Methodology, and 25 percent under the Institutional Methodology. Parents, however, only pay 5.6 percent, or 5 percent, depending on the formula. So, it's probably a better idea to put the money under your name. That holds true for money that your own parents may want to contribute. Consider asking your child's grandparents whether they would mind if you kept the money in your own account.

If your child has filed federal tax returns for two years, has been employed, and has earned at least $4,000 a year, he or she might be considered as independent. That means you wouldn't claim him or her as dependent on your tax forms. As an independent, your child might be eligible for more aid than if he or she is claimed as a dependent on your taxes. Keep in mind that it's illegal for someone to apply falsely for aid as an independent. Be sure to check with an accountant before you make that decision.

THE AWARD LETTER

Once your child has been accepted by a school, he or she will receive an award letter from the school's financial aid office. Review it carefully. It's helpful to understand what will be in it, how to respond, and how to negotiate or appeal. For a typical award letter, see Figure 10.2.

What's in It?

The award letter details how your child's eligibility for government aid was determined, how his or her need for college aid was calculated, and what kind and how much aid is being offered, if any. The aid package may include a combination of grants, loans, scholarships, work-study, and other programs. Any aid your child receives will first go to tuition, fees, and room and board. The rest will be for living expenses, but not for books and supplies. You'll have to provide written permission for that.

Remember that what you care about is whether the aid offered is enough to permit your child to attend that school. In other words, a big award that leaves you paying $15,000 on your own may not be that useful in reality. Why? Although the offer may seem great, you still may not be able to send your child to that school, if the amount you're responsible for is out of your reach.

Figure 10.2   Sample Award Letter

SLM UNIVERSITY
Office of Student Financial Aid

John E. Student	Social Security Number:
25 College-Bound Drive	123-45-6789
University College, VA 20000	

Dear Student:

After reviewing your FAFSA, we are pleased to provide you with
the following financial aid offer. This award is contingent
upon anticipated annual renewal of funding from federal,
state, and private sources. You may accept or decline any of
the awards offered.

Financial Aid Award

Type of Aid	Fall	Spring	Total	Accept	Decline
Federal Pell Grant	600	600	1,200	( )	( )
Federal SEOG	800	800	1,600	( )	( )
SLM Grant	1,000	1,000	2,000	( )	( )
Federal Work-Study Program	700	700	1,400	( )	( )
Federal Perkins Loan	600	600	1,200	( )	( )
Federal Subsidized Stafford Loan	1,300	1,300	2,600	( )	( )
Total	5,000	5,000	10,000		

*Please sign this letter and return it to the financial aid
office within two weeks. Read the enclosed information on how
to apply for and receive the Stafford Loan. If you need
additional funding to supplement this offer, please refer to
the attached list of Additional Funding Options.*

Source: © 2002 Sallie Mae, Inc. Courtesy of Sallie Mae.

How to Respond

Even if your child isn't sure which college he or she will accept, you should accept the aid offer. If you do, that doesn't mean you have to attend the school. But colleges keep to strict deadlines and, if you delay, your child could lose the package. As soon as your child has decided, however, let the financial aid office know if you're going to withdraw.

Negotiations and Appeals

You don't have to jump at the first offer. If your child has been accepted by several schools, weigh the pros and cons of all the offers. If a school wants your child's enrollment badly enough, it might sweeten the initial offer. It's not something financial aid offices broadcast, but they often offer additional aid, if you ask them to. You'll be in the best position to bargain if you can show your child has a better offer from a competitor.

Chances are, you won't have any success at one of the Ivy League or top-tier schools. And, attempts to negotiate might be made even harder, thanks to efforts by a group of selective private colleges and universities to standardize the method they use for determining how much institutional money to award. By agreeing to use the same criteria, such as whether to include a home equity loan as part of the parents' assets, families have even less room to negotiate than before.

But, if you're dealing with a less prestigious place and your child has a strong academic record, you may have a much better chance. Don't worry about seeming crass. The financial aid office understands you just want the best opportunity possible.

If your SAR tells you your child does not qualify for a Pell Grant, don't assume that means you are not eligible to receive any aid. You may be able to receive other money from the state, your college, or a loan. But, you also should try to determine why you were turned down. It could have been because of an error on your part; even something as simple as an incorrect Social Security number can put the kibosh on your eligibility.

If you receive an award, but it's less than you thought you'd get, don't give up. Most schools have an appeals process, which is described in their award letter. If not, ask the financial aid officer how it works. First, though, talk to the financial aid office and try to find out how they analyzed the information you provided and came up with a lower figure. Ask how they calculated such items as your expenses or EFC. If you still feel the aid is lower than it should be, then think about going through an appeal.

Be prepared: This will be your only chance. Make sure you base your arguments on facts and numbers. An appeal, as opposed to a negotiation, must include new information that wasn't included in the original form. If, after the appeal is over, the original offer hasn't been changed, you'll have to accept it, or go to another school.

If you've had a substantial change in your financial situation—for example, a job loss—and the information you supply on the form does not accurately represent your current ability to pay, don't wait for the SAR. Put together a packet of documents proving that your situation has changed and send it to the financial aid office as soon as possible. And, remember: When assembling the information needed to demonstrate your case, more is better.

Reapplying

Unfortunately, even if your child gets aid for one year, you have to reapply for each subsequent year after that. After you've applied for the first time, you'll need to complete a Renewal FAFSA form. Although you'll only have to provide information that's changed from the year before, don't assume things will be status quo. Even fairly modest increases in income can have a big effect.

In the end, however, the financial aid package, while important, should not be the main determinant of which college your child attends. He or she should believe that the academic and social offerings and the physical facilities will provide the best education you can afford. For a better idea of the kind of financial aid package you might expect, and the gap between that financial aid and what you still need to finance, look at Figure 10.3.

Figure 10.3   Financial Aid Package Worksheet

Item	$ Amount
1. **Costs of College** (tuition, room, board, fees)	$
2. **Expected Family Contribution** (parents and students)	$
3. **Financial Need** (subtract item 2 from item 1)	$
4. **Sources of Aid**	
Grants and Scholarships	
Pell	$
FSEOG	
State	
College	
Private	
Work-Study	
Federal Work-Study	
ROTC or Other Military Aid	
Cooperative Education	
Loans	
Perkins	
Stafford (subsidized)	
Stafford (unsubsidized)	
PLUS/SLS	
State	
College	
Commercial	
Sources of Aid Total	$
GAP BETWEEN FINANCIAL NEED AND FINANCIAL AID (subtract item 4 from item 3)	$

CHAPTER 11

Tackling the Financial Aid Application

For most parents, completing the Free Application for Federal Student Aid (FAFSA) form is just about the hardest part of the entire college application process. It has many sections, with questions that seem straightforward—but aren't. In fact, there are many opportunities to make mistakes in each section.

The ordeal of applying for financial aid is so strenuous that an industry of financial aid counselors has emerged to help you work through the procedure, for a fee that can run from $150 to $700 and higher. Fees depend on how extensively you use the service. These advisors will not only fill out the forms, but they also may help negotiate with aid officers and devise strategies for getting the most aid. If you can spend the money, and you're not the best at dealing with forms, it's not a bad idea—as long as you find someone who comes highly recommended. There's no specific training for the job, although financial aid counselors often are former financial aid officers themselves, so references and evidence of their track record are of critical importance. Also, the consultant will have to sign the FAFSA form, which could cause greater scrutiny by financial aid officers.

For those who choose to go it alone, however, it's helpful to understand as much as possible about the elements that go into the school's final calculation, as well as all those numbers you'll need to supply. The more you comprehend, the less the chance you'll make a mistake—and the better the chance of winning at least some aid.

CALCULATING YOUR EFC

Before you do anything, take the time to do your own estimate of your Expected Family Contribution, which was discussed in Chapter 10. It's worth the effort, because the number is of such crucial importance to the outcome of the process. After all, how can you know whether a financial aid office has underestimated that amount unless you've figured it out yourself?

To determine what might be expected of you, your child, and your entire family, look at the worksheets in Figures 11.1, 11.2, and 11.3, and see Tables 1 to 5. With the worksheet in Figure 11.1, you can determine your own expected contribution, using the Federal Methodology. You'll have to include the income protection allowance and the asset protection allowance that apply

Table 1. Social Security (FICA) Tax Allowance

When individual's yearly wage total equals	Allowance per wage earner for wage Social Security (FICA) tax is
$1 to $80,400	7.65% of income earned by each wage earner (maximum $6,150.60 per person)
$80,401 or more	$6,150.60 + 1.45% of income earned above $80,400 by each wage earner

Source: "Table 9. Social Security (FICA) Tax Allowance, 2002–2003." *The College Board College Cost & Financial Aid Handbook 2003.* © 2002 by College Entrance Examination Board. Reprinted with permission. All rights reserved. <www.collegeboard.com>

Table 2. Income Protection Allowance

Family Size* (including student)	Number in College**				
	1	*2*	*3*	*4*	*5*
2	$13,210	$10,950			
3	16,450	14,210	$11,940		
4	20,320	18,060	15,810	$13,550	
5	23,980	21,720	19,470	17,210	$14,960
6	28,050	25,790	23,540	21,280	19,030

*For each additional family member, add $3,170.
**For each additional college student, subtract $2,250.
Source: "Table 10. Income Protection Allowance, 2002–2003." *The College Board College Cost & Financial Aid Handbook 2003.* © 2002 by College Entrance Examination Board. Reprinted with permission. All rights reserved. <www.collegeboard.com>

Figure 11.1   Parents' Expected Contribution Worksheet

2001 income:

1. Father's yearly wages, salaries, tips, and other
    compensation $ _____

2. Mother's yearly wages, salaries, tips, and other
    compensation $ _____

3. All other income of mother and father (dividends,
    interest, Social Security, pensions, welfare, child
    support, etc.). Include IRA/Keogh payments
    and 401(k) $ _____

4. IRS allowable adjustments to income (business
    expenses, interest penalties, alimony paid, etc.).
    Do not include IRA/Keogh payments. $ _____

B. Total income (Add 1, 2, and 3, and subtract 4.) $ _____

Expenses:

5. U.S. income tax parents paid on 2001 income
    (not amount withheld from paycheck) $ _____

6. Social Security (FICA) tax (See Table 1.) $ _____

7. State and other taxes (Enter 8% of B.) $ _____

8. Employment allowance. If two-parent family and
    both parents work, or, if one-parent family, allow
    35% of lower salary to a maximum of $3,000. No
    allowance for a two-parent family in which only
    one parent works. $ _____

9. Income protection allowance (See Table 2.) $ _____

C. Total allowance against income (Add 5, 6, 7, 8, and 9.) $ _____

D. Available income (Subtract C from B.) $ _____

Figure 11.1   (continued)

Assets:

10.   Other real estate equity (Value minus unpaid
      balance on mortgage.) $ _____

11.   Business or farm (Figure total value minus
      indebtedness and then take percentage shown in
      Table 3.) If your family is only part owner of the
      farm or business, list only your share of net value. $ _____

12.   Cash, savings, and checking accounts $ _____

13.   Other investments (current net value) $ _____

E.   Total assets $ _____

Deductions:

F.   Asset protection allowance (See Table 4.) $ _____

G.   Remaining assets (Subtract F from E.) $ _____

H.   Income supplement from assets (Multiply G by 12%;
       if value is negative, enter 0.) $ _____

I.   Adjusted available income (Add D and H.) $ _____

J.   Parents' expected contribution (Multiply I by
       amount given in Table 5.) $ _____

**K.   Parents' expected contribution if more than one
       family member is in college** (Divide J by number of
       family members in college at least half time.) $ _____

Figure 11.2   Student's Expected Contribution Worksheet

Student's 2001 income:

14. Student's yearly wages, salaries, tips, and other
     compensation $ _____

15. Spouse's yearly wages, salaries, tips, and other
     compensation $ _____

16. All other income of student (dividends, interest,
     untaxed income, and benefits) $ _____

L.   Total income (Add 14, 15, and 16.) $ _____

Allowances:

17. U.S. income tax student (and spouse) paid on 2001
     income (not amount withheld from paychecks) $ _____

18. State and other taxes (Enter 4% of L.) $ _____

19. Social Security (FICA) tax (See Table 1.) $ _____

20. Dependent student offset $ _____

M.   Total allowances against student's income
     (Add 17, 18, 19, and 20.) $ _____

N.   Available income (Subtract M from L.) $ _____

Resources:

21. Contribution from income (Line N × 50%.
     Cannot be less than $0.) $ _____

22. Contribution from assets (Multiply the total
     savings and other assets, such as stocks and
     bonds, excluding home equity, by 35%.) $ _____

23. Other gift and scholarships already received $ _____

O.   Total student resources (Add lines 21, 22, and 23.) $ _____

Source: "Worksheet 3. Student's Expected Contribution, 2002–2003." *The College Board College Cost & Financial Aid Handbook 2003.* © 2002 by College Entrance Examination Board. Reprinted with permission. All rights reserved. <www.collegeboard.com>

to your income level, which can be found in Tables 1 to 4, in Figure 11.1. The worksheet in Figure 11.2 will show you your child's expected contribution. Finally, you can use the worksheet in Figure 11.3 to determine your total estimated family contribution. Another approach is to estimate your EFC using

Figure 11.3   Total Family Contribution Worksheet

J. **Parents' expected contribution** (Use figure for
K instead of J if there is more than one family
member in college.) $ _____

O. **Student's expected contribution from resources** $ _____

P. **Total family contribution** (Add J and O.) $ _____

Source: "Worksheet 3. Total Family Contribution, 2002–2003." *The College Board College Cost & Financial Aid Handbook 2003.* © 2002 by College Entrance Examination Board. Reprinted with permission. All rights reserved. <www.collegeboard.com>

Table 3.   Business or Farm Adjustments

Net Worth (NW)	Adjusted Net Worth
Less than $1	$0
$1 to 95,000	$0 + 40% of NW
$95,001 to 285,000	$38,000 + 50% of NW over $95,000
$285,001 to 470,000	$133,000 + 60% of NW over $285,000
$470,001 or more	$244,000 + 100% of NW over $470,000

Source: "Table 11. Business or Farm Adjustments, 2002–2003." *The College Board College Cost & Financial Aid Handbook 2003.* © 2002 by College Entrance Examination Board. Reprinted with permission. All rights reserved. <www.collegeboard.com>

a Web-based calculator, like the one found on the Web site Finaid.org, shown in Figure 11.4.

You may also want to get an idea of how much families of various incomes generally are expected to contribute—and how you compare to them. The sample table shown in Figure 11.5, from the College Board, will give you some sense of how much parents are expected to contribute to college costs, based on their pretax income, assets, and number of children. The Board made the following assumptions when assembling this table:

- The older parent is 45 years old and both parents are employed at equal wages.
- Income is derived solely from both parents' jobs.

Table 4.   Asset Protection Allowance

Older Parent's Age	Two-Parent Family	One-Parent Family
25 or under	$0	$0
26	2,300	1,100
27	4,600	2,200
28	6,900	3,300
29	9,100	4,500
30	11,400	5,600
31	13,700	6,700
32	16,000	7,800
33	18,300	8,900
34	20,600	10,000
35	22,900	11,100
36	25,200	12,200
37	27,400	13,400
38	29,700	14,500
39	32,000	15,600
40	34,300	16,700
41	35,200	17,000
42	36,100	17,400
43	36,700	17,800
44	37,700	18,200
45	38,600	18,600
46	39,600	18,900
47	40,600	19,400
48	41,900	19,900
49	42,900	20,300
50	44,000	20,800
51	45,100	21,200
52	46,500	21,700
53	47,600	22,400
54	49,100	22,900
55	50,300	23,400
56	51,800	24,000
57	53,300	24,700
58	54,900	25,300
59	56,600	26,000
60	58,300	26,600
61	60,000	27,400
62	62,000	28,100
63	63,800	28,900
64	66,000	29,700
65 or over	68,200	30,700

Table 5.   Parents' Expected Contribution

Adjusted Available Income (AAI)	Total Parents' Contribution
Less than $3,409	$750
$3,409 to 11,800	22% of AAI
$11,801 to 14,800	$2,596 + 25% of AAI over $11,800
$14,801 to 17,800	$3,346 + 29% of AAI over $14,800
$17,801 to 20,100	$4,216 + 34% of AAI over $17,800
$20,101 to 23,900	$5,236 + 40% of AAI over $20,100
$23,901 or over	$6,476 + 47% of AAI over $23,900

Source: "Table 12. Parents' Expected Contribution, 2002–2003." *The College Board College Cost & Financial Aid Handbook 2003.* © 2002 by College Entrance Examination Board. Reprinted with permission. All rights reserved. <www.collegeboard.com>

- The family's circumstances are not unusual, and it has no out-of-the-ordinary expenses.
- One undergraduate family member attends college.
- Any equity in the family's home or farm is not included in its net assets for the purpose of determining federal aid eligibility.

FILLING OUT THE FORM

The financial aid forms you obtain from the school your child wants to attend will help you go through the application process step by step. To complete the forms, you should have your bank and brokerage statements available for reference, as well as recent tax forms. That's because the application will ask for information from specific lines on the tax form. If you're not an early bird filer, like most people, you can estimate your answers and correct them later on. (More on that subject follows.) Remember to save everything, in case a school asks you for proof that certain information is correct. You won't get aid until you correct it.

As you can see in Figure 11.6, the form includes seven sections, called steps, plus three worksheets. Steps one, three, and five mostly cover personal information and background, while steps two and four ask the really important questions about finances needed to determine your family's financial need. Steps six and seven involve housekeeping information.

A few words of warning: The form is addressed to the student. So, whenever the words "you" or "your" appear, they refer to your child. And, make sure not to leave an item blank. The financial aid office will figure you just

Figure 11.4   FinAid Calculator

The SmartStudent™ Guide
to Financial Aid

Site Map   About FinAid

Financial Aid Estimation Form

This form is used to prepare an estimate of the Expected Family Contribution (EFC) and
financial need. This is a free service. We do not retain any record of the information you
submit using this form, and have taken steps to ensure your privacy.

Before filling out this form, we strongly recommend that you read the caveats and
instructions.

ntions

stions   Show:
          Detailed Output   ▲▼

Calculators
          Need Analysis Methodology:
Beyond Financial Aid   Federal Methodology   ▲▼

          Use Tables for Award Year:
SEARCH   2002-2003   ▲▼

          Choose "Federal Methodology" to get an estimate of your financial need using a formula
          similar to the Federal Methodology used by the Federal processor and school financial aid
          administrators. Choose "Institutional Methodology" to get an estimate of your financial
          need using a formula similar to the one used by many private colleges and universities.

          Student Status:

          The requirements for a student to be considered "independent" for financial aid purposes
          are very strict. If you aren't genuinely independent, you should select "Dependent
          Student" below. Use the dependency status form to determine whether you are a
          dependent or independent student.

          If you are an independent student, do not fill in the parent information section, but do add
          the salary and assets of your spouse to your own in the student information section and
          provide your family information (not your parents' family information) in the family
          information section.

forgot to answer it and may bounce the form back to you. Finally, don't include any additional information with the forms; it will just be thrown out. If
you need to add documentation, arrange to send it separately.

Here's a play-by-play, line-by-line look at each question:

Lines 1–3: Student's full name. You must include your child's name as
it appears on his or her Social Security card; nicknames are not acceptable.

Lines 4–7: Your address. Make sure you give a permanent address.

Lines 8–9: Social Security number and date of birth. Enter your
child's—not yours—and write clearly; the wrong number will create havoc
in the process.

Figure 11.5 Estimating Parental Contributions

Net Assets: $25,000

Family Size: Parents' Pretax Income	3	4	5	6
		Parental Contribution		
$ 20,000	$ 0	$ 0	$ 0	$ 0
30,000	836	80	0	0
40,000	2,362	1,606	897	97
50,000	4,178	3,205	2,422	1,623
60,000	6,807	5,384	4,265	3,224
70,000	9,547	8,110	6,772	5,414
80,000	12,196	10,759	9,420	7,889
90,000	15,124	13,687	12,348	10,817
100,000	18,064	16,627	15,288	13,757

Net Assets: $50,000

Family Size: Parents' Pretax Income	3	4	5	6
		Parental Contribution		
$ 20,000	$ 0	$ 0	$ 0	$ 0
30,000	1,137	381	0	0
40,000	2,672	1,907	1,197	398
50,000	4,637	3,579	2,741	1,923
60,000	7,450	5,931	4,730	3,601
70,000	10,190	8,753	7,415	5,961
80,000	12,839	11,402	10,063	8,532
90,000	15,767	14,330	12,991	11,460
100,000	18,707	17,270	15,931	14,400

Net Assets: $100,000

Family Size: Parents' Pretax Income	3	4	5	6
		Parental Contribution		
$ 20,000	$ 931	$ 176	$ 0	$ 0
30,000	2,457	1,701	992	192
40,000	4,319	3,313	2,517	1,718
50,000	7,011	5,557	4,412	3,332
60,000	10,270	8,656	7,140	5,587
70,000	13,010	11,573	10,235	8,691
80,000	15,659	14,222	12,883	11,352
90,000	18,587	17,150	15,811	14,280
100,000	21,527	20,090	18,751	17,220

Figure 11.5   Estimating Parental Contributions (continued)

Net Assets: $150,000

Family Size:	3	4	5	6
Parents' Pretax Income		Parental Contribution		
$ 20,000	$ 2,251	$ 1,496	$ 717	$ 0
30,000	4,033	3,079	2,312	1,512
40,000	6,571	5,191	4,112	3,098
50,000	9,831	8,216	6,701	5,216
60,000	13,090	11,476	9,960	8,252
70,000	15,830	14,393	13,055	11,511
80,000	18,479	17,042	15,703	14,172
90,000	21,407	19,970	18,631	17,100
100,000	24,347	22,910	21,571	20,040

Source: "Table 8. Estimated Parents' Contribution, 2002–2003." *The College Board College Cost & Financial Aid Handbook 2003.* © 2002 by College Entrance Examination Board. Reprinted with permission. All rights reserved. <www.collegeboard.com>

Line 10: Your phone number. This is the phone number they will use to contact you.

Lines 11–12: Your driver's license number and state. Fill it in exactly.

Lines 13–14: U.S. citizenship. Indicate "Yes" if your child is a citizen; if not, there are special instructions for noncitizens.

Lines 15–16: Marital status. Enter your child's status as of the day the form is filled out, and appropriate dates.

Lines 17–21: Full-time status. Enter whether your child will be full-time, three-quarters time, half time, less than half time, or not attending. If you are not sure, mark the Full-time/Not sure box.

Lines 22–23: Highest school level completed by parents. Note that you need to fill out only the highest level you and your spouse attained.

Lines 24–26: State of legal residence. Include the abbreviation for the state. Fail to fill that in and, in many cases, you won't receive the application for state aid.

Lines 27–28: Selective Service. Males must generally register with the Selective Service to get federal aid.

Line 29: Degree or certificate. You must indicate the degree or certificate your child will be working on. The application will include the correct code.

Line 30: Grade level. You will find a table in the application with the correct number to use.

Figure 11.6   The Free Application for Federal Student Aid Form

the 2002-2003 FAFSA SM

Free Application for Federal Student Aid
For July 1, 2002 — June 30, 2003

OMB # 1845-0001

Step One: For questions 1-34, leave blank any questions that do not apply to you (the student).

1-3. Your full name (as it appears on your Social Security card)

1. LAST NAME
2. FIRST NAME
3. MIDDLE INITIAL

4-7. Your permanent mailing address

4. NUMBER AND STREET (INCLUDE APT. NUMBER)
5. CITY (AND COUNTRY IF NOT U.S.)
6. STATE
7. ZIP CODE

8. Your Social Security Number
9. Your date of birth
10. Your permanent telephone number

11-12. Your driver's license number and state (if any)

11. LICENSE NUMBER   STATE

13. Are you a U.S. citizen? Pick one. **See page 2.**
   a. Yes, I am a U.S. citizen. **Skip to question 15.**
   b. No, but I am an eligible noncitizen. Fill in question 14.
   c. No, I am not a citizen or eligible noncitizen.

14. ALIEN REGISTRATION NUMBER A

15. What is your marital status as of today?
   I am single, divorced, or widowed
   I am married/remarried
   I am separated

   Month and year you were married, separated, divorced, or widowed
   MONTH YEAR

For each question (17 - 21), please mark whether you will be full-time, 3/4 time, half time, less than half time, or not attending. **See page 2.**

	Full time/Not sure	3/4 time	Half time	Less than half time	Not attending
17. Summer 2002					
18. Fall 2002					
19. Winter 2002-2003					
20. Spring 2003					
21. Summer 2003					

22. Highest school your father completed   Middle school/Jr. High   High school   College or beyond   Other/unknown
23. Highest school your mother completed   Middle school/Jr. High   High school   College or beyond   Other/unknown

24. What is your state of legal residence?   STATE

25. Did you become a legal resident of this state before January 1, 1997?   Yes   No

26. If the answer to question 25 is "No," give month and year you became a legal resident.   MONTH YEAR

27. Are you male? (Most male students must register with Selective Service to get federal aid.)   Yes   No

28. If you are male (age 18-25) and not registered, answer "Yes" and Selective Service will register you.   Yes   No

29. What degree or certificate will you be working on during 2002-2003? **See page 2** and enter the correct number in the box.

30. What will be your grade level when you begin the 2002-2003 school year? **See page 2** and enter the correct number in the box.

31. Will you have a high school diploma or GED before you enroll?   Yes   No
32. Will you have your first bachelor's degree before July 1, 2002?   Yes   No
33. In addition to grants, are you interested in student loans (which you must pay back)?   Yes   No
34. In addition to grants, are you interested in "work-study" (which you earn through work)?   Yes   No

35. **Do not leave this question blank.** Have you ever been convicted of possessing or selling illegal drugs? If you have, answer "Yes," complete and submit this application, and we will send you a worksheet in the mail for you to determine if your conviction affects your eligibility for aid.   No   Yes   **DO NOT LEAVE QUESTION 35 BLANK**

Page 3

For Help — 1-800- 433-3243

Figure 11.6   The Free Application for Federal Student Aid Form (continued)

Step Two: For questions 36-49, report your (the student's) income and assets. If you are married today, report your and your spouse's income and assets, even if you were not married in 2001. Ignore references to "spouse" if you are currently single, separated, divorced, or widowed.

36. For 2001, have you (the student) completed your IRS income tax return or another tax return listed in **question 37**?

   a. I have already completed my return. ○₁   **b.** I will file, but I have not yet completed my return. ○₂   **c.** I'm not going to file. **(Skip to question 42.)** ○₃

37. What income tax return did you file or will you file for 2001?

   a. IRS 1040 .... ○₁
   b. IRS 1040A, 1040EZ, 1040Telefile .... ○₂
   c. A foreign tax return. **See page 2.** .... ○₃
   d. A tax return for Puerto Rico, Guam, American Samoa, the U.S. Virgin Islands, the Marshall Islands, the Federated States of Micronesia, or Palau. **See page 2.** .... ○₄

38. If you have filed or will file a 1040, were you eligible to file a 1040A or 1040EZ? **See page 2.**   Yes ○₁   No ○₂   Don't Know ○₃

For questions 39-51, if the answer is zero or the question does not apply to you, enter 0.

39. What was your (and spouse's) adjusted gross income for 2001? Adjusted gross income is on IRS Form 1040–line 33; 1040A–line 19; 1040EZ–line 4; or Telefile–line I. $ ▢ , ▢▢▢

40. Enter the total amount of your (and spouse's) income tax for 2001. Income tax amount is on IRS Form 1040–lines 47 + 52; 1040A–lines 30 + 34; 1040EZ–line 11; or Telefile–line K(2). $ ▢ , ▢▢▢

41. Enter your (and spouse's) exemptions for 2001. Exemptions are on IRS Form 1040–line 6d or on Form 1040A–line 6d. For Form 1040EZ or Telefile, **see page 2.**   ▢▢

42-43. How much did you (and spouse) earn from working (wages, salaries, tips, etc.) in 2001? Answer this question whether or not you filed a tax return. This information may be on your W-2 forms, or on IRS Form 1040–lines 7 + 12 + 18; 1040A–line 7; or 1040EZ–line 1. Telefilers should use their W-2 forms.   **You (42)** $ ▢ , ▢▢▢   **Your Spouse (43)** $ ▢ , ▢▢▢

Student (and Spouse) Worksheets (44-46)

44-46. Go to page 8 and complete the columns on the left of Worksheets A, B, and C. Enter the student (and spouse) totals in questions 44, 45, and 46, respectively. Even though you may have few of the Worksheet items, check each line carefully.   **Worksheet A (44)** $ ▢ , ▢▢▢   **Worksheet B (45)** $ ▢ , ▢▢▢   **Worksheet C (46)** $ ▢ , ▢▢▢

47. As of today, what is the net worth of your (and spouse's) current **investments**? **See page 2.** $ ▢ , ▢▢▢

48. As of today, what is the net worth of your (and spouse's) current **businesses and/or investment farms**? **See page 2.** Do not include a farm that you live on and operate. $ ▢ , ▢▢▢

49. As of today, what is your (and spouse's) total current balance of **cash, savings, and checking accounts**? Do not include student financial aid. $ ▢ , ▢▢▢

50-51. If you receive veterans' education benefits, for **how many months** from July 1, 2002 through June 30, 2003 will you receive these benefits, and **what amount** will you receive per month? Do not include your spouse's veterans education benefits.   **Months (50)** ▢▢   **Amount (51)** $ ▢▢▢

Step Three: Answer all seven questions in this step.

52. Were you born before January 1, 1979? .... Yes ○₁   No ○₂

53. During the school year 2002-2003, will you be working on a master's or doctorate program (such as an MA, MBA, MD, JD, PhD, EdD, or graduate certificate, etc.)? .... Yes ○₁   No ○₂

54. As of today, are you married? (Answer "Yes" if you are separated but not divorced.) .... Yes ○₁   No ○₂

55. Do you have children who receive more than half of their support from you? .... Yes ○₁   No ○₂

56. Do you have dependents (other than your children or spouse) who live with you and who receive more than half of their support from you, now and through June 30, 2003? .... Yes ○₁   No ○₂

57. Are you an orphan, or are you or were you (until age 18) a ward/dependent of the court? .... Yes ○₁   No ○₂

58. Are you a veteran of the U.S. Armed Forces? **See page 2.** .... Yes ○₁   No ○₂

If you (the student) answer "No" to every question in Step Three, go to Step Four.

If you answer "Yes" to any question in Step Three, skip Step Four and go to Step Five on page 6.

(If you are a health profession student, your school may require you to complete Step Four even if you answered "Yes" in Step Three.)

Figure 11.6 (continued)

Step Four: Complete this step if you (the student) answered "No" to all questions in Step Three.

59. Go to page 7 to determine who is considered a **parent** for this step. What is your parents' marital status as of today?

(Pick one.)   Married/Remarried ○ 1   Single ○ 2   Divorced/Separated ○ 3   Widowed ○ 4

60-63. What are the Social Security Numbers and last names of the parents reporting information on this form? If your parent does not have a Social Security Number, enter 000-00-0000

60. FATHER'S/STEPFATHER'S SOCIAL SECURITY NUMBER

61. FATHER'S/ STEPFATHER'S LAST NAME

62. MOTHER'S/STEPMOTHER'S SOCIAL SECURITY NUMBER

63. MOTHER'S/ STEPMOTHER'S LAST NAME

64. Go to **page 7** to determine how many people are in your parents' household.

65. Go to **page 7** to determine how many in question 64 **(exclude your parents)** will be college students between July 1, 2002 and June 30, 2003.

66. What is your parents' state of legal residence?   STATE

67. Did your parents become legal residents of the state in question 66 before January 1, 1997?   Yes ○ 1   No ○ 2

68. If the answer to question 67 is "No," give the month and year legal residency began for the parent who has lived in the state the longest.   MONTH   YEAR

69. What is the age of your older parent?

70. For 2001, have your parents completed their IRS income tax return or another tax return listed in question 71?

a. My parents have already completed their return. ○ 1
b. My parents will file, but they have not yet completed their return. ○ 2
c. My parents are not going to file. (Skip to question 76.) ○ 3

71. What income tax return did your parents file or will they file for 2001?

a. IRS 1040 .... ○ 1
b. IRS 1040A, 1040EZ, 1040Telefile ...... ○ 2
c. A foreign tax return. See page 2. .... ○ 3

d. A tax return for Puerto Rico, Guam, American Samoa, the U.S. Virgin Islands, the Marshall Islands, the Federated States of Micronesia, or Palau. See page 2. .... ○ 4

72. If your parents have filed or will file a 1040, were they eligible to file a 1040A or 1040EZ? See page 2.   Yes ○ 1   No ○ 2   Don't Know ○ 3

For questions 73 - 83, if the answer is zero or the question does not apply, enter 0.

73. What was your parents' adjusted gross income for 2001? Adjusted gross income is on IRS Form 1040–line 33; 1040A–line 19; 1040EZ–line 4; or Telefile–line I. $

74. Enter the total amount of your parents' income tax for 2001. Income tax amount is on IRS Form 1040–lines 47 + 52; 1040A–lines 30 + 34; 1040EZ–line 11; or Telefile–line K(2). $

75. Enter your parents' exemptions for 2001. Exemptions are on IRS Form 1040–line 6d or on Form 1040A–line 6d. For Form 1040EZ or Telefile, see page 2.

76-77. How much did your parents earn from working (wages, salaries, tips, etc.) in 2001? Answer this question whether or not your parents filed a tax return. This information may be on their W-2 forms, or on IRS Form 1040–lines 7 + 12 + 18; 1040A–line 7; or 1040EZ–line 1. Telefilers should use their W-2 forms.   **Father/ Stepfather (76)** $ **Mother/ Stepmother (77)** $

Parent Worksheets (78-80)

78-80. Go to page 8 and complete the columns on the right of Worksheets A, B, and C. Enter the parent totals in questions 78, 79, and 80, respectively. Even though your parents may have few of the worksheet items, check each line carefully.   **Worksheet A (78)** $ **Worksheet B (79)** $ **Worksheet C (80)** $

81. As of today, what is the net worth of your parents' current **investments**? See page 2. $

82. As of today, what is the net worth of your parents' current **businesses and/or investment farms**? See page 2. Do not include a farm that your parents live on and operate. $

83. As of today, what is your parents' total current balance of **cash, savings, and checking accounts**? $

Now go to Step Six.

Figure 11.6   The Free Application for Federal Student Aid Form (continued)

Step Five: Complete this step only if you (the student) answered "Yes" to any question in Step Three.

84. Go to page 7 to determine how many people are in your (and your spouse's) household.

85. Go to page 7 to determine how many in question 84 will be college students between July 1, 2002 and June 30, 2003.

Step Six: Please tell us which schools should receive your information.

Enter the 6-digit federal school code and your housing plans. Look for the federal school codes at **www.fafsa.ed.gov**, at your college financial aid office, at your public library, or by asking your high school guidance counselor. If you cannot get the federal school code, write in the complete name, address, city, and state of the college. For state aid, you may wish to list your preferred school first.

	1ST FEDERAL SCHOOL CODE	NAME OF COLLEGE	STATE	HOUSING PLANS
86.		OR	ADDRESS AND CITY	**87.** on campus / off campus / with parent
88.	2ND FEDERAL SCHOOL CODE	OR	NAME OF COLLEGE / ADDRESS AND CITY	**89.** on campus / off campus / with parent
90.	3RD FEDERAL SCHOOL CODE	OR	NAME OF COLLEGE / ADDRESS AND CITY	**91.** on campus / off campus / with parent
92.	4TH FEDERAL SCHOOL CODE	OR	NAME OF COLLEGE / ADDRESS AND CITY	**93.** on campus / off campus / with parent
94.	5TH FEDERAL SCHOOL CODE	OR	NAME OF COLLEGE / ADDRESS AND CITY	**95.** on campus / off campus / with parent
96.	6TH FEDERAL SCHOOL CODE	OR	NAME OF COLLEGE / ADDRESS AND CITY	**97.** on campus / off campus / with parent

Step Seven: Please read, sign, and date.

If you are the student, by signing this application you certify that you (1) will use federal and/or state student financial aid only to pay the cost of attending an institution of higher education, (2) are not in default on a federal student loan or have made satisfactory arrangements to repay it, (3) do not owe money back on a federal student grant or have made satisfactory arrangements to repay it, and (4) will notify your school if you default on a federal student loan.

If you are the parent of a student, by signing this application you agree, if asked, to provide information that will verify the accuracy of your completed form. This information may include your U.S. or state income tax forms. Also, you certify that you understand that **the Secretary of Education has the authority to verify information reported on this application with the Internal Revenue Service and other federal agencies.** If you purposely give false or misleading information, you may be fined $20,000, sent to prison, or both.

98. Date this form was completed.

MONTH / DAY / 2002 or 2003

99. Student signature   (Sign in box)

Parent signature (one parent whose information is provided in Step Four)   (Sign in box)

If this form was filled out by someone other than you, your spouse, or your parent(s), that person must complete this part.

Preparer's name, firm, and address

100. Preparer's Social Security Number (or 101)

101. Employer ID number (or 100)

102. Preparer's signature and date

SCHOOL USE ONLY: Federal School Code

D/O

FAA SIGNATURE

MDE USE ONLY:
Special Handle

Page 6   For Help – www.ed.gov/prog_info/SFA/FAFSA

Figure 11.6 (continued)

Notes for questions 59–83 (page 5) **Step Four: Who is considered a parent in this step?**

Read these notes to determine who is considered a parent for purposes of this form. **Answer all questions in Step Four about them,** even if you do not live with them.

If your parents are both living and married to each other, answer the questions about them.

If your parent is widowed or single, answer the questions about that parent. If your widowed parent is remarried as of today, answer the questions about that parent **and** the person whom your parent married (your stepparent).

If your parents are divorced or separated, answer the questions about the parent you lived with more during the past 12 months. (If you did not live with one parent more than the other, give answers about the parent who provided more financial support during the last 12 months, or during the most recent year that you actually received support from a parent.) If this parent is remarried as of today, answer the questions on the rest of this form about that parent **and** the person whom your parent married (your stepparent).

Notes for question 64 (page 5)

Include in your parents' household (see notes, above, for who is considered a parent):
- your parents and yourself, even if you don't live with your parents, and
- your parents' other children if (a) your parents will provide more than half of their support from July 1, 2002 through June 30, 2003 or (b) the children could answer "No" to every question in Step Three on page 4 of this form, and
- other people if they now live with your parents, your parents provide more than half of their support, and your parents will continue to provide more than half of their support from July 1, 2002 through June 30, 2003.

Notes for questions 65 (page 5) **and 85** (page 6)

Always count yourself as a college student. **Do not include your parents.** Include others only if they will attend at least half time in 2002-2003 a program that leads to a college degree or certificate.

Notes for question 84 (page 6)

Include in your (and your spouse's) household:
- yourself (and your spouse, if you have one), and
- your children, if you will provide more than half of their support from July 1, 2002 through June 30, 2003, and
- other people if they now live with you, and you provide more than half of their support, and you will continue to provide more than half of their support from July 1, 2002 through June 30, 2003.

Information on the Privacy Act and use of your Social Security Number

We use the information that you provide on this form to determine if you are eligible to receive federal student financial aid and the amount that you are eligible to receive. Sections 483 and 484 of the Higher Education Act of 1965, as amended, give us the authority to ask you and your parents these questions, and to collect the Social Security Numbers of you and your parents. We use your Social Security Number to verify your identity and retrieve your records, and we may request your Social Security Number again for those purposes.

State and institutional student financial aid programs may also use the information that you provide on this form to determine if you are eligible to receive state and institutional aid and the need that you have for such aid. Therefore, we will disclose the information that you provide on this form to each institution you list in questions 86–97, state agencies in your state of legal residence, and the state agencies of the states in which the colleges that you list in questions 86–97 are located.

If you are applying solely for federal aid, you must answer all of the following questions that apply to you: 1–9, 13–15, 24, 27–28, 31–32, 35, 36–40, 42–49, 52–66, 69–74, 76–85, and 98–99. If you do not answer these questions, you will not receive federal aid.

Without your consent, we may disclose information that you provide to entities under a published "routine use." Under such a routine use, we may disclose information to third parties that we have authorized to assist us in administering the above programs; to other federal agencies under computer matching programs, such as those with the Internal Revenue Service, Social Security Administration, Selective Service System, Immigration and Naturalization Service, and Veterans Administration; to members of Congress if you ask us to help you with student aid questions.

If the federal government, the U.S. Department of Education, or an employee of the U.S. Department of Education is involved in litigation, we may send information to the Department of Justice, or a court or adjudicative body, if the disclosure is related to financial aid and certain conditions are met. In addition, we may send your information to a foreign, federal, state, or local enforcement agency if the information that you submitted indicates a violation or potential violation of law, for which that agency has jurisdiction for investigation or prosecution. Finally, we may send information regarding a claim that is determined to be valid and overdue to a consumer reporting agency. This information includes identifiers from the record; the amount, status, and history of the claim; and the program under which the claim arose.

State Certification

By submitting this application, you are giving your state financial aid agency permission to verify any statement on this form and to obtain income tax information for all persons required to report income on this form.

The Paperwork Reduction Act of 1995

The Paperwork Reduction Act of 1995 says that no one is required to respond to a collection of information unless it displays a valid OMB control number, which for this form is 1845-0001. The time required to complete this form is estimated to be one hour, including time to review instructions, search data resources, gather the data needed, and complete and review the information collection. If you have comments about this estimate or suggestions for improving this form, please write to: U.S. Department of Education, Washington DC 20202-4651.

We may request additional information from you to process your application more efficiently. We will collect this additional information only as needed and on a voluntary basis.

Page 7

Figure 11.6   The Free Application for Federal Student Aid Form (continued)

Worksheets
Calendar Year 2001

Do not mail these worksheets in with your application.
Keep these worksheets; your school may ask to see them.

Student/Spouse | Worksheet A | Parent(s)

For question 44 | | **For question 78**

Student/Spouse		Parent(s)
$	Earned income credit from IRS Form 1040–line 61a; 1040A–line 39a; 1040EZ–line 9a; or Telefile–line L(2).	$
$	Additional child tax credit from IRS Form 1040–line 63 or 1040A–line 40	$
$	Welfare benefits, including Temporary Assistance for Needy Families (TANF). Don't include Food Stamps or subsidized housing.	$
$	Social Security benefits received that were not taxed (such as SSI)	$
$	Enter in question 44.	Enter in question 78. $

Worksheet B

For question 45 | | **For question 79**

Student/Spouse		Parent(s)
$	Payments to tax-deferred pension and savings plans (paid directly or withheld from earnings), including, but not limited to, amounts reported on the W-2 Form in Boxes 12a through 12d, codes D, E, F, G, H, and S	$
$	IRA deductions and payments to self-employed SEP, SIMPLE, and Keogh and other qualified plans from IRS Form 1040–total of lines 23 + 29 or 1040A–line 16	$
$	Child support received for all children. Don't include foster care or adoption payments.	$
$	Tax exempt interest income from IRS Form 1040–line 8b or 1040A–line 8b	$
$	Foreign income exclusion from IRS Form 2555–line 43 or 2555EZ–line 18	$
$	Untaxed portions of IRA distributions from IRS Form 1040–lines (15a minus 15b) or 1040A–lines (11a minus 11b). Exclude rollovers. If negative, enter a zero here.	$
$	Untaxed portions of pensions from IRS Form 1040–lines (16a minus 16b) or 1040A–lines (12a minus 12b). Exclude rollovers. If negative, enter a zero here.	$
$	Credit for federal tax on special fuels from IRS Form 4136–line 10– nonfarmers only	$
$	Housing, food, and other living allowances paid to members of the military, clergy, and others (including cash payments and cash value of benefits)	$
$	Veterans noneducation benefits such as Disability, Death Pension, or Dependency & Indemnity Compensation (DIC) and/or VA Educational Work-Study allowances	$
$	Any other untaxed income or benefits not reported elsewhere on Worksheets A and B, such as worker's compensation, untaxed portions of railroad retirement benefits, Black Lung Benefits, disability, etc. **Don't include** student aid, Workforce Investment Act educational benefits, or benefits from flexible spending arrangements, e.g., cafeteria plans.	$
$	Cash received, or any money paid on your behalf, not reported elsewhere on this form	XXXXXXXX
	Enter in question 45.	Enter in question 79.

Worksheet C

For question 46 | | **For question 80**

Student/Spouse		Parent(s)
$	Education credits (Hope and Lifetime Learning tax credits) from IRS Form 1040-line 46 or 1040A-line 29	$
$	Child support **paid** because of divorce or separation. Don't include support for children in your (or your parents') household, as reported in question 84 (or question 64 for your parents).	$
$	Taxable earnings from Federal Work-Study or other need-based work programs	$
$	Student grant, scholarship, fellowship, and assistantship aid, including AmeriCorps awards, that was reported to the IRS in your (or your parents') adjusted gross income	$
$	Enter in question 46.	Enter in question 80. $

Page 8

Lines 31–32: High school diploma, GED, and B.A. Fill in "Yes" or "No" in the appropriate box.

Lines 33–34: Interest in student loans and work-study. If you mark "Yes," it won't result in any less grant money.

Line 35: Conviction for illegal drug possession. They mean what they say: Do not leave the space blank.

Lines 36–38: Student tax returns. If the student does not have to file income taxes, you can skip to line 39. Otherwise, you need to indicate whether your child will file and what type of tax return that will involve.

Line 39: Student's AGI. If your child has any, you must fill in his or her adjusted gross income, which is key to determining how much your family will be expected to contribute from your income to college costs. The application tells you on which line of the IRS form you'll find that number; don't mix it up with the line for the income tax total.

Line 40: Student's federal income tax. This asks for the amount of federal income tax paid, if any. Make sure to include the total federal tax liability. Taxes reduce the amount of money you and your child are expected to contribute. If you under-report, the formula will assume there is more available income at your disposal than you really have.

Line 41: Student's tax exemptions. This asks you to enter the amount of your child's exemptions, if he or she has filed an income tax return.

Lines 42–43: Earned income from work. Students must fill this in even if they did not file a tax return. It is used, among other things, to determine the Social Security tax, which also reduces the available income for the EFC.

Lines 44–46: Worksheets. You are expected to use the worksheets on page 8 of the application to calculate the answers to these questions. The worksheets are aimed at determining untaxed income and benefits and other items used to assess your child's financial need.

Line 47: Current investments. This asks for the net worth of your child's current investments, defined as the current value of these holdings minus outstanding debt. The application provides a definition of which investments should be included. Be sure to include custodial accounts in the student's name, even if he or she can't use the money yet.

Line 48: Net worth of business or farm. Again, the application gives you a definition of what is included in determining this figure. Note that they're interested in a farm used for investment purposes, not one you live on and operate.

Line 49: Current balance of cash, savings, and checking accounts. Be sure to exclude student financial aid in the figure.

Lines 50–51: Veterans education benefits. This asks for how many months your child will receive VA benefits and how much they will come to.

Lines 52–58: Date of birth, number of dependents, and related questions. These are a series of questions that determine whether your child is considered an independent or a veteran. If you answer "Yes" to any of the questions, you skip Step Four. If you answer "No" to all the questions—the situation in most cases—then you must complete that step. Note that in line 58, which asks whether your child is a veteran, he or she must have served on active duty, with an honorable discharge; it doesn't count if he or she is just in training.

Line 59: Parents' marital status. The application provides information to help you determine who is considered a parent for this step. For example, if a widowed or divorced parent is remarried, then all answers must pertain to that parent and stepparent. For a divorced parent, answer questions about the parent your child lived with more during the past 12 months. If your child spent the same amount of time with each parent, then provide answers about the one who provided more financial support.

Lines 60–63: Parents' Social Security numbers and last names. Remember that information for stepparents also must be included.

Line 64: Number of people in your household. The application includes information to help you figure this one out. For example, if grandparents or grandchildren are living in your home and you're providing more than 50 percent of their support, count them as part of the household. The more people there are in your household, the more income will be sheltered from the aid formula.

Line 65: Number of college students in household. The larger the number, the more income will be sheltered from the EFC.

Lines 66–68: State of legal residence and date when you became a resident. It's important to fill these questions in correctly, so your child is eligible for state aid.

Line 69: Age of older parent. The closer you are to retirement, the more your EFC will be reduced.

Line 70: Completion of IRS tax return. This lets them know whether you are including estimated figures or the real thing.

Lines 71–72: What type of income tax return you filed and eligibility for 1040A or 1040EZ. You have to indicate what type of form you will file or filed. The application provides information to help you.

Line 73: Parents' AGI. Like line 39, this item is of crucial importance to determining your EFC. Again, if you're divorced or separated, the parent whom your child primarily lived with over the past year is the one responsible for filling out the form. If you're remarried, your spouse's income should be included, even if he or she isn't actually pitching in to pay for college costs.

Lines 74–75: Total income tax paid and exemptions. The application tells you which line on the IRS form to look at.

Lines 76–77: Earnings from working. Like lines 43–44, this number is used to determine the Social Security tax and other allowances.

Lines 78–80: Worksheets. You'll need to include such items as workers' compensation and payments to tax-deferred pension plans made for the previous year. They are considered to be part of your AGI, although such contributions from previous years are considered assets, and not included in your EFC.

Line 81: Current investments. As in line 47, you will calculate the total of your real estate and other investments, this time for yourself, rather than your child. Prepaid tuition plans are not considered to be part of a parent's assets, nor are pensions and the cash value of a life insurance policy. Note: It's important for everyone to fill this out. Some states and schools will use the information for determining their own aid.

Line 82: Net worth of businesses and investment farms. This one is like line 48, but for yourself.

Line 83: Current balance of cash, savings, and checking accounts. As in line 49, don't include financial aid. To reduce this number, consider paying some big bills.

Lines 84–85: Number of people in household and who will be in college. You answer this only if you answered "Yes" to any question in Step Three.

Lines 86–96: List of schools to receive your financial aid information. You can list up to six schools. Be sure to include their federal school code, which you can get from various places, including <www.fafsa.ed.gov>, the college's financial aid office, or your child's high school guidance counselor.

Lines 98–99: Date of application and signatures. Make sure everyone signs the form. If a third party helped prepare the form—even if he or she was unpaid—that person must sign in the appropriate spot. Otherwise, it could be interpreted as a sign that the individual encouraged you to use false or misleading information.

The Matter of Mistakes

The FAFSA form is a potential minefield of errors. Parents often incorrectly answer the most seemingly simple items, such as Social Security number—they fill in their Social Security number when they should enter the child's—or even date of birth. Mistakes can result in the need for aid offices to reprocess applications. By the time they get to your corrected form, they may not have as much money left, and your child will end up with a lower award.

Still, there is some controversy over the issue of whether to fill out the form with estimated answers, or wait until you've filed your income tax return, so you know the numbers are correct. On the one hand, time is of utmost importance. On the other, if you complete the form incorrectly, you'll slow down the process even more. In the end, one view holds that it comes down to a matter of complexity. "The more complicated your financial situation, the more you should consider waiting," is the advice of Seppy Basili, vice president of precollege planning at Kaplan Publishing. The bottom line: Read all instructions carefully. This is not a time to skim. If you have questions, don't hesitate to call the financial aid office for help.

Verification

Every year, U.S. Department of Education processors choose families for a process known as verification. It's meant to make sure applicants don't include false information and that everyone gets their fair share of aid. Some are randomly selected, others are chosen because information on the FAFSA is inconsistent with other information reported on the application. If you're one of the lucky ones, you'll have to give your financial aid office documentation to show the application is accurate. The sooner you verify the data, the sooner you'll be able to receive financial aid, so a speedy response is advisable.

RESOURCES

Books

Don't Miss Out: The Ambitious Student's Guide to Financial Aid, by Anna and Robert Leider (Octameron Press, P.O. Box 2748, Alexandria, VA 22301; 703-836-5480; www.octameron.com). Detailed descriptions of qualifications for financial aid. Also lists many sources of government and private aid. Contains complete tables and worksheets for family contribution under Federal Methodology.

Financial Aid Financer: Expert Answers to College Financing Questions (Octameron Press, P.O. Box 2748, Alexandria, VA 22301; 703-836-5480; www.octameron .com). Explains how to apply for financial aid, how to put together a financial aid package, strategies for financing college, and financing strategies for graduate students.

Financial Aid Officers: What They Do to You and for You, by Donald Moore (Octameron Press, P.O. Box 2748, Alexandria, VA 22301; 703-836-5480; www .octameron.com). Describes who financial aid officers are and their role in granting students financial aid. Helps you fill out a financial aid application and explains how applications are processed.

The Government Financial Aid Book: The Insider's Guide to State and Federal Government Grants and Loans, by Student Financial Services (Perpetual Press, P.O.

Box 30414, Lansing, MI 48909-7914; 800-444-4226; www.readersndex.com). A variety of federal and state financial aid programs exist to help students pay for college, but if the proper procedures are not followed when applying for them, your application can be disqualified. This book simplifies the application process by helping the reader understand each program and by providing detailed instructions and tips for completing forms. Internet instructions to access the latest federal aid policies are included.

Paying for College without Going Broke, by Kalman A. Chany and Geoff Martz (Princeton Review, 2315 Broadway, New York, NY 10024; 800-2-REVIEW [800-273-8439]; www.review.com). This book helps the reader plan ahead to improve the chances of getting financial aid, calculate aid eligibility before applying to colleges, complete financial aid forms, negotiate with financial aid offices, and learn about educational tax breaks.

Software

Financial Aid (EFC) (Octameron Associates, P.O. Box 2748, Alexandria, VA 22301; 703-836-3480; www.octameron.com). A simple software program designed to help you compute your EFC to college costs. By changing the income or assets that your family reports, you easily can see how your expected contribution changes. Also may help you to find ways to lower your EFC and qualify for more student aid.

Trade Association

The National Association of Student Financial Aid Administrators (1129 20th St., N.W., Suite 400, Washington, DC 20036; 202-785-0453; www.nasfaa.org). Represents more than 10,000 financial aid professionals at more than 3,000 colleges, universities, and career schools.

Web Sites

Collegeboard. Helps with the financial aid process. This site offers calculators, scholarship searches, and useful facts. <www.collegeboard.com>

Department of Education's (DOE) Office of Postsecondary Education. The federal government's site allows you to file your FAFSA online. The site offers detailed instructions on filling out the form, and is loaded with links to colleges and other financial aid–related Web sites. Part of this site is called FAFSA Express, at <www .ed.gov/offices/OPE/express.html>, which allows you to complete and electronically submit the FAFSA form and get it processed quicker than the old-fashioned paper form. If you have questions about filling out these forms, you can call the FAFSA Service Center at 800-801-0576. The site also has information on the DOE's Direct Loan program at <www.ed.gov/offices/OPE/DirectLoan/>. <www.ed.gov/offices /OPE/Students>

Federal Student Financial Assistance Program. On this Department of Education Web site, students can apply for financial aid online. They even can electronically sign the application forms on completion. All the worksheets can be downloaded from the Web site. <www.fafsa.ed.gov>

FinAid. A public service site that provides information about college loans, scholarships, and grants. Assists you with financial aid applications, demystifies the paperwork, and provides forms and instructions. Includes calculators to help determine how much money you will need and what loan payments will be. Has advice on college admissions and jobs. <www.finaid.org>

The Princeton Review. The site offers a tool called the FAFSA Worksheet. When you enter the information, each question is explained so you understand how best to allocate your resources to ensure maximum eligibility. <www.review.com>

CHAPTER 12

Using Your Computer to Finance Your Child's Education

When it comes to the process of figuring out how to pay for college, today's parents and students have one big advantage over previous generations: the Internet. Indeed, the computer can make the search for financial aid much more efficient and productive than the old-fashioned way of wading through books and filling out applications and financial aid forms by hand. There are enormous resources available through the Internet to help you calculate how much financial aid you will need, and to help you find as much as possible.

In fact, you can use the Web just about every step of the way. From deciding which schools to try for to finding out about government grants, it's there. And, you'll find a lot more than just information. Many applications also can be completed online.

Perhaps the biggest advantage is the ability to search. With the Web, you can search a database using specific criteria, making the process of looking for possible scholarships considerably more efficient than it used to be. Of course, time is money. The faster you can get the information, the faster you can get your applications in—and, hopefully, find the money you need.

SEARCHING FOR SCHOOLS

The Web makes it a lot easier to survey the landscape of schools and decide which ones to consider. Using a variety of search engines, you and your child can evaluate schools on the basis of criteria that are particularly important to you. For example, at collegeboard.com, you answer a comprehensive series of questions, pinpointing, for example, whether your child would prefer a school in an urban area or a small liberal arts school. Next, the site produces a list of colleges that match your answers. There's also an option called "Like Finder," which allows you to locate places that are similar to schools you already know you like. With College Quest, at <www.collegequest.com>, you can get information about colleges and do side-by-side comparisons. After you put together a list of schools to consider, you then can take a virtual tour of the campuses. Most colleges and universities have elaborate Web sites allowing you to visit their campus online, and also find out about course offerings and the amount of financial aid available. It certainly is a lot cheaper and less time consuming to tour several colleges online than it is to go to each in person. Only, be careful: Many sites are nothing more than Web-based promotional material. If you really think you're interested in applying, a real-life visit is probably a good idea.

Applying

Once your child is ready to apply, you also can do that online. School sites often include applications you can print out and fill out manually, or that you can submit over the Web. If the schools your child is applying to are some of the 209 colleges and universities that accept a standard form called the Common Application, you can fill out the document electronically at <www .commonapp.org>. For a look at this Web site, see Figure 12.1. A number of sites, such as <www.collegenet.com>, also serve as electronic hosts to hundreds of college applications that can be filled out online.

Figuring Out Costs

Many college and financial aid Web sites contain calculators that help you figure out how much colleges will expect parents to pay, how much will be provided in financial aid—depending on the parents' financial circumstances —and what kind of loan repayment schedule you can expect. They also help you set up a savings plan. One site often referred to as one of the best is <www.finaid.org>. Its many calculators allow you to do everything from determining how much you might get in federal aid to what your loan repayment schedule should be. Consider the Savings Plan Designer. With it, you can figure out how much money to contribute each month to an interest-bearing bank account or investment fund to reach a particular savings goal. You plug in the amount of your current savings, a specific rate of return on investment, the number of years your child has to go until starting college, and how often you want to make the contributions, along with your savings goal and the current cost of a particular college. For a better look, see Figure 12.2.

Figure 12.1   Commonapp.org Web Site

Welcome to the 2002-2003 Common App Online!

Why would you apply any other way?

Home | Register | Login | College Info | Forms | FAQ | Instructions | Feedback

Welcome!

The Common Application is the recommended form of 230 selective colleges and universities for admission to their undergraduate programs. Many of these institutions use the form exclusively. All give equal consideration to the Common Application and the college's own form. With 230 colleges and universities to choose from and one easy form to fill out, why would you apply any other way?

Please Note: The 2002-03 Common Application should be used by students to apply for the fall 2003 and spring 2004 college sessions.

College Information

Get information on the 230 Common Application Colleges and Universities!

Register

Ready to get started? Click here to register and start applying!

Download Forms

Download additional report and evaluation forms in PDF format!

Login

Registered users click here log in and work on your application.

Instructions

Instructions for completing the application.

Forgot Your Password

Forgot your user name or password? Click here to have it mailed to you.

Frequently Asked Questions

Click here for a list of common questions.

Feedback

Contact us with your questions, comments, or suggestions

Legal Stuff

Minimum Browser Requirement:
Netscape Navigator 4.7 or Microsoft Internet Explorer 5.0;
Adobe Acrobat Reader 4.05 or later
© 1996-2002 ApplicationsOnline LLC. All rights reserved.

Source: Used with permission of the Common Application, Inc.

Figure 12.2   FinAid's Savings Plan Designer

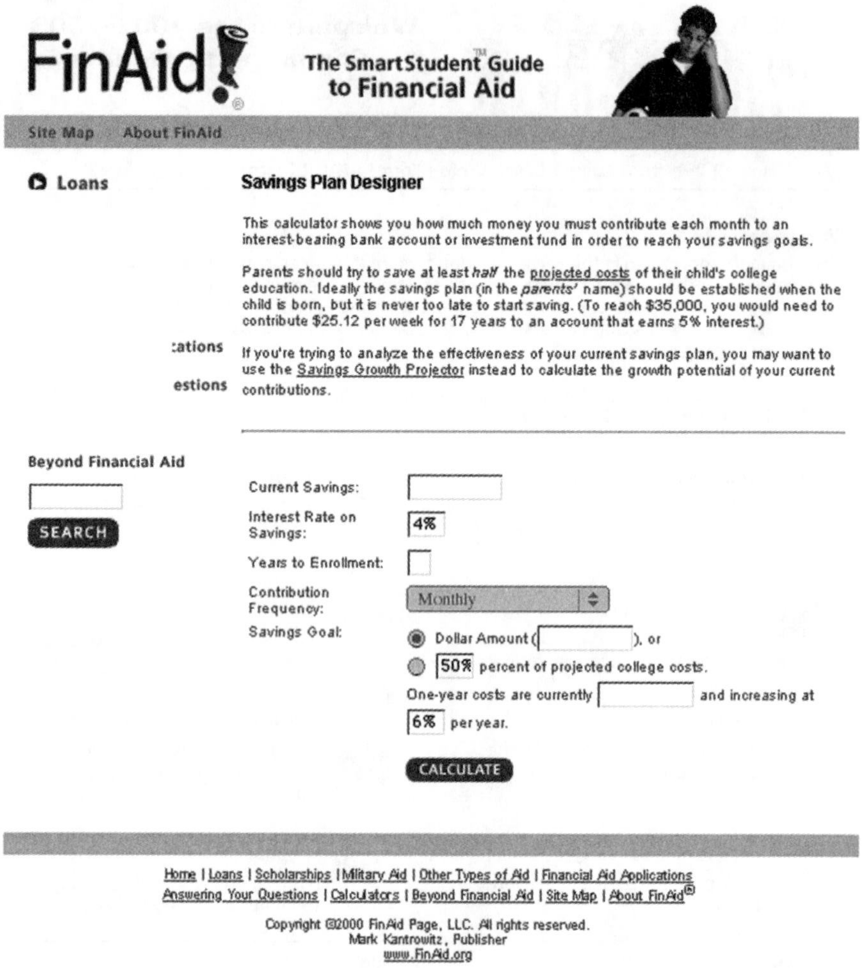

LOOKING FOR AID

To get a thorough overview of federal grants and loans, start with the U.S. Department of Education's site at <www.ed.gov/studentaid>. There are also many other Web sites containing mountains of information on scholarships, grants, and loans that your child may be able to qualify for. National Scholarship Research Service (www.fastaid.com), for example, the oldest private sector scholarship database, allows you to plug in information about your grade point average, ethnic background, special interests, and the like, and then provides a list of potential scholarships that fit those criteria. There are also several CD-ROMs that allow you to search for scholarships that your child might have a good chance of getting. These discs often are sold along with scholarship listing books.

APPLYING FOR AID

Of course, you also can apply for financial aid online. For federal aid, you can fill out the Free Application for Federal Student Aid form at <www.fafsa.ed.gov>. You and your child will need to get a personal identification number (PIN), which you can request from <www.pin.ed.gov>. You use your PIN to sign your FAFSA application electronically. If you have questions about your PIN, you also can call 800-433-3243. It's a good idea, however, to print out a copy of your application for your records, in case the school asks you to show that the information on your FAFSA is correct.

Many private schools require that you fill out another form, the CSS/ Financial Aid PROFILE. You either can complete it on paper or you can choose to fill it out electronically at <www.collegeboard.org/profile.html>.

RESOURCES

The following is a list of Web sites that can help you with all aspects of the process of financing a college education:

@theU. This site offers online applications for financial aid along with online loan calculators. Students also can buy their textbooks at this site, earning UniBucks worth up to 5 percent of the purchase price. The student's personal UniBucks are tracked and accessed via the ATM. Once earned, UniBucks can be applied to your student loan account serviced at UNIPAC or any other financial institution you designate. Parents, family members, and friends can establish their own @theU accounts. UniBucks from those accounts can then be transferred to the student's account. <www.attheu.com>

CampusTours.com. This site allows you to tour any of the thousands of colleges in the site's database. It offers a photo tour, a panoramic 360-degree tour of principal areas on campus, the college's own Web site, and Web cams on some campuses providing live photos, updating every minute of the day. <www.campustours.com>

Collegeboard. Helps with the financial aid process. This site offers calculators, scholarship searches, and useful facts. <www.collegeboard.com>

CollegeClub. A general student site with lots of information and help for students, including a scholarship search engine and a loan finder. <www.collegeclub.com>

College Express. This site presents information on hundreds of private colleges and universities. It also has an extensive section on the financial aid process, including the best ways to apply for federal and college-based aid and how to negotiate a lower tuition cost from the school. <www.collegexpress.com>

CollegeLearning.com. College Learning has partnerships with more than 100 accredited colleges and universities that offer a range of for-credit and noncredit distance courses. Courses are delivered via the Internet, television, CD-ROM, videotape, audiotape, videoconferencing, or other media. <www.collegelearning.com>

CollegeNet. CollegeNet lets applicants complete, file, and pay for their admissions applications entirely over the Internet. <www.collegenet.com>

College Parents of America. This is a member site; membership costs $25. The site provides members with information on saving strategies, financial aid, education tax credits and deductions, and other ways to help pay for college. Also offers members special values and discounts on items such as computers, books, college guides, and study-abroad programs. <www.collegeparents.org>

College Savings Plans Network. This network is designed to administer college savings plans. College savings plans allow participants to save money in a special college savings account on behalf of a designated beneficiary's qualified higher education expenses. Contributions can vary, depending on the individual's savings goals. The plans offer a variable rate of return, although some programs guarantee a minimum rate of return. The College Savings Plans Network is an affiliate to the National Association of State Treasurers. <www.collegesavings.org>

Department of Education's (DOE) Office of Postsecondary Education. The federal government's site allows you to file your FAFSA online. The site offers detailed instructions on filling out the form, and is loaded with links to colleges and other financial aid–related Web sites. Part of this site is called FAFSA Express, at <www.ed.gov/offices/OPE/express.html>, which allows you to complete and electronically submit the FAFSA form and get it processed quicker than the old-fashioned paper form. If you have questions about filling out these forms, you can call the FAFSA Service Center at 800-801-0576. The site also has information on the DOE's Direct Loan program at <www.ed.gov/offices/OPE/DirectLoan/>. <www.ed.gov/offices /OPE/Students>

Ed-X. This site creates its own multimedia learning content and offers consulting on the online marketing of learning content to third parties. <www.ed-x.com>

Embark.com. This site offers an admission service to colleges, graduate schools, business schools, and law schools. It also offers online degrees and certificates. Helps prepare for standardized tests and offers student loans, credit cards, and online banking for students. <www.embark.com>

eStudent Loan. Students or parents can compare student loans and apply online. The site starts out by asking you to select the type of student you are, or your child is; that is, an undergraduate or a graduate student. The site will then give you a list of lenders based on your state, intended college or university, and other factors. <www.estudentloan.com>

FastWeb. This site allows you to conduct a personalized search of potential loans and scholarships you or your child may qualify for. You fill in a detailed form about you or your child, and the site searches its vast database for financing options, with the details about each program. For more information on FastWeb, call 800-327-8932. <www.fastweb.com>

Federal Student Financial Assistance Program. On this U.S. Department of Education Web site, students can apply for financial aid online. They even can electronically sign the application forms on completion. All the worksheets can be downloaded from the Web site. <www.fafsa.ed.gov>

Fidelity. On Fidelity's College Planning section, you will find a concise explanation of Section 529 college savings plans, along with comparisons of those plans with custodian, brokerage, Education IRA, and prepaid tuition plans. <fidelity.com>

FinAid. A public service site that provides information about college loans, scholarships, and grants. Assists you with financial aid applications, demystifies the paperwork, and provides forms and instructions. Includes calculators to help determine how much money you will need and what loan payments will be. Has advice on college admissions and jobs. <www.finaid.org>

Internet Student Loans Company. On this site, you can learn about the various types of student loans available. You can apply for a private loan online, and the site claims that they will have the loan approved or otherwise in five minutes. You also can apply for a federal undergraduate Stafford Loan or a federal PLUS Loan online. <www.istudentloan.com>

Mind Edge. Provides resources for personal development, distance learning, continuing education, and on-campus and corporate training courses. <www.mindedge .com>

MyRoad.com. This site allows the student to explore majors, find a college, research careers, and discover what careers suit their individual talents. Guides you to develop your own plan for your education and subsequent career. <www.myroad.com>

National Scholarship Research Service. The world's largest and oldest private sector scholarship database. Students also can compare available loans and apply online for a student loan. <www.fastaid.com>

Parent Soup Guide to College Planning. This site for parents has extensive resources on finding the best college and financing a child's college education. <www .parent.soup.com>

Peterson's Education Center. The publisher of many financial aid books has a useful site explaining the entire process. There is a college admissions calendar reminding you of various filing deadlines, plus a glossary of terms and definitions of various types of financial aid. <www.petersons.com>

R1Edu.org. This site directs students to participating institutions' distance learning course information. It is not a degree-granting institution. <www.r1edu.org>

RSP Funding Focus. Reference Service Press provides a one-stop information resource for scholarships, fellowships, loans, grants, awards, and internships. The site features a financial aid library, a listing of state financial aid agencies, and a mailing list you can get on that provides a free electronic newsletter filled with the latest information about financial aid programs. You also can contact RSP at 5000 Windplay Dr., Suite 4, Eldorado Hills, CA 95762; 916-939-9620. RSP also publishes 19 books, including *Financial Aid for the Disabled and Their Families* and *High School Senior's Guide to Merit and Other No-Need Funding.* <www.rspfunding.com>

Saving for College.com. This site provides a lot of information about Section 529 college savings plans. Includes details of all the state government college financing plans. Just select your state and the information comes up. <www.savingforcollege .com>

Scholarship Resource Network Express. A search engine and database of private scholarships designed to assist students in identifying sources for undergraduate through postgraduate study. <www.srnexpress.com>

Student Credit. Students can learn about credit, credit reports, and credit repair, and can apply for a number of major bank student credit cards. These cards are designed especially for students, usually with no annual fee, some with e-mail reminders about their account balance, and some with ATM access. <www.studentcredit.com>

Studentmarket.com. This site has a good student loan education section. You can apply online for prequalification and an information kit. You also can apply online for a student Discover, American Express, or CapitalOne credit card. The site has a number of offers for students for long distance telephone rates, software, computers, clothing, and jobs. <www.studentmarket.com>

TextBooksatCost.com. Offers textbooks at discounted prices. Includes a free service for students to advertise used textbooks on the site for other students to buy or swap. <www.textbooksatcost.com>

TIAA-CREF. Serves as investment manager for state-sponsored college savings programs, Education IRAs, prepaid tuition plans, and other college loans. TIAA-CREF charges an annual fee of .8 percent of account assets for its services. <www .tiaa-cref.org>

U.S. News and World Report. The *U.S. News and World Report*'s annual college edition provides a list of what the magazine evaluates as the best college values. Another part of the site guides you through the financial aid process. It answers frequently asked questions about financing college. The site also lists other financial aid Web sites, offers a loan center, and much more. <www.usnews.com>

VarsityBooks.com. Online college bookstore that offers to identify the books you need once you select your college and program. You then can buy those books your professors have recommended for your courses. <www.varsitybooks.com>

Vault.com. An online source for career and internship information. <www .vault.com>

Wiredscholar.com. A comprehensive site from Sallie Mae, with everything from a college-matching service to tools for calculating loans. <wiredscholar.com>

CHAPTER 13

Other Borrowing Alternatives and Ways to Cut College Costs

S till coming up short? You have other options. One is borrowing from yourself. You may not realize it, but you may have accumulated substantial equity in certain assets, meant for other purposes, that you can borrow against. And, you can do so at a lower interest rate and with less hassle than applying for government, college, or commercial loans. For many middle-class families who don't qualify for much aid, it's often a useful alternative.

Another possibility is to reduce your total costs. For example, your child may be able to reduce the number of credits needed in order to graduate. If, for example, he or she starts out from the get-go with college credits, fewer classes will be needed to graduate, and you lower the price tag. In some cases, your child may be able to earn a degree in a shorter period of time.

Other avenues to explore include attending a community college. Or, what about applying to a school in Canada? The country has many top-quality schools and, with the strong U.S. dollar, the cost of education comes at bargain-basement prices. Many Canadian schools are offering attractive packages to U.S. students.

BORROWING FROM YOURSELF

The most obvious places to look for equity include your home, your company's savings plan, and your life insurance policy. But, borrowing against these assets comes with a price—sometimes a heavy one. After all, they all involve areas of vital importance. Don't make these moves unless you're sure you can repay.

Your Home

If you have paid down your mortgage and built up substantial equity in your home, you may be able to receive a home equity line of credit or loan. A home equity loan charges a low interest rate and allows you to repay it as quickly or as slowly as you wish, as long as you meet each month's minimum payment. Most financial institutions, such as banks, savings and loans, brokerage firms, finance companies, credit unions, and others, have entered the home equity market.

In effect, a home equity loan is a second mortgage on your home. You generally can borrow up to 80 percent of the appraised value of your home, minus whatever you still owe on your first mortgage. For example, if your home is worth $100,000 and you owe $20,000 on your mortgage, you might receive a home equity line of credit for $60,000, as your lender subtracts your $20,000 owed on the first mortgage from your $80,000 worth of equity. At the same time, with many lenders offering home equity, you may be able to find one willing to approve 90 percent, or even 100 percent, but at a somewhat higher interest rate.

An extra bonus is that all borrowing up to $100,000 is tax deductible on your federal and state income tax returns, except if the money is used to purchase tax-exempt bonds or single-premium life insurance. Thanks to that deduction, many people limit themselves to that amount. If you qualify, however, banks will lend much more.

Loan versus Credit Line

You have two choices when you're borrowing against your home equity: taking out a line of credit or a loan. With the line of credit, you can tap it when you have to. If you need a few thousand dollars one semester, the money is there. The loan, however, comes in a lump sum, so you have one shot to estimate how much you'll need. Plus, you have to pay interest starting from the moment you take out the loan.

Flexibility

One of the biggest appeals to borrowing against your home equity is its flexibility. You can tap the credit line simply by writing a check, although some lenders levy an annual fee or a transaction charge every time you write a check on your credit line. You also can pay back the loan as quickly or as slowly as you like, as long as you meet the minimum payment each month. In theory, you must repay outstanding balances in five or ten years in one balloon payment. In practice, the bank probably will not require the balloon payment as long as you pay the minimum due. Keep in mind, however, that the longer you take to repay, the more in interest you'll also accumulate. Figure 13.1 gives you a better idea of what that might amount to.

Interest Rates

The other big attraction of home equity loans is low interest rates. Because the loans are less risky for banks—they are backed by your home as collateral—you benefit by paying a much lower interest rate than you would on credit cards or most other kinds of loans. Home equity credit lines, however, typically charge a variable rate one to three percentage points above the prime lending rate. In many cases, home equity lenders will start you off with an introductory rate of one-half to one percentage point below the prime rate for six months to as long as one year. Home equity lines of credit can there-

---

Figure 13.1   Home Equity Payments

Here's how your interest payments might be affected by longer repayment schedules. The table assumes a fully amortizing $50,000 fixed-rate loan, with no late fees or prepayment fees, and that the loan is carried through full term.*

Years of Repayment	4% Interest Rate Monthly Payment	Total Interest Paid
5	$ 920.80	$ 5,248.00
10	506.24	10,748.80
15	369.88	16,578.40

Years of Repayment	6% Interest Rate Monthly Payment	Total Interest Paid
5	$ 966.60	$ 7,996.00
10	555.13	16,615.60
15	421.98	25,956.40

Years of Repayment	8% Interest Rate Monthly Payment	Total Interest Paid
5	$1,013.76	$10,825.60
10	606.67	22,800.40
15	477.90	36,022.00

*These rates assume no other fees or additional charges in connection with obtaining a loan. Fees and charges may vary by lender and will change the payment amounts shown.
Source: FleetBoston Financial Corp.

fore offer extremely attractive rates when the prime rate is low, but subject you to much higher interest costs if the prime shoots up.

Qualifying and Costs

Like other mortgages, qualifying for a loan involves a complicated and not inexpensive process. First, you will qualify not only on the value of your home, but also on your creditworthiness. For instance, you must prove that you have a regular source of income to repay a home equity loan. You also will usually need a home appraisal and must pay legal and application fees and closing costs. In addition, the lender may collect an annual fee of up to $50 to maintain the account.

The largest up-front cost, called points, is really an add-on fee in the form of prepaid interest to the lender. One point equals 1 percent of the credit line you open. For example, if you establish a $100,000 home equity line of credit, one point would total $1,000 due at the time your loan closes. Some lenders charge two or three points, which would amount to $2,000 or $3,000 on a $100,000 loan. Nonetheless, competition in the marketplace has induced some lenders to offer no-points home equity lines of credits and loans, though such loans may charge higher interest rates than loans requiring points.

Make sure to shop for the best rate. A difference of just a few points can mean several thousand dollars more or less in how much you'll have to repay, so it's worth doing a thorough job. You can check out rates and points at Web sites such as Bankrate.com, shown in Figure 13.2, which lets you search for the best rates in your area.

A Word of Caution

Tapping your home equity provides a flexible, easy way to borrow money. But, you have to be cautious. First, the interest is tax-deductible only if you itemize deductions. If you take the standard deduction, because your total deductions are less than $4,550 if you're filing individually, or $7,600 if you're filing as a couple, you aren't allowed to take a deduction for your home equity loan. Also, be careful not to take out too big a credit line. Even if you don't use it, other lenders may include the full amount as part of your total outstanding debt. That may mean you would be rejected for other loans, such as credit cards and car loans. Most important, however, remember that your home is on the line; if you default, the bank will foreclose.

Your Company Savings Plan

If you have participated for several years in a salary reduction or profit-sharing plan at work, such as a 401(k), you probably have accumulated a substantial sum of money. Most employers will let you borrow against that

Figure 13.2 Bankrate.com Web Site

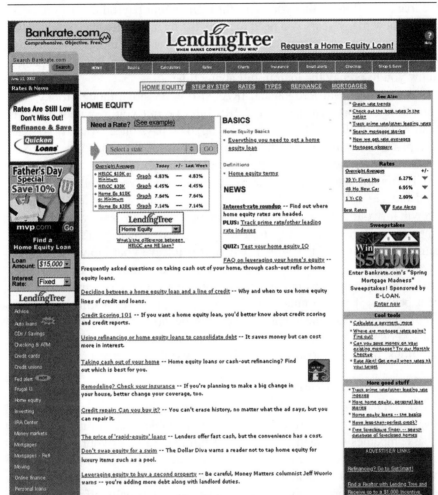

Source: Bankrate.com.

money. Interest rates charged on such loans often are quite favorable at one or two percentage points above the prime rate.

Most companies allow you to borrow a certain amount of the assets accumulated in your 401(k) plan up to $50,000. Often, you must shift the amount of funds you want to borrow into an extremely conservative investment option, such as a Guaranteed Investment Contract (GIC), for the duration of the loan. Because your company wants to make sure that you repay the loan, it will insist that you do so through regular payroll deductions. You choose how many years you need to repay the loan, usually from one to five. The longer you take to pay off the loan, the lower your monthly payments, but the higher your interest costs over the life of the loan. Most companies allow you to prepay the loan in full at any time.

Borrowing from Keoghs and IRAs also is possible, though tricky, and should be a short-term last resort. IRS rules permit you to withdraw from your Keogh or IRA without penalty for up to 60 days once a year. If you fail to replace the money within those two months, you must pay income taxes on the borrowed amount, plus a 10 percent penalty.

Borrowing against your retirement savings, however, should be considered only as a last resort. These plans are designed to provide long-term growth for your golden years, not to pay huge college costs for your children. The more you take out to pay for college, the less growth you'll get in your retirement nest egg. Also, with a 401(k), if you leave your job voluntarily or involuntarily, money you borrowed becomes due within 60 days. If you're unable to pay, you must pay income tax on the amount, along with a 10 percent penalty, if you're under age 55. While you're investigating options at your company, ask the employee benefits department whether your firm makes college loans to employees. Some companies, particularly large corporations, offer such loans at attractive, below-market interest rates.

Your Life Insurance

If you have amassed a large amount of cash value in your insurance policy, you usually can borrow against it at a favorable interest rate. All insurance companies will lend cash up to the full face value of your policy at an interest rate from as little as 5 percent to as much as 15 percent. Some older policies permitted loans at a guaranteed rate of 5 percent as long as the policy remained in force. Policies issued more recently usually offer a variable-rate loan tied to some index of interest rates, such as the prime rate or yields on Treasury securities. Like other consumer interest, the finance charges you pay on a life insurance loan are not deductible.

All you must do to borrow from your policy is to inform your insurance agent how much money you want, and he or she will process your loan application. You need not explain your plans for the loan proceeds, and no one will check your credit record. You should receive a check within a few days or weeks.

Again, consider this as a last resort. Your death benefit is automatically reduced by the amount you borrow, so if you die while the loan is outstanding, your heirs receive less of a payout from the insurer. Some companies also lower the return they credit you on your cash value by the amount of your loan. Therefore, the cash value remaining in your policy might grow more slowly than if you hadn't borrowed. The bottom line: Don't borrow so much that you seriously impair your insurance coverage.

COST-CUTTING MEASURES

If borrowing against your assets seems risky, there are a number of other routes you can take to reduce the total amount you will have to pay.

Graduate in Three Years

One way to cut costs is for your child to attend a school that lets students graduate in three years. Some schools have formal programs that allow students to do this. In some cases, students generally don't have to attend summer sessions or take a heavier course load. Some examples include:

- *Southern New Hampshire University, Manchester, New Hampshire* <www.snhu.edu>. The program, for Business Administration majors only, was developed with a grant from the U.S. Department of Education. Students must apply to the program, which accepts about 30 students a year. Basically, you pay the regular cost of tuition, fees, and room and board, which is $25,000, but you pay it only for three years, instead of four.
- *Southern Oregon University, Ashland, Oregon* <www.sou.edu>. To be accepted, a student must have had a 3.4 GPA in high school or a score of 1,150 on the SAT1 or 25 on the ACT. About ten departments participate. Students pay the regular cost of tuition and fees—$3,550 for Oregon residents and $10,970 for nonresidents—for each of the three years they attend school.
- *Northern Arizona University, Flagstaff, Arizona* <www.nau.edu>. Students take 18 hours a semester for six semesters, plus 12 hours of summer school. You'll have to pay the regular tuition and fees, which are $2,346 for in-state residents and $8,778 for out-of-state residents, plus summer school. You can reduce costs further if your child attends a community college over the summer instead. Many, but not all, departments participate in the program. The program, warn admissions officers, isn't for everyone, but if your child knows what he or she wants to study, and is willing to forgo a lot of extracurricular activities, it may be the right move.

Of course, it's also possible for your child to cobble together his or her own three-year program, by taking a heavier course load and, perhaps, attending summer school. But, it's a tough road, and not something that a lot of students can handle. In many cases, the savings may not be worth the ordeal your child will have to go through.

Take Advanced Placement

Another possibility is for your child to take Advanced Placement (AP) courses in high school, which would qualify him or her to take an AP exam, administered by the College Board. Most colleges will award course credit to students who get a 3 or 4 on the exam, depending on the college. For a look at the courses now offered, see Figure 13.3.

Policies regarding AP credit vary widely. Not every institution will grant credit, for example. Instead, they may just allow students to skip certain entry-level courses, without allowing them to take a reduced course load. Or, they may simply use them as part of the college application process, and give no course credit at all. Check with the school to find out what their policy is.

Take CLEP Tests

Your child also may be able to take College-Level Examination Program (CLEP) tests. These exams, also sponsored by the College Board, are another way to get course credit. Again, school policies differ from one institution to the next, so you need to check with the school to see which exams they recognize and what other requirements they may have. You'll probably find the CLEP policy in the general catalog, under a heading such as Credit-by-Examination, Advanced Standing, Advanced Placement, or External Degree Program. Some colleges limit the total amount of credit your child can earn through exams. And, not all schools award the same amount of credit. Your child also may have to pass a departmental test, in addition to the exam, to earn credit.

Attend a Community College

Community colleges can provide your child with an excellent education —at a fraction of the cost of a four-year school. The average cost of tuition and fees at one of the 1,166 community colleges in North America is $1,518—a bargain. For a sample of community colleges and what they cost, see Figure 13.4. When your child has earned his or her associate degree, he or she can then transfer to a four-year school, and graduate along with the rest of the class, at a fraction of the cost that everyone else had to pay.

What's your child's chance of transferring into a four-year school? Pretty good, because 25 percent of community college students transfer to such schools. Your child will have a particularly good shot at a public university. For example, in California and Florida, public institutions have to give preference to students transferring from in-state community colleges. Colorado,

Figure 13.3   Advanced Placement Subjects

Here is a list of AP subjects currently offered:

Art History	Human Geography
Biology	International English Language (APIEL)
Calculus AB & BC	Latin
Chemistry	Music Theory
Computer Science	Physics
Economics	Psychology
English	Spanish
Environmental Science	Statistics
European History	Studio Art
French	U.S. History
German	World History
Government & Politics	

Figure 13.4   Tuition and Fees at Community Colleges

School	*Tuition and Fees*
Clatsop Community College Astoria, Oregon www.clatsop.cc.or.us	$1,512 in-state $3,672 out-of-state
Ellsworth Community College Iowa Falls, Iowa www.iavalley.cc.ia.us/ecc	$2,670 in-state $4,680 out-of-state
Holyoke Community College Holyoke, Massachusetts www.hcc.mass.edu	$1,756 in-state $6,700 out-of-state
Itasca Community College Grand Rapids, Minnesota www.cc.mn.us	$2,583 in-state $4,731 out-of-state
Pensacola Junior College Pensacola, Florida www.pjc.cc.fl.us	$1,456 in-state $5,180 out-of-state

Massachusetts, and Wisconsin actually guarantee admission to a public university in the state for graduates of community colleges who have met certain academic standards. In addition, private schools also have recently increased the number of transfers from community colleges with new scholarship programs targeted specifically at graduates with associate's degrees.

Go to Canada

There are a number of top-quality schools over the border that rival the Ivy Leagues in the level of education they provide. And, they cost around $10,000 to $16,000 per year—a good $25,000 less than your typical U.S. Ivy League school or its equivalent. Some examples include McGill University in Montreal, Queen's University in Kingston, Ontario, and the University of Toronto. Remember: You also can use money in your 529 plan to pay for tuition at many Canadian schools. The competition is just as stiff as it is for a similar school here, however, so getting accepted is by no means guaranteed.

Pay in Installments

One way to lighten the financial burden is to sign up for a tuition payment plan, letting you pay in monthly installments. Usually, there is no interest charged, but there may be a minimal enrollment fee. You won't reduce costs, but you may find it easier to pay the bill.

RESOURCES

Book

Insurance for Dummies, by Jack Kingelmann (Hungry Minds, 10475 Crosspoint Blvd., Indianapolis, IN 46256l; 800-434-3422; www.hungryminds.com). Another easy-to-understand primer on the basics of insurance.

Software

APCD (College Board, 45 Columbus Ave., New York, NY 10023; 800-323-7155; collegeboard.com). Available from the College Board through mail order, this CD-ROM includes practice exams and tutorials for Advanced Placement tests.

Quicken (Intuit, 2535 Garcia Ave., Mountain View, CA 94043; 650-944-6000; www.qfn.com). You can use this financial software program to calculate a loan repayment schedule for your home equity loan.

Trade Associations/National Services

American Association of Community Colleges (One Dupont Circle, N.W., Suite 410, Washington, DC 20036; 202-728-0200; www.aacc.nche.edu/). The trade association for community colleges can provide you with information about colleges in your area, costs, financial aid, and other information.

American Council of Life Insurers (1001 Pennsylvania Ave., N.W., 5th Floor South, Washington, DC 20004-2599; 202-624-2000; www.acli.com/). A trade group of life insurance companies that lobbies on life insurance, long-term-care insurance, disability income insurance, and retirement savings matters. Upon written request, they will send a free copy of "What You Should Know about Buying Life Insurance," which is also downloadable from the Web site.

National Insurance Consumers Hotline (800-942-4242). This toll-free service provides information about all kinds of insurance questions.

Federal Government Regulator

Federal Trade Commission (6th St. and Pennsylvania Ave., N.W., Washington, DC 20580; 202-326-3650; www.ftc.gov). Will send a free copy of the following brochures, which also are available online in full text at <www.ftc.gov>: "Getting a Loan: Your Home as Security," "Home Equity Credit Lines," and "Home Equity Scams: Borrowers Beware!"

Web Sites

Bankrate.com. Search for the best bank loan rates and deals in your area. <www.bankrate.com>

Collegeboard.com. The site provides a fount of information, including an explanation of how Advanced Placement and the College-Level Examination Program work, descriptions of the exams, and which schools accept AP and CLEP exam credits. <collegeboard.com>

The Community College Web. You'll find an index of community colleges around the world. Search alphabetically, by location, or by key words. <www.mcli.dist.maricopa.edu/cc/index.html>

Federal Consumer Information Center. Part of the U.S. General Services Administration, this site has a detailed online brochure about life insurance. <www.pueblo.gsa.gov>

Federal Reserve. The Fed's site has a section on home equity loans, including how to find one and a comparison with traditional second mortgages. <www.federalreserve.gov>

Federal Trade Commission. Web site includes an online brochure about home equity and the pros and cons, as well as home equity scams. <www.ftc.gov>

Kiplinger.com. You'll find a lengthy explanation of home equity loans, as well as the best rates in your area and a glossary. <www.kiplinger.com>

Two-Year College Directory. Contact information for every community college in the United States. <cset.sp.utoledo.edu/twoyrcol.html>

Appendix: 529 College Savings Plans by State

This is a snapshot of all the 529 savings plans offered. Unless otherwise noted, they include an age-based investment program among the investments you can choose from; that means it automatically adjusts the allocation of funds as your child gets nearer to graduation. Also, all are offered to nonresidents, unless otherwise noted. Finally, remember that in most cases you can't choose specific funds.

ALABAMA

Alabama College Education Savings Program
Plan under development

ALASKA

University of Alaska College Savings Plan/T. Rowe Price College Savings Plan/ Manulife College Savings Plan
Manager: T. Rowe Price/T.Rowe Price/T. Rowe Price and Manulife Financial
Contact: 866-277-1005/800-369-3641/866-222-7498, www.uacollegesavings.com/ www.troweprice.com/www.manulifecollegesavings.com
No. investment options: 12/11/10
Name of funds: T. Rowe Price Summit Cash Reserve Fund, T. Rowe Price Spectrum Income Fund, T. Rowe Price Equity Index 500 Index Fund, T. Rowe Price Blue Chip Growth Fund, T. Rowe Price Value Fund, T. Rowe Price Mid-Cap Growth Fund, T. Rowe Price Small-Cap Stock Fund, T. Rowe Price International Stock Fund, T. Rowe Price U.S. Bond Index Fund/T. Rowe Price Blue Chip Growth Fund, MFS Massachusetts Growth Stock Fund A, T. Rowe Price Value Fund, Davis New York Venture Fund A, T. Rowe Price Mid-Cap Value, AIM Aggressive Growth Fund A, Templeton Foreign Fund A, Oppenheimer International Growth Fund A, T. Rowe Price Spectrum Income Fund, T. Rowe Price Summit Cash Reserve Fund, T. Rowe Price Short-Term Bond Fund, Pimco Total Return Bond Fund Admin., T. Rowe Price

Science and Technology Fund, T. Rowe Price Health Sciences Fund, T. Rowe Price Financial Services Fund

Max. investment: $250,000 maximum account total

Min. investment: $250, $50 monthly under certain circumstances

State tax deduction: No

Additional: Alaska has no state income tax. For state residents and students attending Alaska schools, UA Savings plan will make up the difference if portfolio falls short of tuition.

ARIZONA

Arizona Family College Savings Program/Arizona Family College Savings Program/ Waddell & Reed InvestEd Plan

Manager: Securities Management & Research/College Savings Bank/Waddell & Reed

Contact: 888-667-3239/800-888-2723/888-923-3355, www.smrinvest.com/ arizona.collegesavings.com/www.waddell.com

No. investment options: 10/1 (CollegeSure CD)/3

Name of funds: SM&R Alger Technology Fund, SM&R Alger Aggressive Growth Fund, SM&R Alger Small-Cap Fund, SM&R Alger Growth Fund, SM&R Alger Equity Income Fund, SM&R Alger Balanced Fund, SM&R Government Bond Fund, SM&R Alger Primary Fund, SM&R Alger Money Market Fund/Waddell & Reed Advisors Core Investment Fund, Waddell & Reed Advisors Value Fund, Waddell & Reed Advisors International Growth Fund, Waddell & Reed Advisors Small-Cap Fund, Waddell & Reed Advisors Vanguard Fund, Waddell & Reed Advisors New Concepts Fund, Waddell & Reed Advisors Bond Fund, Waddell & Reed Advisors Government Securities Fund, Waddell & Reed Advisors High Income Fund, Waddell & Reed Advisors Cash Management Fund

Max. investment: $177,000 maximum account total

Min. investment: $20 to $50 per mutual fund/$250, $25 per pay period for automatic deductions, $100 per month/$500 or $50 initially, $25 a month

State tax deduction: No

Additional: College Savings Bank offers a CollegeSure CD that grows at the same rate as a predetermined index of college costs; no age-based program available in CollegeSure CD plan.

ARKANSAS

GIFT College Investing Plan

Manager: Mercury Advisors

Contact: 877-615-4116, www.thegiftplan.com

No. investment options: 5

Name of funds: Mercury Growth Opportunity Fund, Mercury Large-Cap Core Fund, Mercury U.S. Small-Cap Growth Fund, Mercury U.S. High Yield Fund, Mercury International Fund, Mercury Aggregate Bond Yield Fund, Templeton Foreign Fund, Franklin Total Return Fund, Franklin Balance Sheet Investment Fund, Franklin Blue Chip Fund, Franklin Equity Income Fund, Mutual Shares Fund

Max. investment: $245,000 maximum account total

Min. investment: $250 residents, $1,000 nonresidents

State tax deduction: No

CALIFORNIA
Golden State ScholarShare College Savings Trust
Manager: TIAA-CREF
Contact: 877-728-4338, www.scholarshare.com
No. of investment options: 4
Name of funds: Institutional Growth Equity, Institutional Growth and Income, Institutional Equity Index, Institutional International Equity, Institutional Bond Fund, Institutional Money Market Fund, Institutional Social Change Equity Option
Max. investment: $124,799 to $174,648 maximum account total depending on age
Min. investment: $25, $15 for payroll deduction plan
State tax deduction: No

COLORADO
Scholars Choice College Savings Program
Manager: Salomon Smith Barney
Contact: 800-478-5651 in-state, 888-572-4652; out-of-state, www.scholars-choice.com
No. investment options: 5
Name of funds: Salomon Smith Barney Investor Value Fund, Salomon Smith Barney Large-Cap Growth Fund, Salomon Smith Barney Small-Cap Growth Fund, Salomon Smith Barney Short-Term High-Grade Bond Fund, Salomon Smith Barney Cash Portfolio Fund, Salomon Smith Barney Investment Grade Bond Fund, Salomon AFG Europe Pacific Growth Fund, Salomon MFS Government Securities Fund
Max. investment: $235,000 maximum account total
Min. investment: $25, subsequent $15
State tax deduction: Yes
Additional: State tax deduction is unlimited.

CONNECTICUT
Connecticut Higher Education Trust
Manager: TIAA-CREF
Contact: 888-799-CHET, www.aboutchet.com
No. investment options: 3
Name of funds: Institutional Equity Index Fund, Institutional International Equity Fund, Institutional Bond Fund, Institutional Money Market Fund, Institutional Growth and Income Fund
Max. investment: $235,000 maximum account total
Min. investment: $25, $15 per pay period for automatic deposits
State tax deduction: No

DELAWARE
Delaware College Investment Plan
Manager: Fidelity Investments
Contact: 800-544-1655, www.fidelity.com
No. investment options: 12
Name of funds: Fidelity Blue Chip Growth Fund, Fidelity Disciplined Equity Fund, Fidelity Equity Income Fund, Fidelity Fund, Fidelity Growth and Income Fund, Fidelity Growth Company Fund, Fidelity OTC Fund, Fidelity Diversified International

Fund, Fidelity Overseas Fund, Fidelity Government Income Fund, Fidelity Interme-
diate Bond Fund, Fidelity Investment Grade Bond Fund, Fidelity Capital and In-
come Fund, Fidelity Cash Reserves Fund, Fidelity Short-Term Bond Fund
Max. investment: $250,000 maximum account total
Min. investment: $500, $50 after
State tax deduction: No

FLORIDA

Florida College Savings Plan
Manager: TIAA-CREF
Contact: 800-552-4723, www.floridaprepaidcollege.com
Plan under development

GEORGIA

Georgia Higher Education Savings Plan
Manager: TIAA-CREF
Contact: 877-424-4377, www.gacollegesaving.org
No. investment options: 5
Name of funds: Institutional International Equity Fund, Institutional Growth Equity
Fund, Institutional Growth and Income Fund, Institutional Bond Fund, Institutional
Money Market Fund, Institutional Equity Index Fund
Max. investment: $235,000
Min. investment: $25
State tax deduction: $2,000

HAWAII

Hawaii College Savings Program
Plan under development

IDAHO

Idaho College Savings Program
Manager: TIAA-CREF
Contact: 866-433-2533, www.idsaves.org
No. investment options: 3
Name of funds: Institutional Growth Fund, Institutional International Equity Fund,
Institutional Growth and Income Fund, Institutional Bond Fund, Institutional Money
Market Fund
Max. investment: $235,000 maximum account total
Min. investment: $24, $15 per pay period for automatic deposits
State tax deduction: Yes, $4,000 per year, $8,000 married couples filing jointly

ILLINOIS

Bright Start College Savings Program
Manager: Salomon Smith Barney
Contact: 877-432-8777, www.brightstartsavings.com
No. investment options: 3
Name of funds: Salomon Smith Barney Large-Cap Value Fund, Salomon Smith Bar-
ney Large Capitalization Growth Fund, Salomon Smith Barney Investment Grade

Bond Fund, Salomon Smith Barney Short-Term High-Grade Bond Fund, Salomon Smith Barney Cash Portfolio Fund, Salomon Smith Barney Small-Cap Core Fund
Max. investment: $235,000 maximum account balance total
Min. investment: $25 initial, $15 after
State tax deduction: Yes
Additional: State tax deduction is unlimited.

INDIANA
College Choice 529 Plan
Manager: One Group Services Co.
Contact: 866-400-7526, www.collegechoiceplan.com
No. investment options: 7
Name of funds: One Group Equity Index Fund, One Group Large-Cap Growth Fund, One Group Large-Cap Value Fund, One Group Mid-Cap Value Fund, One Group Mid-Cap Growth Fund, One Group Small-Cap Value Fund, One Group Small-Cap Growth Fund, One Group Diversified International Fund, One Group Bond Fund, One Group Intermediate Bond Fund, One Group High-Yield Bond Fund, One Group Prime Money Market Fund
Max. investment: $236,750
Min. investment: $50 initial, at least $25 after
State tax deduction: No

IOWA
College Savings Iowa
Manager: State Treasurer and Vanguard
Contact: 888-672-9116, www.collegesavingsiowa.com
No. investment options: 5
Name of funds: Vanguard Institutional Index Fund, Vanguard Extended Market Index Fund Institutional Shares, Vanguard Institutional Developed Market Index Fund, Vanguard Total Market Bond Index Fund Institutional Shares
Max. investment: $146,000 maximum account total
Min. investment: $50 total in one year
State tax deduction: up to $2,180

KANSAS
Learning Quest Education Savings Program
Manager: American Century
Contact: 800-579-2203, www.learningquestsavings.com
No. investment options: 22
Name of funds: American Century Growth Select, American Century Vista, American Century Heritage, American Century Income and Growth, American Century Equity Growth, American Century Large-Cap Value, American Century Value, American Century Equity Income, American Century Diversified Bond, American Century Premium Money Market
Max. investment: $235,000 maximum account total
Min. investment: $500 initial Kansas residents, $2,500 nonresidents, $50 after
State tax deduction: up to $2,000, $4,000 married couples filing jointly

KENTUCKY

Kentucky Education Savings Plan Trust
Manager: TIAA-CREF
Contact: 877-598-7878, www.kentuckytrust.org
No. investment options: 2
Name of funds: Institutional Bond Fund, Institutional Equity Index Fund, Institutional Growth and Income Fund, Institutional International Equity Fund, Institutional Growth Fund, Institutional Money Market Fund
Max. investment: $235,000 maximum account total
Min. investment: $25, $15 per pay period for automatic deposits
State tax deduction: No
Additional: Account owner or beneficiary must have current or former residence or employment in Kentucky, or family member with current or former residence in Kentucky.

LOUISIANA

Student Tuition Assistance and Revenue Trust
Manager: State Treasurer
Contact: 800-259-5626, www.osfa.state.la.us
No. investment options: 1
Name of funds: Invests in various fixed-rate securities
Max. investment: $173,065 maximum account total
Min Investment: $10
State tax deduction: up to $2,400 a year
Additional: Account owner or beneficiary must be Louisiana resident; does not offer age-based investment program; state may offer a partial match to contributors at some income levels.

MAINE

NextGen College Investing Plan
Manager: Merrill Lynch
Contact: 877-463-9843, www.nextgenplan.com
No. investment options: 15 through broker/4 direct
Name of funds: Direct series—Merrill Lynch Vista Value Fund, Merrill Lynch Fundamental Growth Fund, Merrill Lynch Large-Cap Core Fund, Merrill Lynch S&P 500 Index, Merrill Lynch Small-Cap Value Fund, Merrill Lynch Small-Cap Growth Fund, Merrill Lynch International Equity Fund, Merrill Lynch International Index Fund, Merrill Lynch Bond Fund, Merrill Lynch Core Bond or High-Income Portfolio Fund
Max. investment: $235,000 maximum account total
Min. investment: $250 lump sum or $50 per month for automatic deposits
State tax deduction: No

MARYLAND

College Savings Plans of Maryland—College Investment Plan
Manager: T. Rowe Price
Contact: 888-463-4723, www.collegesavingsmd.org

No. investment options: 10

Name of funds: T. Rowe Price Equity Index 500 Fund, T. Rowe Price Blue Chip Growth Fund, T. Rowe Price Value Fund, T. Rowe Price Mid-Cap Growth Fund, T. Rowe Price Small-Cap Stock Fund, T. Rowe Price International Stock Fund, T. Rowe Price Spectrum Income Fund, T. Rowe Price Summit Cash Reserve Fund, T. Rowe Price Short-Term Bond Fund

Max. investment: $175,000 maximum account total

Min. investment: $250 lump sum or $25 per month for automatic deposits

State tax deduction: up to $2,500

Additional: Nonqualified withdrawals include no interest for first three years; penalty of 50% of program's investment return after.

MASSACHUSETTS

U.Fund College Investing Plan

Manager: Fidelity Investments

Contact: 800-544-2776, www.fidelity.com

No. investment options: 11

Name of funds: Fidelity Blue Chip Growth Fund, Fidelity Disciplined Equity Fund, Fidelity Dividend Growth Fund, Fidelity Equity Income Fund, Fidelity Equity Income II Fund, Fidelity Fund, Fidelity Growth and Income Fund, Fidelity Growth Company Fund, Fidelity OTC Portfolio Fund, Fidelity Spartan Index Fund, Fidelity Diversified International Fund, Fidelity Overseas Fund, Fidelity Government Income Fund, Intermediate Bond Fund, Fidelity Investment Grade Bond Fund, Fidelity Capital and Income Fund, Fidelity Cash Reserves Money Market Fund, Fidelity Short-Term Bond Fund

Max. investment: $230,000 maximum account total

Min. investment: $1,000 initial or $50 per month for automatic deposits

State tax deduction: No

MICHIGAN

Michigan Education Savings Program

Manager: TIAA-CREF

Contact: 877-861-6377, www.misaves.com

No. investment options: 3

Name of funds: Institutional Bond Fund, Institutional Money Market Fund, Institutional Growth and Income Fund, Institutional International Equity Fund, Institutional Growth Fund, Institutional Equity Index Fund

Max. investment: $235,000 maximum account total

Min. investment: $25, $15 per pay period for automatic deposits

State tax deduction: up to $5,000 per year: $10,000 for married couples filing jointly

Additional: Will match $1 for every $3 you contribute up to $200, if the plan is for a child six years old or younger and the family income is $80,000 or less.

MINNESOTA

Minnesota College Savings Plan

Manager: TIAA-CREF

Contact: 877-338-4646, mnsaves.org

No. investment options: 3
Name of funds: Institutional Growth Fund, Institutional Growth and Income Fund, Institutional Equity Index Fund, Institutional International Equity Fund, Institutional Bond Fund, Institutional Money Market Fund
Max. investment: $235,000 maximum account total
Min. Investment: $25, $15 per payroll for automatic deposits
State tax deduction: Up to $5,000 per year, $10,000 married couples filing jointly

MISSISSIPPI

Mississippi Affordable College Savings
Manager: TIAA-CREF
Contact: 800-486-3670, www.collegesavingsms.com
No. investment options: 3
Name of funds: Institutional Equity Index Fund, Institutional Growth and Income Fund, Institutional International Fund, Institutional Bond Fund, Institutional Money Market Fund
Max. investment: $235,000 maximum account total
Min. investment: $25, $15 payroll deduction deposits
State tax deduction: up to $10,000, $20,000 for married couples filing jointly

MISSOURI

Missouri Saving for Tuition Program
Manager: TIAA-CREF
Contact: 888-414-6678, www.missourimost.org
No. investment options: 3
Name of funds: Institutional Equity Index Fund, Institutional Growth Fund, Institutional International Equity Fund, Institutional Growth and Income Fund, Institutional Bond Fund, Institutional Money Market Fund
Max. investment: $235,000 maximum account total
Min. investment: $25, $15 per payroll for automatic deposits
State tax deduction: $8,000 per year per taxpayer
Additional: Qualified withdrawals can be taken 12 months after account is opened.

MONTANA

Montana Family Education Savings Program
Manager: College Savings Bank
Contact: 800-888-2723, montana.collegesavings.com
No. investment options: 1
Name of fund: CollegeSure CD
Max. investment: $177,000 maximum account total
Min. investment: $250, $25 payroll for automatic deposit, $100 per month or $250 per quarter
State tax deduction: up to $3,000 per year, $6,000 for married couples filing jointly
Additional: CollegeSure CD, with interest rate pegged to a national index of college costs; state tax deduction recaptured if account is withdrawn within three years of opening; penalties for nonresidents if withdrawal before maturity.

NEBRASKA
College Savings Plan of Nebraska/AIM College Savings Plan/TD Waterhouse College Savings
Manager: Union Bank & Trust/AIM Funds/Union Bank & Trust
Contact: 888-993-3746/877-246-7526/877-408-4644, www.PlanForCollegenow .com/www.aimfunds.com/tdwaterhouse.com
No. investment options: 10
Name of funds: American Century Equity Income Fund, American Century Income and Growth Fund, Fidelity Advisors Equity Growth Fund, Fidelity Diversified International Fund, Janus Enterprise Fund, Pimco Total Return Fund, T. Rowe Price Foreign Equity Fund, Vanguard Prime Money Market Fund, Vanguard Total Bond Market Index Fund, Vanguard Total International Stock Index Fund, Vanguard Extended Market Index Fund/AIM Basic Value Fund, AIM Blue Chip Fund, Aim Constellation Fund, AIM International Equity Fund, AIM Intermediate Government Fund, AIM International Value Fund, AIM Mid-Cap Equity Fund, AIM Small-Cap Growth Fund, AIM Cash Reserves Fund/American Century Equity Income Fund, American Century Income and Growth Fund, Fidelity Advisor Equity Growth Fund, Fidelity Diversified International Fund, Janus Enterprise Fund, T. Rowe Price Foreign Equity Fund, State Street 500 Index Fund, Vanguard Prime Money Market Fund, Vanguard Total Bond Market Index Fund, Vanguard Total International Stock Index Fund, Vanguard Extended Market Index Fund, Pimco Total Return Fund
Max. investment: $250,000 maximum account balance
Min. investment: None/$50 initially, $24 automatic deposit/None
State tax deduction: up to $1,000 per year

NEVADA
American Skandia College Savings Program/America's College Savings Plan
Manager: Strong Capital Management and American Skandia/Strong Capital Management
Contact: 800-SKANDIA/877-529-5295, www.americanskandia.com/ www.americas529plan.com
No. investment options: 6/4
Name of funds: American Skandia Advisor Funds, Neuberger-Berman Mid-Cap Growth Fund, ASAF Gabelli Small-Cap Value Fund, ASAF Gabelli All-Cap Value Fund, ASAF Invesco Equity Income Fund, ASAF Marsico Capital Growth Fund, ASAF PBHG Small-Cap Growth Fund, ASAF Pimco Total Return Bond Fund, ASAF Federated High-Yield Bond Fund, ASAF Money Market Fund, ASAF Strong International Equity Fund, Strong Government Securities Fund, Strong Corporate Bond Fund/ Strong Growth Fund, Strong Advisor Small-Cap Value Fund, Strong Corporate Bond Fund, Strong Opportunity Fund, Strong Advisor U.S. Value Fund, Strong Short-Term Bond Fund, Strong Government Securities Fund, Strong Ultra Short-Term Income Fund
Max. investment: $246,000 maximum account balance
Min. investment: $250 initial, $50 with automatic deposits, $50 after
State tax deduction: No
Additional: Nevada does not have a state income tax.

NEW HAMPSHIRE
UNIQUE College Investing Plan
Manager: Fidelity Investments
Contact: 800-544-1722, www.fidelity.com/unique
No. investment options: 11
Name of funds: Fidelity Blue Chip Growth Fund, Fidelity Disciplined Equity Fund, Fidelity Dividend Growth Fund, Fidelity Equity Income Fund, Fidelity Fund, Fidelity Growth and Income Fund, Fidelity Growth Company Fund, Fidelity OTC Portfolio Fund, Fidelity Diversified International Fund, Fidelity Overseas Fund, Fidelity Government Income Fund, Fidelity Intermediate Bond Fund, Fidelity Investment Grade Bond Fund, Fidelity Capital and Income Fund, Fidelity Cash Reserves Money Market Fund, Fidelity Short-Term Bond Fund, Fidelity Small-Cap Independence Fund
Max. investment: $233,240 maximum account balance
Min. investment: $1,000 or $50 per month for automatic deposits
State tax deduction: No

NEW JERSEY
New Jersey Better Educational Savings Trust
Manager: State Treasurer
Contact: 877-4NJBEST, www.hesaa.org/students/njbest
No. investment options: 1
Name of funds: Invested in trust of stocks and fixed income instruments
Max. investment: $185,000 maximum account total
Min. investment: $25 per month, $300 annually until account reaches $1,200
State tax deduction: No
Additional: Account owner or beneficiary must be state resident.

NEW MEXICO
The Education Plan's College Savings Program/Scholar'sEdge/CollegeSense 529 Higher Education Savings Plan/Arrive Education Savings Plan
Manager: Schoolhouse Capital/Schoolhouse Capital, OppenheimerFunds/Schoolhouse Capital, New York Life Investment Management/Prudential, Sun America and Evergreen
Contact: 800-499-7581/800-845-5044/866-529-7367/877-277-4838/www.tepnm .com/www.scholarsedge529.com/www.collegesense.com/arrive529.com
No. investment options: 8
Name of funds: SSGA High-Yield Bond Fund, Invesco Small Company Growth Fund, Janus Advisory Growth and Income Fund, Janus Advisory International Fund, MFS Value A Fund, SSGA International Growth Opportunities Fund, SSGA Growth and Income Fund, SSGA Bond Market Fund/Oppenheimer Capital Appreciation, State Street Growth and Income, Oppenheimer Quest Value, Oppenheimer Mid-Cap Fund, Oppenheimer Quest Capital Value Fund, State Street Bond Market, Oppenheimer U.S. Government Trust, Oppenheimer Main Street Small-Cap Fund, OGA Growth & Income Fund, SSGA International Growth Opportunities Fund, SSGA Bond Market Fund, Oppenheimer International Growth Fund, State Street High

Yield Bond Fund, State Street Bond Market Fund, Oppenheimer U.S. Government Trust Fund, Oppenheimer Money Market Fund/MainStay Capital Appreciation Fund A, Mainstay Value Fund A, MainStay International Equity Fund A, SSGA Growth and Income Fund, SSGA Bond Market Fund, SSGA International Growth Opportunities Fund, J.P. Morgan Capital Growth Fund A, J.P. Morgan Capital Dynamic Small Cap Fund A, Eclipse Core Bond Plus Fund, Eclipse Money Market Fund Service, SSGA International Growth Opportunity Fund, Prudential International Value, Evergreen Small-Cap Value, Evergreen Growth Fund, Jennison Equity Opportunity Fund, Sun America Growth Opportunities Fund, Evergreen Capital Growth Fund, Sun America Focus Growth and Income, Jennison Growth, Prudential Total Return Bond Fund, Prudential Stable Value Offering I, Evergreen Core Bond Fund, Prudential Stable Value Offering II, Sun America GNMA Fund

Max. investment: $251,000 maximum account total

Min. investment: $250, $100 after, $25 per month for automatic deposits/$250 initially, $100 after or $25 a month for automatic deposits/$250 or $25 a month or $75 a quarter

State tax deduction: Yes

Additional: Unlimited tax deduction

NEW YORK

New York's College Savings Program

Manager: TIAA-CREF

Contact: 877-697-2837, www.nysaves.com

No. investment options: 4

Name of funds: New York College Savings Growth Fund, New York College Savings Bond Fund, New York College Savings Money Market Fund, Institutional Equity Index

Max. investment: up to $235,000 maximum account total

Min. investment: $25, $15 per pay period for automatic deposits

State tax deduction: up to $5,000 per year, $10,000 for married couples filing jointly

Additional: No qualified withdrawals in first 36 months

NORTH CAROLINA

North Carolina's National College Savings Program/Seligman CollegeHorizon-Funds

Manager: College Foundation Inc./College Foundation Inc. and J.&W. Seligman

Contact: 800-600-3453/800-600-3453, www.cfnc.org/savings/ www.seligman529.com

No. investment options: 4 (residents), 1 (nonresidents)

Name of funds: For residents and nonresidents: Seligman Capital Fund, Seligman Cash Management Fund, Seligman Common Stock Fund, Seligman Communications and Information Fund, Seligman Emerging Markets Fund, Seligman Frontier Fund, Seligman Global Growth Fund, Seligman Global Smaller Companies Fund, Seligman Growth Fund, Seligman High-Yield Bond Series, Seligman International Growth Fund, Seligman Investment Grade Fixed Income Fund, Seligman Large-Cap Value Fund, Seligman Small-Cap Value Fund. For residents: Evergreen Core Equity

Fund, Evergreen Small-Cap Value Fund, Evergreen International Growth Fund, Evergreen Core Bond Fund, Wachovia TIPS Portfolio, AAA Bond Fund managed by state treasurer, North Carolina Mutual Capital Management Group's Focused Equity Portfolios and Legg Mason Value Trust

Max. investment: $268,804 maximum account total

Min. investment: $5/$250 initially, $100 later, $25 automatic payroll deposit, $100 automatic bank deposit

State tax deduction: No

Additional: Only option for nonresidents is Seligman.

NORTH DAKOTA

College SAVE

Manager: Morgan Stanley

Contact: 866-728-3529, www.collegesave4u.com

No. investment options: 5

Name of funds: Morgan Stanley Growth Fund, Morgan Stanley S&P 500 Index Fund, Van Kampen Aggressive Growth Fund, Morgan Stanley Small-Cap Growth Fund, Morgan Stanley International Fund, Morgan Stanley U.S. Government Securities Trust, Morgan Stanley Short-Term U.S. Treasury Trust, Morgan Stanley Liquid Asset Fund

Max. investment: $269,000 maximum account total

Min. investment: $25, $300 account balance by end of first year

State tax deduction: No

OHIO

Ohio CollegeAdvantage Savings Plan

Manager: Putnam Investments

Contact: 800-233-6734, www.collegeadvantage.com

No. investment options: 14

Name of funds: Putnam Voyager Fund, Putnam Growth and Income Fund, Putnam High-Yield Trust II, Putnam International Growth Fund, Putnam International Voyager, Putnam Income, Putnam New Opportunities, Putnam New Value, Putnam Capital Opportunities, Putnam Investors Fund, Putnam Money Market Fund

Max. investment: $232,000 maximum account total

Min. investment: $15

State tax deduction: up to $2,000 per year

OKLAHOMA

Oklahoma College Savings Plan

Manager: TIAA-CREF

Contact: 877-654,7284, www.ok4saving.org

No. investment options: 3

Name of funds: Institutional Growth Fund, Institutional Growth and Income Fund, Institutional Equity Index Fund, Institutional International Equity Fund, Institutional Bond Fund, Institutional Money Market Fund

Max. investment: up to $235,000 maximum account total

Min. investment: $25, $15 automatic payroll deposit

State tax deduction: up to $2,500 per year
Additional: Qualified withdrawals may not be taken in first 12 months.

OREGON
Oregon College Savings Plan
Manager: Strong Capital Management
Contact: 866-772-8464, www.oregoncollegesavings.com
No. investment options: 6
Name of funds: Strong Growth Fund, Strong Growth and Income, Strong Index 500 Fund, Strong Opportunity Fund, Strong Corporate Bond Fund, Strong Short-Term Bond Fund, Strong Ultra-Short Income Fund, First American International Fund, First American Equity Income Fund, First American Small-Cap Value Fund, First American Fixed Income Fund, First American Intermediate-Term Bond Fund, First American Prime Obligations Fund, First American Equity Index, First American Small-Cap Index, First American Mid-Cap Index
Max. investment: up to $250,000 maximum account total
Min. investment: $250 initially, $25 after, $25 automatic investment or payroll deduction
State tax deduction: up to $2,000, $1,000 for married couples filing separately

PENNSYLVANIA
Manager: NA
Contact: 800-440-4000, patap.org
No. investment options: NA
Max. investment: up to $260,000 maximum account total
Min. investment: NA
State tax deduction: No

RHODE ISLAND
CollegeBoundfund
Manager: Alliance Capital Management
Contact: 888-324-5057, www.collegeboundfund.com
No. investment options: 15
Name of funds: Alliance Growth and Income Fund, Alliance Mid-Cap Growth Fund, Alliance Premier Growth Fund, Alliance Institutional Quasar Fund, Alliance Technology Fund, Alliance Quality Bond Fund, Alliance U.S. Government Bond Fund, Alliance High-Yield Fund, Alliance Exchange Reserves Fund, Alliance Bernstein International Value Fund, Alliance Bernstein Small-Cap Value Fund, Alliance Principal Protection Income Fund
Max. investment: Up to $265,620
Min. investment: $250 initially, $50 later
State tax deduction: No
Additional: Nonresidents incur higher costs of broker-sold shares.

SOUTH CAROLINA
Future Scholar 529 College Savings Plan
Manager: Bank of America Advisors
Contact: 888-244-5674, www.futurescholar.com

No. investment options: 9/15 (nonresidents)
Name of funds: *Residents:* Nations Large-Cap Index Fund, Nations Mid-Cap Index Fund, Nations Small-Cap Index Fund, Nations International Value Fund, Nations Bond Fund, Nations Short-Term Income Fund, Nations Cash Reserves Fund. *Nonresidents:* Nations Value Fund, Nations Strategic Growth Fund, Nations Marsico Focused Equities Fund, Nations Mid-Cap Growth Fund, Nations Small Company Fund, Nations International Value Fund, Nations Bond Fund, Nations Short-Term Income Fund, Nations High-Yield Bond Fund, Nations Cash Reserves Fund
Max. investment: $250,000 maximum account total
Min. investment: $250 if not done through automatic deposit
State tax deduction: No limit
Additional: Opens nationally May 1.

SOUTH DAKOTA
Plan under development

TENNESSEE
Tennessee's BEST Savings Plan
Manager: TIAA-CREF
Contact: 888-486-2378, www.tnbest.org
No. investment options: 2
Name of funds: Institutional Growth Fund, Institutional Growth and Income Fund, Institutional Equity Index Fund, Institutional International Equity Fund, Institutional Bond Fund, Institutional Money Market Fund
Max. investment: Up to $235,000 maximum account total
Min. investment: $25, $15 automatic payroll deposit
State tax deduction: No

TEXAS
Plan under development

UTAH
Utah Educational Savings Plan Trust
Manager: Vanguard
Contact: 800-418-2551, www.uesp.org
No. investment options: 4
Name of funds: Vanguard Institutional Index Fund, Vanguard Total Bond Market Index Fund Institutional Shares, Public Treasurers Investment Fund
Max. investment: Up to $176,000 maximum account total
Min. investment: $25, at least $300 a year
State tax deduction: Up to $1,410 per year, $2,820 for married couple
Additional: Qualified withdrawals must generally begin by age 22 and four months.

VERMONT
Vermont Higher Education Investment Plan
Manager: TIAA-CREF
Contact: 800-637-5860, www.vsac.org
No. investment options: 3

Name of funds: Institutional Growth Fund, Institutional International Equity Fund, Institutional Growth and Income Fund, Institutional Bond Fund, Institutional Money Market Fund
Max. investment: Up to $240,100 maximum account total
Min. investment: $25, $15 per pay period for automatic payroll deposits
State tax deduction: No

VIRGINIA
Virginia Education Savings Trust/College America
Manager: Virginia College Savings Plan Board/American Funds
Contact: 888-567-0540/800-421-4120, www.virginia529.com/www.americanfunds.com
No. investment options: 12/21
Name of funds: Vanguard 500 Index Fund, Rothschild Small/Mid-Cap Domestic Equity Fund, Vanguard Small-Cap Domestic Equity Fund, American Funds Non-U.S. Equity Fund, Templeton Foreign Equity Series Fund, Fixed, Western Asset Management Fixed Income Fund, Pimco Stable Value Fund, Vanguard Life Strategies Growth Fund, Vanguard Life Strategies Moderate Growth Fund, Vanguard Life Strategies Income Fund, Vanguard Prime Money Market Fund/American Funds AMCAP Fund, American Funds EuroPacific Fund, American Funds The Growth Fund of America, American Funds The New Economy Fund, American Funds New Perspective Fund, American Funds New World Fund, American Funds Small-Cap World Fund, American Funds American Mutual Fund, American Funds Capital World Growth and Income Fund, American Funds Fundamental Investors Fund, American Funds The Investment Company of America, American Funds Washington Mutual Investors, American Funds Capital Income Builder, American Funds The Income Fund of America, American Funds American Balanced Fund, American Funds American High-Income Trust, American Funds The Bond Fund of America, American Funds Capital World Bond Fund, American Funds Intermediate Bond Fund of America, American Funds U.S. Government Securities Fund, American Funds The Cash Management Trust of America
Max. investment: $250,000 maximum account total
Min. investment: $25, $250 minimum first 12 months/$250 initial, $50 a month after
State tax deduction: Up to $2,000 per year
Additional: Investor selects funds individually in College America plan.

WASHINGTON
Plan under development

WASHINGTON, D.C.
Plan under development

WEST VIRGINIA
Smart 529
Manager: The Hartford
Contact: 866-574-3542, www.hartfordinvestor.com
No. investment options: 9

Name of funds: The Hartford Dividend and Growth 529 Fund, The Hartford Stock 529 Fund, The Hartford Global Leaders 529 Fund, The Hartford Mid-Cap 529 Fund, The Hartford Capital Appreciation 529 Fund, The Hartford Advisers 529 Fund, The Hartford Bond Income Strategy 529 Fund, The Hartford Money Market 529 Fund
Max. investment: $265,620
Min. investment: $500 initial, $50 after
State tax deduction: No limit

WISCONSIN
EdVest College Savings Program/Tomorrow's Scholar
Manager: Strong Capital Management/Strong Capital Management and American Express
Contact: 888-338-3789/866-677-6933, ww.edvest.com/tomorrowsscholar.com
No. investment options: 7/6
Name of funds: Strong Index 500 Fund, Strong Advisor Bond Fund, Strong Government Securities Fund, Strong Short-Term Bond Fund, Strong Ultra Short-Term Income Fund, Strong Growth Fund, Strong Advisor U.S. Value, Strong Opportunity Fund, Strong Overseas Fund/AXP Diversified Equity Fund, AXP Equity Select Fund, AXP Federal Income Fund, AXP International Fund, AXP New Dimensions Fund, AXP Bond Fund, AXP Cash Management Fund, Strong Ultra Short-Term Income Fund, Strong Corporate Bond Fund, Strong Advisor U.S. Value Fund, Strong Government Securities Fund, Strong Growth Fund, Strong Opportunity Fund, Strong Short-Term Bond Fund
Max. investment: Up to $246,000 account total
Min. investment: $250, or $25 per month/$250, waived with $25 automatic investment plan
State tax deduction: Up to $3,000 per year

WYOMING
College Achievement Plan
Manager: Mercury Advisors
Contact: 877-529-2655, www.collegeachievementplan.com
No. investment options: 5
Name of funds: Mercury Large-Cap Core Fund, Mercury Small-Cap Value Fund, Mercury U.S. Small-Cap Growth Fund, Mercury U.S. High-Yield Fund, Mercury International Fund, MFS Capital Opportunities Fund, MFS Strategic Growth Fund, MFS Research International Fund, MFS Bond Fund, Summit Cash Reserve Fund
Max. investment: Up to $245,000 maximum account total
Min. investment: $1,000 non residents, $250 state residents, $50 later
State tax deduction: No
Additional: Wyoming does not have a state income tax.

General Resources

The following is a list of general or additional resources you can use to help finance a college education:

Books

College Money Handbook (Peterson's Publishing, Princeton Pike Corporate Center, 2000 Lennox Dr., P.O. Box 67005, Lawrenceville, NJ 08648; 800-338-3282; www.petersons.com). Helps identify sources of college financing. Includes a CD-ROM to help you estimate college costs. Profiles hundreds of colleges and what financial aid they have to offer.

Discounts and Deals at the Nation's 360 Best Colleges: The Parent Soup Financial Aid and College Guide, by Bruce G. Hammond (Western Publishing Co., P.O. Box 1228, North Platte, NE 69103; 800-951-6700; www.wespub.com). Combines financial aid information with a detailed guide to the nation's best colleges. Reveals which colleges offer the best need-based aid, which give the biggest merit scholarships, and how to qualify for scholarships and discounts.

Essential Finance Series: Financial Aid for College, by Marc Robinson and Ronald W. Johnson (Dorling Kindersley Publishing, 501 Mason Rd., Lavergne, IN 37086; 877-342-5357, 212-213-4800; www.usstore.dk.com/shop/). Questionnaires assess the reader's financial status, and charts and graphs track cash flow. Helps reader learn how to live debt-free, invest in the stock market, and pay for a child's education.

The Fiske Guide to Colleges, by Edward B. Fiske (Times Books, Random House, 201 E. 50th St., New York, NY 10022; 212-751-2600, 800-733-3000; www.randomhouse.com). The most frequently asked questions about attending college, from academics to social life. Includes a section on getting a first-rate education at public university prices.

Funding a College Education: Finding the Right School for Your Child and the Right Fit for Your Budget, by Alice Drum and Richard Kneedler (Harvard Business School Publishing, 300 N. Beacon St., 4th Floor, Watertown MA 02472; 800-988-0886; www.hbsp.harvard.edu). Targeted to parents, this book explains how to negotiate the maze of available education choices and financial aid options. Provides worksheets to help assess family resources and explain the different types of colleges with the different types of aid, loans, and scholarships.

Kiplinger's Financing College: How Much You'll Really Have to Pay—and How to Get the Money (Kiplinger Books, 1729 H St., N.W., Washington, DC 20006; 202-887-6431; www.kiplinger.com). A comprehensive look at the full range of college financing issues, from savings plans to applying for financial aid.

Last Minute College Financing: It's Never Too Late to Prepare for the Future, by Daniel J. Cassidy (Career Press, P.O. Box 687, Franklin Lakes, NJ 07417; 201-848-0310; www.careerpress.com). Explains how to save for your child's college expenses, how to make your savings grow, how to estimate how much money will be needed, and how to locate sources.

Paying for Your Child's College Education, by Marguerite Smith (Time Warner, 3 Center Plaza, Boston, MA 02108; 800-343-9204; www.timewarner.com). From *Money* magazine; offers precise short- and long-term plans, helpful graphs, and worksheets to help parents.

Peterson's Competitive College (Peterson's Publishing, Princeton Pike Corporate Center, 2000 Lennox Dr., P.O. Box 67005, Lawrenceville, NJ 08648; 800-338-3282; www.petersons.com). Presents in-depth profiles of more than 350 U.S. colleges and universities that attract the world's best students.

Peterson's Insider's Guide to Paying for College: Find Out How to Get More Money for College, by Don M. Betterton (Peterson's Publishing, Princeton Pike Corporate Center, 2000 Lennox Dr., P.O. Box 67005, Lawrenceville, NJ 08648; 800-338-3282; www.petersons.com). Takes each type of student and sets them up with as many financial aid avenues as possible. Describes many options for each type of student.

Tips on Financial Aid for College (Council of Better Business Bureaus, 4200 Wilson Blvd., Suite 800, Arlington, VA 22203; 703-276-0100; www.bbb.org). A helpful brochure, which can be downloaded from the Web, explaining different kinds of college financial aid and how to apply for them.

Trade Associations and Companies Specializing in College Financing

ACT Inc. (formerly American College Testing) (2201 N. Dodge St., P.O. Box 168, Iowa City, IA 52243; 319-337-1000; www.act.org). Administers tests and advises financial aid administrators and students. Publishes the *ACTIVITY* newsletter for counselors, admissions officers, and teachers. Processes the Free Application for Federal Student Aid (FAFSA).

American Distance Education Consortium (c218 Animal Science Building, Lincoln, NE 68583; 402-472-7000; www.adec.edu). This is an international consortium of state and land grant institutions providing economic distance education programs and services via the latest and most appropriate information technologies.

The College Board (45 Columbus Ave., New York, NY 10023-6992; 212-713-8000; www.collegeboard.org). Publishes many books on financing college. The three most popular are *College Costs & Financial Aid Handbook; Meeting College Costs: What You Need to Know Before Your Child and Your Money Leave Home;* and the *College Board Scholarship Handbook.* Another book, designed for adult students, is *Financing Your College Degree.* Also offers a college search program, College Explorer, on a CD-ROM, which comes with the *College Handbook,* and Fundfinder. Also on the CD is the *Scholarship Handbook.* These allow you to match your characteristics against a database of thousands of scholarship sources. Also sponsors a loan program called CollegeCredit (call 703-707-8999 for more information). The Board's College Scholarship Service also administers the CSS/Financial Aid PROFILE program, used by many colleges to help determine a student's need for financial aid.

Distance Education & Training Council (1601 18th St., N.W., Suite 2, Washington, DC 20009; 202-234-5100; www.detc.org). The accrediting agency for correspondence schools, which provide lessons for home study, sometimes for degrees. When you complete a lesson, you mail it to the school, where a professor corrects, grades, and comments on your work. The assignment is then returned to you, and you move on to the next lesson in the course. Subjects taught by correspondence schools include advertising, bookkeeping, cartooning, desktop publishing, engine tune-up, floristry, gemology, hotel operations, interior decorating, jewelry sales, kindergarten instruction, landscaping, music appreciation, nutrition, oil painting, paralegal work, robotics, screenwriting, travel, VCR repair, window display, and yacht design. Its *Directory of Accredited Institutions* can tell you where to find a home-study course teaching the subject in which you are interested. Other free publications offered by the Council include "What Does Accreditation Mean to You?" and "Using Your Distance Education to Earn an Academic Degree."

Federal Government Regulators

U.S. Department of Education (Federal Student Aid Program; 400 Maryland Ave., S.W., Washington, DC 20202; 800-433-3243; www.ed.gov). Oversees all federal aid programs. Will send brochures titled "Looking for Student Aid," "Funding Your Education," and "The Student Guide: Financial Aid from the U.S. Department of Education," which explains Pell grants, FSEOGs, college work-study programs, Perkins loans, Stafford loans, and PLUS and SLS loans. Also publishes a useful guide titled *Preparing Your Child for College: A Resource Book for Parents,* available free from the Consumer Information Center (Pueblo, CO 81009). The guide answers questions about college, such as why your child may want to attend college, how to choose a school, and how to finance a college education. It also lists sources of further information about educational financing programs. For information on the

Education Department's direct loan origination and consolidation program, call the Federal Direct Student Loan Origination Center at 800-557-7392 or 800-557-7394. If you already have an existing loan and have a question about it, you can call the Direct Loan Servicing Center at 800-848-0979.

Web Sites

@theU. This site offers online applications for financial aid along with online loan calculators. Students also can buy their textbooks at this site, earning UniBucks worth up to 5 percent of the purchase price. The student's personal UniBucks are tracked and accessed via the ATM. Once earned, UniBucks can be applied to your student loan account serviced at UNIPAC or any other financial institution you designate. Parents, family members, and friends can establish their own @theU accounts and the UniBucks from those accounts can be transferred to the student's account. <www.attheu.com>

CollegeClub. A general student site with lots of information and help for students, including a scholarship search engine and a loan finder. <www.collegeclub.com>

College Express. This site presents information on hundreds of private colleges and universities. It also has an extensive section on the financial aid process, including the best ways to apply for federal and college-based aid and how to negotiate a lower tuition cost from the school. <www.collegexpress.com>

CollegeLearning.com. College Learning has partnerships with more than 100 accredited colleges and universities that offer a range of for-credit and noncredit distance courses. Courses are delivered via the Internet, television, CD-ROM, videotape, audiotape, videoconferencing, or other media. <www.collegelearning.com>

College Parents of America. This is a member site; membership costs $25. The site provides members information on saving strategies, financial aid, education tax credits and deductions, and other ways to help pay for college. Also offers members special values and discounts on items such as computers, books, college guides, and study-abroad programs. <www.collegeparents.org>

Ed-X. This site creates its own multimedia learning content and offers consulting on the online marketing of learning content to third parties. <www.ed-x.com>

Embark.com. This site offers an admission service to colleges, graduate schools, business schools, and law schools. It also offers online degrees and certificates. Helps prepare for standardized tests and offers student loans, credit cards, and online banking for students. <www.embark.com>

Mind Edge. Provides resources for personal development, distance learning, continuing education, and on-campus and corporate training courses. <www.mindedge .com>

MyRoad.com. This site allows the student to explore majors, find a college, research careers, and discover what careers suit their individual talents. Guides you to develop your own plan for your education and subsequent career. <www.myroad .com>

Parent Soup Guide to College Planning. This site for parents has extensive re-sources on finding the best college and financing college education. <www.parent .soup.com>

Peterson's Education Center. The publisher of many financial aid books has a useful site explaining the entire process. There is a college admissions calendar re-minding you of various filing deadlines, a glossary of terms, and definitions of var-ious types of financial aid. <www.petersons.com>

R1Edu.org. This site directs students to participating institutions' distance learn-ing course information. It is not a degree-granting institution. <www.r1edu.org>

RSP Funding Focus. Reference Service Press provides a one-stop information re-source for scholarships, fellowships, loans, grants, awards, and internships. The site features a financial aid library, a listing of state financial aid agencies, and a mailing list you can get on that provides a free electronic newsletter filled with the latest in-formation about financial aid programs. You also can contact RSP at 5000 Windplay Dr., Suite 4, Eldorado Hills, CA 95762; 916-939-9620. RSP also publishes 19 books, including *Financial Aid for the Disabled and Their Families* and *High School Senior's Guide to Merit and Other No-Need Funding.* <www.rspfunding.com>

Student Credit. Students can learn about credit, credit reports, and credit repair, and can apply for a number of major bank student credit cards. These cards are de-signed especially for students, usually with no annual fee, some with e-mail reminders about their account balance, and some with ATM access. <www.studentcredit.com>

Studentmarket.com. Has a good student loan education section. You can apply online for prequalification and an information kit. You can apply online for a student Discover, American Express, or CapitalOne credit card. The site has a number of of-fers for students for long distance telephone rates, software, computers, clothing, and jobs. <www.studentmarket.com>

U.S. News & World Report. The *U.S. News and World Report*'s annual college edition provides a list of what the magazine evaluates as the best college values. An-other part of the site guides you through the financial aid process. It answers fre-quently asked questions about financing college. The site also lists other financial aid Web sites, offers a loan center, and much more. <www.usnews.com>

VarsityBooks.com. Online college bookstore that offers to identify the books you need once you select your college and program. You then can buy those books your professors have recommended for your courses. <www.varsitybooks.com>

Vault.com. An online source of career and internship information. <www.vault. com>

Index

Bulk Pricing Information

For special discounts on
20 or more copies of
Everyone's Money Book on College,
call Dearborn Trade Special Sales
at 800-621-9621, extension 4455,
or e-mail bermel@dearborn.com.
You'll receive great service
and top discounts.

For added visibility, please
consider our custom cover service,
which highlights your firm's name
and logo on the cover.
We are also an excellent resource
for dynamic and
knowledgeable speakers.